Praise for *World Class*

"Teru's personal experiences abroad with her children breathe life into the data and research compiled over many years by the Organisation for Economic Co-operation and Development (OECD). This is a wakeup call for families, policy-makers and educational institutions."

—Andreas Schleicher, director for education and skills at the OECD

"Teru Clavel is the voice of twenty-first century education. She has lived the bigger picture and generously shares how her experiences match leading research. We should pay attention—and adjust."

—Arne Duncan, former Secretary of Education
under President Barack Obama

"Teru Clavel questions and challenges the educational system, and moves her family around the globe for over a decade to redefine and reassess what education means to them. This book changed me. It's a must-read."

—Angela C. Santomero, creator of *Blue's Clues*
and *Daniel Tiger's Neighborhood*

"Look no further. This is an indispensable guide for parents who are seeking insight into a myriad of education strategies around the world. The international comparisons and well-researched strategies were eye-opening to me as a parent of four."

—Senator Richard Blumenthal

"*World Class* captures the central importance of community and equity within educational systems. Teru's journey brings best practices from around the world and places them inside American homes and schools. It is time to accept the competitive nature of our global economy and adapt accordingly for our future collective security."

—Nick Melvoin, board member of the
Los Angeles Unified School District

"A thoughtful combination memoir and manual . . . [Clavel's] personal narrative is studded with lists of useful tips about choosing schools and hiring tutors, for parents who must advocate for their children and supplement gaps in their educations."

—*Publishers Weekly*

"An upbeat chronicle of [Clavel's] children's school experiences in Hong Kong, Shanghai, and Tokyo and a harsh critique of American education . . . [offering] advice about vetting schools and enriching children's education."

—*Kirkus Reviews*

"An intriguing volume on the differences in global education."

—*Library Journal*

World Class

*One Mother's Journey Halfway
Around the Globe in Search of the
Best Education for Her Children*

TERU CLAVEL

ATRIA PAPERBACK
New York   London   Toronto   Sydney   New Delhi

ATRIA
PAPERBACK

An Imprint of Simon & Schuster, Inc.
1230 Avenue of the Americas
New York, NY 10020

First Atria Paperback edition October 2020

ATRIA PAPERBACK and colophon are trademarks of Simon & Schuster, Inc.

For information about special discounts for bulk purchases, please contact Simon & Schuster Special Sales at 1-866-506-1949 or business@simonandschuster.com.

The Simon & Schuster Speakers Bureau can bring authors to your live event. For more information or to book an event, contact the Simon & Schuster Speakers Bureau at 1-866-248-3049 or visit our website at www.simonspeakers.com.

Design by Jill Putorti

Manufactured in the United States of America

1 3 5 7 9 10 8 6 4 2

The Library of Congress has cataloged the hardcover edition as follows:

Names: Clavel, Teru, author.
Title: World class : one mother's journey halfway around the globe in search of the best education for her children / Teru Clavel.
Description: First. | New York : Atria Books, [2019] | Includes bibliographical references.
Identifiers: LCCN 2019010134 (print) | LCCN 2019981143 (ebook) | ISBN 9781501192975 (hardcover) | ISBN 9781501192999 (ebook)
Subjects: LCSH: Comparative education. | Education—United States. | Education—Asia.
Classification: LCC LB43 .C53 2019 (print) | LCC LB43 (ebook) | DDC 370.9—dc23
LC record available at https://lccn.loc.gov/2019010134
LC ebook record available at https://lccn.loc.gov/2019981143

ISBN 978-1-5011-9297-5
ISBN 978-1-5011-9298-2 (pbk)
ISBN 978-1-5011-9299-9 (ebook)

For the greatest educators in my life:
my three children—James, Charles, and Victoria—
and my mother, Sachiko.
Thank you for inspiring me to write this book.
I love you always and forever.

Contents

CONTENTS

World
Class

Introduction

Three's Company

The house phone rang, and I ran to the kitchen to get it. It was 9:00 p.m.

"Hello?" I said.

"Hel-lo," said an automated voice. "This is the Palo Alto Unified School District. We are calling to inform you that your student was absent from school today." I spun around to glare at James, my oldest child, who had just started eighth grade, his second year in our new district. Then my phone buzzed with a new email alert and a text communicating the same message.

"James, you cut school today?!"

"Of course not, Mama," he replied. "Why would you ask me that?" I immediately felt guilty for accusing him, but it hadn't occurred to me that the school might have gotten it wrong.

This was the first week of school, and by the end of it, James was mistakenly marked absent three days. On the fourth day, he was sent to the principal's office—and missed an entire class while they figured out they had the wrong James. This was a wholly different experience from the one we'd had in our last school overseas, where I grew accustomed to receiving calls from my children's classroom teachers in the evening to discuss their progress. But here in Palo Alto, California's top-rated school district, these regular calls confirmed my sense that something was very,

very wrong. Were my kids even safe in school? What if they never made it to class? Would I hear about it? After all, *the school had waited until 9:00 p.m. to let me know they hadn't seen him all day!*

It exemplified perfectly our educational experience in Palo Alto. My children were getting lost in a district I came to believe was struggling with a systemic lack of oversight, where students' academic—let alone social and emotional—needs were getting lost in bureaucratic failures.

No wonder this was the first time in ten years that my kids didn't love school. They didn't even want to go to school anymore.

Welcome back to America.

This was our first time back in the United States after living abroad for a decade. Ten years earlier, called by the promise of adventure—and avoiding the uber-competitive rat race that is preschool admissions in New York City—my husband and I uprooted our preordained life in our hometown and moved halfway across the world to Hong Kong.

I didn't know exactly what I was looking for when we got on that plane as a family with two toddler sons. And I didn't know what to expect. But I *did* want my kids to be worldly, compassionate, inspired, and passionate about learning. I wanted them to be exposed to different cultures and develop empathy for different ways of thinking.

The years we spent abroad, starting in Hong Kong, then Shanghai, and then Tokyo, opened our eyes to new experiences and ideas in ways I could never have anticipated. Perhaps the biggest surprise of all was how well all of my children—three of them by the time we returned to the States—thrived in the distinct culture and education system in China and Japan. Instead of enrolling my kids in international schools meant to attract English-speaking expatriate families, I sent them to the local public schools. They transitioned from new culture to new culture, from public school to public school. Schools in Asia often seemed bare-bones and institutional from the outside, lacking heat, indoor toilets, and the technology that is almost inevitable at their

American counterparts. Yet these schools ultimately gave my children some of the best educational experiences I could have hoped for.

As I saw how different, yet immensely effective, the school systems were in Asia, I was motivated to further my own education. While living in Shanghai, I returned to school for a master's degree in comparative international education and became an education journalist and speaker in Tokyo.

The result was that *I* got quite the schooling over those ten years. My master's course work, coupled with my firsthand experience as a parent of children enrolled in public schools in China and Japan, was eye-opening. I witnessed how the old-school education practices that had long fallen out of vogue in the United States, like rote memorization, gave my children an unparalleled knowledge base. I saw how the cultural priorities in China, like competitive learning, and in Japan, like the whole child philosophy and the way the community watches out for children, allowed me to trust the education system in a way my friends back home couldn't.

But I hadn't realized how sharp the contrast was until we returned home, and it became sadly apparent that our top-rated public school was nowhere near able to pick up where the Asian schools left off. By then, my sons were placing two years ahead in math, and their California schools weren't prepared to challenge them. My middle son, Charles, had no fewer than five teachers in the course of fifth grade. Coming from the structure, rigor, and tried-and-true pedagogical methodologies I'd seen in China and Japan, this felt unnervingly chaotic. And I realized that this messy system is something that every American parent must wrestle with. Many of us don't know any other way—there's proof education can work so much better.

Thanks to our immersive experience in Asia, I know what public schools are capable of and that we should do better by our children. I believe we can.

My goal with this book is to empower you, my readers, to take the educational philosophies and practices that work so well in China and

Japan and incorporate them in your own homes and classrooms. I want you to better understand how the education system works in the United States, so that you can more effectively advocate for your child. I want to offer you the tools to give your children a truly world-class education.

But first, I'll tell you a bit more about me.

One of my first assignments for my master's was to take a deep dive into my personal educational history to reflect on my own personal subjectivity, which could color my studies and learning. My professors called it the lens through which we see things: facing my upbringing would help me to understand my own background and biases. As you read this book, I ask you to think about your educational lens. Whatever your beliefs may be, I ask that you stay open to new ideas and unfamiliar practices you may find here.

Like religion and politics, education is one of the most contentious dinner table topics; we all have our own experiences that we can blindly and staunchly defend. Yet as disparate as they may be, we *all* strive to do right by our children—and that includes giving them the best possible education—while working through our pasts.

Because I inevitably bring a particular lens and perspective to writing this book, it seems only right to let you know what my childhood and education were like. Here is my lens.

For the first five years of my life, I lived in suburban Greenwich, Connecticut, with my parents: a Japanese immigrant mother who barely spoke English and a doting American father who was twenty-five years her senior. My father was nearing retirement at the time they separated, and I moved to Manhattan with my mother at the end of first grade, where she became a real estate broker and investor.

My mom was completely hands-off about my formal education, partly because she didn't speak English but mostly because the US education system was culturally foreign to her. I missed lots of school events because she couldn't understand the notices. From the beginning, I was expected to be responsible for all my own homework, studying, and projects. As an immigrant in the United States on a green card, she endeavored to raise me to be a "self-sufficient survivor." She would say, "You never know when I could drop dead." (She's always been blunt.)

Every weeknight, I practiced the piano and studied Japanese with her by my side. She took me to a music conservatory every Friday after school and to Japanese school every Saturday. I had little time for playing with friends. I always felt a little out of place socially anyway; I was the only person in my grade whose second language was English (my first is Japanese), and I attended public school in Japan every summer, which also made me feel different.

For as long as I can remember, I was the poster child for school international days, teaching classmates perfunctory origami lessons. And like the stereotypical Asian, I won talent shows with the most recognizable or complicated piano pieces in my repertoire at the time. But I was envious of the most entertaining skits, like Jake Donovan and his fourth-grade boy band, who donned towels and lip-synched the Go-Go's "We Got the Beat." Jake was so cool, even imitating Belinda Carlisle.

In many ways, his was the world I wished I belonged to. Without many social connections and without siblings, I spent a good amount of time alone. Although my mother limited my television time, I snuck in my fair share when she went out in the evenings. Jack, Janet, and Chrissy on *Three's Company* were like friends to me. TV gave me a priceless sneak peek into American culture beyond my small circle of friends and classmates. At home, we lived as a Japanese family, speaking the language and eating rice with chopsticks. I may have been born American, but I was always aware that I didn't quite fit in.

I studied *The Brady Bunch* and *Family Ties* to get clues about what typical American families were like. I called my dad "Pa" like Laura Ingalls Wilder on *Little House on the Prairie* did. I wanted freckles and braids just like Melissa Gilbert on that show and went through a stage when I wore a bonnet to sleep. These shows rounded out my education. TV offered me a connection to what I wistfully thought of as a "normal life" in the United States. So please indulge me here, as each of my chapters is named after one of my favorite TV shows.

My mother, born in ravaged post–World War II Japan, worked incredibly hard to be admitted to university in Tokyo, making herself a complete outlier as a woman of that era in Japan. She invested every cent in her only child—me, a generation and world apart—to yield the highest outcomes, like she had produced for herself. Meanwhile, my father doted on me like a loving grandfather on our weekend visits, spoiling and rarely disciplining me—a sharp contrast to my mother's love that was so focused on my achievements. In addition to his love, I also experienced his slowly declining health. On May 19, 1986, while I was in seventh grade, he passed away.

Shortly after that, my mother's financial issues forced us to move to the suburbs, and I attended Rye Country Day, a private school in Westchester County, New York. School began to feel like a chore—a means to an end. It had to do with figuring out how to get A's to make it to a good college. I did well enough to be accepted at an Ivy League college. But I had somehow made it that far without having developed much intellectual curiosity. I also managed to graduate from high school never having taken a European history, geography, or physics class. I felt like I cheated the system.

It was in Asia, not the United States, where I began to see critically outside of my own experience. Zooming out to see the bigger global picture, I gained an appreciation and understanding of all the wonders and pitfalls of the US system. It taught me that it was possible to give my children the best parts of my upbringing—growing up bilingual, bicultural, and resilient—but also to help them take ownership of their education, love learning, and love school, which I had not done.

My master's program was the most challenging and exhilarating two-year academic experience of my life, rocking my view of everything I thought I understood about privilege and opportunity. That's what planted the seeds for this book.

I expected to learn about other countries' educational systems, but I was surprised to learn so much about my own. I grew increasingly disillusioned by our educational system, which keeps the wealthy on top while stacking up barriers in front of the majority. How could we compete on a global level if we were not developing leadership equally and fairly among our overall population, instead of just from a privileged few? Worse, how can this leadership guide the nation if it can't relate to the experiences of average working people? The belief that education is the "great equalizer" felt like nonsense. Until that point, I'd never stopped to imagine what my life might have been like if I'd been born into poverty, with parents (or foster parents, or other guardians) who didn't or couldn't support my learning. I'd never seriously examined my own privilege before. Understanding the barriers to education and the inequalities—at home and throughout the rest of the world—made me see things more clearly.

Ironically, it was when I landed back in America in 2016, in time for my children to start second, fifth, and seventh grades, that I experienced the worst culture shock of my life. We came back to a world with erectile dysfunction commercials during family programming, a blazing inferno of a presidential election, and a culture that worships football players but rejects science. After spending years in cultures where it's cool to be smart, I had almost forgotten how different attitudes are here.

The most disappointing part was the school district itself, which was ranked the number one school district in California. Because the United States lacks a centralized federal policy for almost every aspect of public education, each state has its own funding formula for public schools. Districts can draw on local tax revenues to supplement what they receive in federal and state funds. This gives wealthier districts more leeway in hiring teachers; they can offer higher salaries to more qualified candidates, while districts in tax-poor areas cannot. It had never before occurred to me to question the way our educational dollars are spent so unevenly among different districts, even ones that are right next to each other.

So much about what we encountered in Palo Alto made me want to pull my hair out—technology overuse in the classroom, low academic expectations, wasteful expenditures instead of investment in teacher professional development, high teacher turnover, corporate influence over public education—that I realized I needed to do something about it. That something is this book.

To write this book, I drew on my experiences and graduate education, but I also spoke to thought leaders and educators to get their perspectives at seemingly countless education conferences throughout the United States. I discussed the challenges facing our schools with professors in our colleges of education, school principals, teachers, PTA leaders, school board members, state legislators, and our nation's legislators on Capitol Hill. While in Palo Alto, I also took advantage of the experts in my own backyard at Stanford University. I feel privileged to have been able to speak with some of the top minds in the country about the challenges facing our education system. They have given me hope, and they have pushed me to look deeper for long-lasting solutions to our most complex educational problems.

In addition, I visited schools all over the country to see what's working and what isn't. I traveled to schools in Palo Alto and nearby Los Angeles; in New York City and elsewhere in New York State; in Utah, Florida, Texas, and Washington, DC. I toured thriving and struggling public schools, including charter schools and magnet schools. I visited some of the country's most elite private schools in New York City and boarding schools in New England.

The United States is a wonderfully diverse nation, where life can be very different from one area to the next. Each child's education is determined not at the federal or even state level but often at the district/local and school and even classroom level. Because of our country's size and demographics, no one solution can meet the needs of every individual, every family, and every community. But there's a lot to be learned from the nations that have surpassed us in education, helping us to shift our perspectives.

During our time in Asia, all three of my kids loved learning; they became trilingual (English, Mandarin, and Japanese) and multicultural. Ultimately, the alternatingly crushing and euphorically rewarding experience transformed me into a stronger and far more empathetic woman and mother than I ever thought I could be.

To be sure, no school system is perfect. Even at the best schools along our travels there were downsides. In Shanghai, there was a lack of creativity, and in Tokyo, gender-based expectations of girls limited their aspirations about possible career paths. And the pressure and demands that Japanese schools place on mothers is hugely problematic for working moms. The common theme I found in Asia was a reverence for education that is cemented by a unified team of teachers, parents, and students. I learned to appreciate seeing preschoolers sitting at desks, engrossed in academic puzzles. I grew to find joy seeing my children following the opposite of a personalized learning curriculum; instead, every student in the entire nation in the same grade learned the same material at the same time. Children's success is not left to chance, corporate interests, or the socioeconomic backgrounds of their parents.

The Chinese and Japanese high school graduates I've met are literate, independent, hardworking, and disciplined. Their knowledge comes from well-respected teachers, high expectations, mastery of content, and problem solving. They finish middle school two academic years ahead of US students in math.[1]

Schools in top-performing countries teach to mastery. That was the big *aha!* for me: in the United States, whether students score a 58 or a 98 on a test, they all move on to the next lesson just the same.

Children also learn different social values in Asia. In Japan, students take care of their own schools: they are the janitors and lunch servers, and every day they have classroom chores to attend to in addition to their studies. They're also expected to get around on their own by the time they start elementary school at age six; they walk to and from school and take public buses and trains unsupervised, a freedom that most American parents couldn't imagine for safety's sake—or legal reasons. One Maryland couple nearly lost custody of their children for letting them visit a park alone in 2015![2]

By the end of our journey, we had lived in three of the world's top global economies: the United States, China, and Japan. Each of these countries plays a tremendous role in the financial, industrial, and technological systems we all depend on. And the outcomes of their respective education systems support the economic success of these countries and our greater world. Both Shanghai (the City of Shanghai participated separately in 2009 and 2012) and Japan have consistently earned top scores on the Programme for International Student Assessment (PISA), an international test administered by the Organisation for Economic Co-operation and Development (OECD) every three years.

In the 2015 test, US students scored slightly above average in reading (497 points out of 600) and science (496) compared to other OECD nations, and 20 points below the OECD average in math (470). Japan scored 516, 538, and 532, respectively.[3]

There are legitimate concerns that the place of the United States as a global leader will fall if we can't reconceptualize our education system to offer all citizens a fair shake at top-quality schooling. Show me a school, and I'll show you that country's future.

At the end of our decade of nomadic living, I knew it was time to bring our family back home to the United States.

I wanted to instill in my children an intrinsic sense of their identity as US citizens and to appreciate how that citizenship afforded us opportunities to live overseas. After returning, however, I found myself longing for the days when my children came home with graphite all over their sleeves from writing all day, teachers seemed to know my children better than I did, and the popular kids were the smart kids. I don't have all the answers about how to fix our educational ills, but I can provide a unique perspective, backed up by academic research and personal and professional observations, on the local school systems in three top-performing nations.

Along with sharing my family's experiences in this book, I also provide practical and actionable advice so you can take what I learned and make it work for you. I explain the ins and outs of school districts, demystify what to look for when evaluating a school, and suggest ways to enhance your children's school learning with valuable home activities and supplemental programs. I realize that not all of this advice will be useful for every reader, so take what you want from this book—what feels right for you and your family. I want you to feel truly empowered when it comes to your child's education.

My hope is that by reading this book you will come away with ideas for how to improve the educational experiences of the children in your lives, whether you're a parent, teacher, grandparent, or even a bystander on the subway. And I hope to make you laugh a bit along the way as you share my moments of stumbling, falling, and picking myself back up.

This is the book I wish I'd had before we boarded that plane to Hong Kong. You don't have to spend a decade abroad to gain this knowledge. I did, and I'm ready to share.

NEW YORK

2006

James: About 2 years old

Charles: About 8 months old

CHAPTER 1

The Wonder Years

The Wild World of NYC Preschools

M y husband, Alex, and I were at an authentic hole-in-the-wall Thai restaurant in the Murray Hill section of Manhattan having dinner with a couple looking to buy an apartment in New York. Despite priding myself on being the most worldly in the bunch, I was embarrassed to be the only one who couldn't get through the tom yung goong soup without tearing up from the spice.

"We want to be within a few blocks of Brick Church," the woman explained. "We've already started going there."

Right away, I knew why: they were both highly educated, ambitious Harvard Business School graduates with a newborn baby girl. A lot of the time, what followed was talked about coyly with a little restraint, but not today. "We're just going there for the preschool," she said with a New Jersey accent, loud enough for the entire restaurant to hear. "It says that to qualify for preference, families must have joined the church at least two years prior to November 1 of the year they are applying. So we're on time!"

I forced a smile that hid my sense of resignation. The Brick Presbyterian Church ran one of New York City's most exclusive preschools, and the city did not offer universal public pre-K at that time. Some NYC preschools are reputedly harder to get into than Stanford (which now has an annual 4 percent acceptance rate), and that may be true. Thou-

3

sands of parents apply each year, and some schools have fewer than thirty openings a year, including the ones reserved for church members and legacy kids (kids whose parents or siblings went to the school). Applying for preschool in New York is a competitive, Olympic-sized sport.

But joining a church so your kid can go to school there later? Ugh. I was pretty sure they weren't Presbyterian before.

More to the point, the school spelled it out clearly: you not only had to be a member of the church but a "financially contributing member" for at least two years to get preference into the preschool. Even then there were no guarantees. So this couple could buy an apartment in the "right" location, switch religions, throw big checks into the collection plate each Sunday, and still possibly not get a spot. It felt that they were selling their souls to get their kid into preschool—and their daughter was only five months old at the time!

That didn't seem to faze them.

"She'll go to Brick, and then Spence or Chapin for kindergarten," the woman declared. These are two of New York's most exclusive all-girls' schools. "I mean," she continued, "it's all about the exmissions."

Exmissions. The taboo word for where the kids get admitted after they finish preschool. Most NYC private preschools have an exmissions staff that works with parents to guide them on how to write "first-choice" letters, addressing which of their child's strengths to emphasize and which weaknesses could be framed as positives, and which ongoing school would be the best match.

"Then our daughter can go on to Harvard, like we did!" Well, she didn't actually say this, but she may as well have. She was beaming with pride as she was setting her wheels in motion. Her husband didn't beam back. He was stoically British, and she was a boisterous American. Despite the fact that both were still using their Harvard email addresses a decade after graduation—the email version of vanity plates—it was an odd pairing. She went on about how the preschool was going to set their daughter up for life because it was connected to the best schools. Finally she said, "Garrod! Stop kicking me under the table!"

4

I felt like we were in a *Saturday Night Live* skit.

And the thing is, as ill as I felt about the whole thing and as much as I wanted to bolt out of the restaurant, I didn't hate her for it. They were doing exactly what they aspired to do. They were making it in Frank Sinatra's "if you can make it here, you'll make it anywhere" New York. They had their eye on the prize, and that's the *only* way to get ahead in this city. I got it.

My aspirations for my family were different. I didn't know exactly what they were yet; I just knew by my visceral reaction to this couple that I needed to change the preordained path I was starting down with my two children, where they would face no real-life hiccups.

I had two little boys—a baby and a toddler—and I would be lying if I said I wasn't getting nervous about the whole school thing. I had thought that our midtown apartment wasn't close enough to most of the "good" preschools uptown. I had also started asking my husband if we should move. It was hard not to get caught up in the craziness, even when I knew it was craziness, because what other option did we have?

All I knew about education came from growing up in New York City. How did parents in other places navigate this time in their kids' lives? Were moms in Oregon also trying to navigate which preschools their one-year-old would go to and how they'd finagle their way in?

We were competing with every other parent around who was moderately to obscenely wealthy, some of whom could pledge major donations to the school prior to admissions (which, of course, schools all say has no bearing on acceptances. *Clearly*). We were even competing with celebrities.

Aside from that, parents also hired counselors to guide them through the preschool application process. For $150 to $400 an hour, some parents hire a private coach to guide them through the applications. For preschool! This counseling runs the gamut depending on what you are willing or able to spend. You can hire a consultant who will know how to get your six- and sometimes seven-figure donation into the right hands at the right school, or you can work with a consultant just to help you figure out how to apply to a New York City public middle school.

In addition to hiring consultants, parents had their kids take "preschool prep" classes so they'd do better in interviews—even for interviews for admission to preschool. Sometimes they call it a playdate, but it's clearly an interview. Most of the time they talk to the kids with the parents in the room; a couple of schools bring the kids to a different room while the parents quietly have heart palpitations in fear of how Avery or June is going to screw up her chances of finger painting at *this* elite academy. Heaven help her if she proves that she isn't reliably potty-trained.

Some preschools want docile kids. Some are looking for creative thinkers. They all want bright kids, of course. And each school has a cutoff date for birth dates. Some will take only 3.1s or 3.4s. I never understood if that meant 3 years and 1 month old or 3 and a tenth years old.

There are private preschool admission workshops that run more than a year in advance. And a directory of Manhattan's private preschools, with more than four hundred pages, is available on Amazon. *People are not messing around here.* They are asking former US presidents to write letters of recommendation. They're hiring ghostwriters to write admissions essays. They're trying to get their toddlers to learn an instrument or a second language just so they can claim a special skill to stand out among the other applicants.

Not only is it extremely difficult to get into these schools, there's also huge competition *just to get an application.* When I was starting this process in 2004, before the age of online applications, there was one simple system: the day after Labor Day, you had to call the admissions line at each preschool just to request an application. The school limited the number of applications because each completed application (with application fee—*cha-ching!*) also meant a tour of the school and potentially a family interview. The administrators simply didn't have the time to do that for the thousands of people who would apply for the very limited open slots.

You needed to have other people helping you to cover your list of potential preschools. Your best friend might call Bank Street, Madison Avenue Presbyterian, and Christ Church, while your mother-in-law covered Episcopal, Brick, and All Souls, and you handled Horace Mann, Montessori, and, of course, the 92nd Street Y if you're Jewish.

You had to figure these things out early. Without a plan, your child would never get into the right school and would never become the neurosurgeon she could have been.

It was important. This was our children's future on the line.

What I believed intuitively then—and would later verify as a fact—was that socioeconomic status is the most important factor in a child's education in the United States. People with a lot of money can send their kids to the best private school or live in areas with great public schools and supplement their kids' education with outside enrichment opportunities, starting from birth. People with little money or education may not know how to direct their children toward academic excellence; they also likely don't have a genuine choice about which schools their kids will attend.

Students in the United States are affected by socioeconomic backgrounds more than students from other developed nations are. According to Miles Corak, an economics professor at the City University of New York, the intergenerational earnings elasticity (IGE) has gone up in the United States. The IGE measures the correlation between parents' income and their children's income in later life. Ideally, the number would be zero, which would mean their children's earning capacity wasn't depending on their parents'; this would indicate that everyone has equal access to mobility. The US IGE has increased from less than 0.3 fifty years ago to nearly 0.5 today, which is higher than in almost every other developed economy.[1]

A 2015 report from the Pew Charitable Trusts and the Russell Sage Foundation went even further in examining the IGE in the United

States. The authors estimated that there is indeed a high correlation between parents' income and their children's income in the United States today. For adults in the 50th to 90th percentile for income, their male adult children have an IGE of 0.68 and their female children, 0.63. The report concludes that "approximately two-thirds of parental income differences within this region of the income distribution persist into the next generation."[2]

Schools are one important way to intervene in cycles of inequality. If all schools are funded equitably, we will see major differences in outcomes. By "equitably," I don't mean that every school gets the same exact funding; each school should be funded according to the needs of its particular student population.

With equitable funding, top teachers will be more likely to work in impoverished areas, and all students will have access to appropriate resources to support their mental, physical, emotional, and social growth, according to their needs. Every student can thrive and grow. Based on my experiences in China and Japan, where teachers are widely respected and supported with adequate economic resources, I suggest this is possible in the United States as well.

The Hamilton Project, an economic policy initiative based at the Brookings Institution, delved deeper into the relationship between poverty and education in the United States. They found that kids living in poverty score worse on standardized tests, have lower graduation rates, and are far less likely to go to college, which means that their earning potential is significantly reduced.[3] The difference is striking: *less than 25 percent* of fourth graders who qualify for free or reduced-price lunch at school scored proficiently on the standardized math exam, whereas about 60 percent of other fourth graders score at or above proficiency levels. In other words, the vast majority of low-income kids are failing to meet standards—whether they get promoted to the next grade or not (and they usually do, even when they're not ready to move on).

Performance among kids in low-income households dropped when they made up more of the school's population. When just a few kids qualified for free lunch in a school, those kids performed better than those in districts where low income is the norm.

So how are US schools funded? Ninety percent of money for education comes from state and local budgets,[4] so less tax money is available in impoverished areas. Schools are counting on scarce federal dollars (less than 10 percent of the total for every school in the United States on average) to make up some of the difference. There are *huge* differences in educational spending per student when you add up state, local, and federal dollars—for example, New York ($21,206 per year on the primary and secondary levels) versus Utah ($6,575) and North Carolina ($8,687)—even after accounting for cost of living differences.[5] Some districts spend their education dollars wisely, on, say, teacher training and textbooks, and others blow it on bells and whistles like bouncy chairs (to be discussed in Chapter 12).

Spending on public education in the United States took a nosedive after the Great Recession beginning in 2007. By 2015, three-quarters of the education cuts carried out between 2009 and 2013 were restored, mostly in the form of increased local and state taxes collected. Federal contributions have remained steady at just below 10 percent. As with the distribution of education funding in general, the uptick in funding has not been distributed evenly among states and districts. For example, California raised its education spending 10 percent between 2013 and 2015, but it still spends $1,000 less per student than the national average.[6]

While it is easy to point to economic inequality generally as the source of our troubled education system, we can pinpoint where disparities contribute most to educational gaps. Many factors are at play here—for example:

- **Preschool.** Getting a jump on learning by engaging young children's brains as early as possible has been proven to have a major impact on kids. According to researchers at Harvard's Center on the Developing Child, "more than 1 million new neural connections form every second" in a child's first few years.[7] Take advantage of your child's amazing potential for development in his or her early years. You can pick a preschool with an academic focus, or make sure you're providing academic support at home.

- **Teacher training.** Every teacher should be well qualified to teach students with a variety of learning styles, backgrounds, and challenges. It's hard to attract well-qualified teachers to impoverished areas: it can be more challenging to teach kids who are starting at a lower point, schools in low-income areas are often less secure, and teachers don't want to receive a lower salary. As it is, in 2017, the OECD reported that US middle school teachers on average made less than 60 percent of the salary of those in other professions with the same level of education; this number falls well below the OECD average of 88 percent.[8] In addition, in the face of shortages, US schools in most states lower standards for teachers, granting emergency credentials that typically require only a bachelor's degree and no teaching experience. You can guess how that turns out. (I'll come back to this in Chapter 9.)

- **Parental involvement.** Parents are becoming more involved with their children's education, but there are still challenges. Often parents have a single-minded focus on supporting their children's *schools* (via the PTA, for example), while not attending directly to their kids' *learning*.[9] Also, parental involvement can look quite different outside the school setting. Parents who can afford it may enroll their kids in private lessons, tutoring programs, educational camps, and so on, extending their finances to the limit. Some parents take out loans and work second jobs to pay for these programs. In addition, many towns and cities have free enrichment programs at museums, libraries, and even on school grounds when classes aren't in session.

- **Kids' responsibilities.** Kids living in poverty often have extra responsibilities compared to other kids; they may be expected to do more work around the house, babysit siblings, run errands, even work outside the home. They may also have additional stresses; if they're worried about where they're going to sleep or whether they're going to eat that night, it's understandably more difficult for them to focus on schoolwork.

Back in New York, I had narrowed our choices down to academic preschools as opposed to play-based, Montessori, or progressive schools. It was what I felt most comfortable with and what I felt I could best support at home.

Although there were no guarantees, my husband and I were much more likely than many others to get our kids into our preferred ongoing schools later simply by riding the wave of our parents' choices—an unfortunate truth about our elitist and nonmeritocratic educational system.

My family had significant advantages that made me less worried about our school options in New York City. I had lived in New York since second grade and had attended Dalton, one of the nation's best private schools, through middle school. My husband's family was dripping with academic credentials; he had attended Trinity, another of the best private schools in the country. It's sort of the Ivy League of K–12, and many parents want their kids to go there because they often lead to Ivy League colleges. It had worked for my husband and me (we wound up at, respectively, Princeton and Dartmouth), and I figured it would work for our kids too.

Being an alumnus carried weight, which was why we were suddenly getting so many playdate requests. Conversations with acquaintances from work and social groups with young kids would inevitably find their way to it:

Little Timothy's mom: Where did you grow up?
Me: In New York City, actually.
Little Timothy's mom: Oh, really? Where did you go to school?
Me: Dalton.

Little Timothy's mom: How nice! [Pause.] You know, I've been meaning to ask you and your family to come over for dinner. Are you free on Friday night?

I was fooled the first couple of times into thinking these were real invitations to connect just for the sake of friendship, but before long, I realized these parents were often courting us to find out if we could pull any strings for their kids. *Why would I do that when I'm stressing about how to get my own kid in during the same year?* I wondered.

At least we got some nice home-cooked meals in the process.

These experiences were only slightly less shocking than dinner parties where parents discussed how much donation money it took to get kids into the Ivies. Right after "Please pass the butter," came "How much does it take to get into Harvard?"

"Legacy gives you a leg up, but if you give a bone, your chances go up to 75 percent." (*Bone* is code for $1 million.)

"When you give $5 million to Harvard, you get a nice letter of thanks, but if you give even $500,000 to Middlebury, the president flies to your house to thank you."

"It's much cheaper to get into Dartmouth, though, right? Teru, how much do you have to give to get in there?"

"I don't know," I mumbled. It was jarring to hear it put out there so openly. I wanted to believe the majority of students got in based on their academic credentials, despite mounting evidence that money and athletics were key—and that status begets status.

When the *Wall Street Journal* analyzed the data for the University of Notre Dame, the University of Virginia, and Georgetown University, reporters found that legacy applicants have twice the odds of acceptance compared to the overall applicant pool; that rises to four times the odds at Princeton. But Harvard "wins" this race, with legacy applicants admitted at *five times* higher rates.[10] Certainly many of these kids do have the credentials to be admitted owing to the high level of academic attainment of their parents, but so do many other applicants. At a time when many top schools claim to be diversifying, this preference for legacy applicants is a smoke-and-mirrors game that favors keeping the status quo in place, which means that the wealthy will continue taking up spots at elite schools. And this is also at a time when US university tuitions are skyrocketing and increasingly cost prohibitive.

Education has the potential to be the great equalizer. Horace Mann, the nineteenth-century education reformer influential in the creation of US public schools, believed that a good education was a birthright of all children and would create social harmony. (Ironically, tuition at the highly esteemed private Horace Mann School in New York City is $51,000 per year as of this writing.) Education becomes an equalizer only when *equitable* resources are applied to all schools, not when the wealthy districts get all the best teachers, best libraries, and so on.

Former Connecticut governor Dannel Malloy talked to *U.S. News & World Report* about why Connecticut ranks so well in education (number three in the country in college readiness of high school students, number one in twelfth-grade literacy, and number three in overall education of the populace at large), and he pointed first to its preschool enrollment, which is ranked second in the country.[11] "I've been a big advocate of pre-K," he said, "and closing the gap between people who can otherwise afford to pay privately for pre-K and those folks who live largely in urban areas but some rural areas who have not been able to send their children to pre-K. We've created thousands of additional education spots for them because we know that the best educational buck spent is in the early years. Having kids start school earlier leads to better results at 12th grade."

He's absolutely right: kids' brains are most primed to learn when they're very young, and yet we do little to take advantage of that time. Preschool shouldn't be optional in this country. Why do kids in wealthy families get to start their schooling up to three years earlier than kids whose parents can't afford private preschool if there are no free pre-school spots available? If we're ever going to live up to the idea that education is the great equalizer, it starts there: providing an equal start with qualified teachers for all.

Children who go to school earlier than kindergarten have signifi-cantly better outcomes than children who do not, all the way through adulthood. A recent analysis of twenty-two high-quality studies from 1960 through 2016 found that children who attend early childhood education (ECE), defined as any schooling from birth to age five, go on to have lower rates of special education placement (a difference of 8 percentage points), lower rates of grade repetition (7.9 percentage points difference), and higher high school graduation rates (9.4 per-centage points difference).[12] Of course, people who graduate from high school and beyond tend to earn more than those who do not, so what you earn as an adult can be traced back partly to what you learned be-fore you were five years old. Researchers estimate a minimum rate of return of three to four dollars for every dollar spent on early childhood education.[13]

In the United States, the median annual salary of ECE teachers is $28,990 a year,[14] a figure not likely to tempt those who could earn more in other fields. The average education level of an ECE teacher is a two-year associate's degree.

In addition, preschool programs are different in different states, with some reaching a far greater percentage of the low-income stu-dent population through programs like Head Start, others with more limited hours, using different curricula, and so on. Head Start is a com-prehensive federal program that offers low-income parents access to free preschool, in addition to health and nutrition services. According to a 2016 report from the Hamilton Project, Head Start increased high school graduation by participants up to 20 percentage points.[15]

Formal education at a school and learning at home in a child's early years literally sets a child up to learn for the rest of her life. We cannot recover the early years of a child's brain development.

To be honest, I hadn't substantially researched the significance of preschool when my first kid reached preschool age. I learned a lot of this information along the way, especially after my oldest, James, started preschool. In the process of writing this book, I have been able to combine my knowledge from enrolling my three kids in preschools in three countries, along with academic research. Here, I offer my suggestions for getting ready for the preschool years.

Prepping for Preschool

- Enroll your kids in an academic preschool if you do not plan to supplement academics at home. (For tips on supplementing at home, see Chapter 5, pages 78–79.)
- Look for ways to support your child's learning (academic, social, emotional) at home and at school.
- Read. Read. Read. All the time to your child. From an actual paper book. And discuss, even when you think she can't yet. Make eye contact, and use expression.
- Make free time for creative and unstructured play.
- Look for free preschool spots in your district well in advance of your child's start date.
- Seek out enrichment activities through local libraries, museums, community centers, concert halls, religious organizations, and so on, many of them free and open to the public.
- Form or join a parent support network for all the latest and greatest gossip, finds, and tips. You may find a group for your school on Facebook, but plan in-person meet-ups rather than relying on online posts. You'll learn insider scoops that people would never post in public. Introduce yourself to familiar-looking parents and expand your network to share issues and build resources.
- Learn about the elementary kindergarten curriculum in your district. What skills and activities can you practice with your child at home to

help her smoothly transition into kindergarten? For example, how familiar should she be with the alphabet? How high is she expected to count?

- Stay on top of the curricular pipeline and learning expectations from kindergarten (and through high school!). Ask teachers on day one for the curriculum for the year, and ask how it's followed or modified. Ask how children are assessed, which textbooks and resources will be used, and how you can support the learning at home.

The New York City private school culture made me want to scream. I listened to parents bad-mouth little children who got into the "good" preschools ("She's not even smart!"). I heard mothers act sweet to each other and then tear each other apart privately for applying here or there. At the same time, I felt insecure enough to get sucked into it. *What choice do I have?* I wondered.

I'm not sure if those preschool parents were proud of trying to pull strings to get advantages for their kids, but when everyone seems to be doing it, then you're *dis*advantaging your kid if you don't, right? And, frankly, we all do whatever we can to help our kids. But how was I supposed to teach my kids a moral code if *this* is what was all around us? Was I going to let them absorb the lesson that entitlement starts in preschool? That kids born into rich families get to skip the line and grab spaces at colleges they didn't necessarily earn their way into? That the most "successful" kids never have to deal with failures or frustrations?

Even John Allman, the headmaster of the esteemed and monied private school Trinity, openly acknowledged the issue in a bombshell letter to parents in 2017, referenced in a September 22, 2017, article in the *New York Times*: "Can Prep Schools Fight the Class War?" In it, Allman called for renewed efforts to build community by teaching children to "serve the common good and to give generously to others for the rest of their lives." Without more work toward socially redeeming purposes, he worried that parents look at Trinity as a "credentialing factory" and that its students will wind up as adults on "a comfortable perch atop a cognitive elite that is self-serving, callous, and spiritually barren." He even went so far as to worry that Trinity had become no more than a "very, very, very expensive finishing school" for the majority of its students.

These schools can create and sustain a pipeline, a path to top universities, and those who follow this path can eventually wind up with a job that pays at least as well as their wealthy parents' jobs. The pipeline isn't just about learning. It is also about access to more advantages. But there needs to be more awareness and social responsibility to the greater community.

The list of donors and current parents at some preschools is a who's who of Wall Street. I wasn't comfortable as a child or now as a parent surrounding my kids with privilege and excess, pressured to measure up socially. Yet I felt like I was swirling around in a vortex, getting closer and closer to the center. I resisted the pressure to insert my kids into a system that perpetuates inequality. I felt lucky to have escaped my own childhood without adopting those same values myself. But I didn't know how to get out without giving up on the idea of my children getting the best education. And I wasn't sure what "the best" education even really meant.

My own schooling at Dalton and later at Rye Country Day was excellent—the best money could buy. I felt confident taking tests and filling out applications for college. I won awards. I had the social capital to know who to ask for answers for any question I had.

On the flip side, along with that elevated education came snobbery and elitism all around me: black-tie bat mitzvahs at the Plaza Hotel in Manhattan on the weekend, holiday cards from classmates' families showing them in front of the Taj Mahal or at the Louvre on extravagant vacations, and a disdain for any of the 99 percenters who didn't have live-in housekeepers. And I remember the devastating personal blows I had to deal with, like my father's poor health and then his death, which made me feel even more different. Being bicultural and raised by a single immigrant mother added a deeper and sometimes painful dimension to my life. My schools were not diverse by any stretch of the imagination and made no effort to change their student body. I didn't wish the same experiences for my children, but I wanted my privileged Caucasian-looking children to earn grit their own way. I also wanted to raise them to embrace people from different cultures as their equals, in a way I never felt accepted as a child.

I wanted to give them experiences money *couldn't* buy, that would teach them culture, independence, and all the things kids don't learn when their parents are "networking" their childhood. But how could I?

It seemed that their whole future was preordained based on making the right chess moves now, even when those moves felt wrong. Why was I was falling into lockstep with the crowd around me? I'd never been a follower before, and my circumstances made me question everything.

Many people flee New York City when they have kids. They arrive there after college graduation for jobs, but then they get married, settle down, and wind up at a crossroads: Do they stay in this uber-competitive world, move to the suburbs, or go back to their hometown to raise kids? In New York, either you get out or you declare, "Game on!" and bare your teeth. But we had nowhere to go. This *was* our hometown.

Then Alex came home one day and dropped a bomb.

"I got an offer for a huge promotion."

"That's fantastic!"

"It's in Hong Kong."

I breathed in and out. Once.

"Let's go!"

That's all it took. I didn't need to think it through or weigh the pros and cons. I wanted a way off the crazy Manhattan ride, and this was it. Hong Kong! How better to completely shake things up? We could give our kids experiences money couldn't buy, and my children could start their education in a place I was familiar with: Asia. What could be better?

It was so spur of the moment that I didn't even know what I expected to find. But Hong Kong didn't scare me at all because as a kid I'd spent summers in Japan visiting my grandmother, and I loved it; I figured Hong Kong would be very similar. Japan had its downsides, of course—it's largely culturally homogeneous, with often inflexible gender roles—but I respected it a lot because of its community-driven values and work ethic. It's what led me to be an Asian studies major in college. (There were obviously big gaps in my education, considering I couldn't imagine much of a difference between Tokyo and Hong Kong. I discovered later just how ill informed I was.)

Alex had also majored in Asian studies. He studied Mandarin long before many people in the United States realized they should learn it. China seemed of little importance to the global economy when he was in school, and it was unusual for a white guy to learn the language. But he was a bit of a quirky intellectual.

When we'd met at a mutual friend's wedding in 2001, he wasted no time letting me know his intentions that night: "If this goes well, we'll be living in China one day." Neither of us realized it would come to fruition five years and two babies later.

Hong Kong was not mainland China, but it was the gateway to Asia—a place lots of people describe as vibrant and modern. Alex was going to be the managing director of a Morgan Stanley division there—a position normally reserved for much older employees. It came with not only a significant salary bump but big housing perks. Little did they know that we would have made the move without any incentives at all just to get off the track we were on. The hunt for a New York City private preschool does things to a person. I joined many of my friends who left the city around the same time for various reasons; I just did it in a more dramatic way.

I wasn't expecting to live in Hong Kong forever: we'd spend a few years overseas and then come back to New York, I'd guessed, after skipping over the nerve-racking school competition. But I didn't mind that it was open-ended. It felt like a terrific adventure. We boxed up our apartment, packed our bags, and off we went.

This starry-eyed excitement was hindered only slightly when I found out that taking a two-year-old and an infant on a sixteen-hour international flight rates somewhere between waking up with a spider in your mouth and bathing in a tub of thumbtacks. But we got through it.

We were headed to a four-bedroom apartment on the water in scenic Repulse Bay, and I just knew it was the best thing we'd ever done. It was going to be *cultural*. It was going to be *genuine*. It was going to be *magical*.

And it totally was . . . for maybe twenty-four hours.

HONG KONG

2006–2010

James: About 2 to 6 years old

Charles: About 8 months to 4 years old

Victoria: 0 to 16 months old

CHAPTER 2

Gilligan's Island

*Stranded on a Tropical Island
with a Strange Cast of Characters*

Hong Kong is a densely populated subtropical area south of mainland China with a little of everything: beaches, hiking trails, skyscrapers. Only 7 percent of the island is zoned for housing, so the majority of residents live in apartments on a tiny part of the land.[1]

In early spring 2006, as we were planning our big move, Alex and I were on a tour of housing options and schools. Thankfully, as part of Alex's work assignment, the housing costs were being covered by his office.

We decided on a beautiful waterfront building that was all expatriate (expat, for short) housing, and many of the people living there had connections to Morgan Stanley. The building had all sorts of amenities on the property: gym, pool, tennis court, concierge.

During the tour with a real estate agent, we moved through the kitchen into a small L-shaped and cavelike room about the size of a pantry with no windows. The real estate agent informed me that it was the "helper room." *Is it even big enough for a mattress?* I wondered.

"I know what it looks like, but trust me. You should see where they come from!"

The agent said that line as if she'd said it hundreds of times before, every time an expat's jaw dropped. All the expats have live-in helpers, she informed us. Most come from the Philippines, some from Thailand

and Indonesia. Her explanation did not make me feel any better: "The help earn much more here."

"Helpers love to work for American families. You'll have your pick when you're ready to do interviews," she said.

"What do they do?" I asked.

"They care for the children, but they're also there for whatever you need—housekeeping, cooking, errands, anything. That's why we just call them 'helpers.'"

Morgan Stanley was picking up this wildly priced housing tab, and we would cover the helper. Helpers worked six days a week (except Sundays and holidays). I soon found out that some people hired more than one, so there was never a day without a helper.

"You just have to sponsor their visas, and they can't share a bedroom with a boy who's sixteen years old or above—but that doesn't apply to you," the agent explained. Sponsoring a visa meant committing to employ, house, and feed the person for two years. I let her words sink in. It was a luxury we could never afford in New York. It didn't seem so outrageous here, but it still felt questionable.

When we moved to Hong Kong a couple of months later, I quickly fell into a community full of friendly people who couldn't wait to introduce themselves. It was overwhelmingly welcoming, and I made lifelong friends during the four years we spent there. Since there's so much turnover in the expat communities, you constantly need to make new social contacts. It's a way of life.

Soon after moving in, the boys and I were invited to a mommy lunch at another expat's house. It was a casual midday invitation (or so I thought), and I showed up in a T-shirt and worn J. Crew khakis, hair still wet from the shower. Every other woman was in head-to-toe Chanel or the like, and I about died.

Oh no. Should I tell them that one of my kids got carsick on the way and bolt? Or that our clothing had yet to arrive from New York?

It was a multicourse sit-down affair with about five other women.

Where are all the kids? I wondered. The host had invited me and the kids, so I imagined everyone else got the same invitation.

Then, seemingly out of nowhere, a helper appeared.

"Sit and eat your lunch," she said. "I will take the children."

She swooped up James and Charles, my older and younger sons, respectively, and took them to an adjacent room that looked like a child's dining room and play space. I surveyed the rooms in amazement at the way the adults were so carefree. I noticed there were so many helpers that I wondered if they outnumbered the kids. Just about every child had a personal helper. Although I was already considering hiring a helper, this cemented my decision. And I realized I was going to have to do it soon if I wanted to have any social life.

I sat down and tried to relax, but within a couple of minutes, Charles was crying for me. He'd never been left with a stranger before and wasn't fond of the idea at all. I ended up eating at the kiddie table in the kiddie room, reassessing my life. Was I supposed to feel like Baby, Jennifer Grey's character in *Dirty Dancing*, stuck in the corner? We had left New York City to get away from the excess and social hierarchy, but this was more excessive than anything I had experienced there.

Within a few months, James started preschool at a for-profit international school taught partly in English and partly in Mandarin. Cantonese is the local language in Hong Kong, but because Alex spoke Mandarin, we felt we could support it at home.

I hadn't put too much study into preschools in Hong Kong. I chose the international school our broker and fellow expats told us was the best around where we lived. It hadn't yet occurred to me what international schools were all about. They're typically schools for expat children with classes that do not follow the national curriculum of the host country but rather the national curriculum of one's home country (whose government may subsidize its costs) or an internationally certified plan like the International Baccalaureate (IB). Typically these schools offer small class sizes and teach classes in English or the native language of the host nation. They're often far more expensive than local private preschools.

I was delighted to find that there was no application process, no finagling for position. You just send in your check, and you're in. We'd made an appointment to see a public Mandarin school, but we backed out when we got to the building. It was nicknamed The Prison, and for good reason—it was a bare-bones, run-down building that may have had barbed wire around the roof. Having visited the school, Alex and I turned to each other and agreed we would never send our children there.

Little did I know.

James attended Tutor Time for a year. It was a well-run school, but I grew increasingly concerned that he wasn't getting the immersive experience I had hoped for. Learning a second language isn't easy when you're surrounded by kids who speak English; it was slow going. I didn't have much to compare it to except my own youth, when I spoke only Japanese at home and then only English in school, which allowed me to become fluent in both. I worried that Tutor Time was an artificial construct in the middle of Hong Kong, which is *itself* an artificial construct—essentially a city-state island created by the British Empire for trade and finance, still politically conflicted with a sense of identity as either a part of China or not.

Who would my children become in this environment, where Western values, with a dash of Mandarin on the side, were king? Was this the Hong Kong experience I wanted them to have?

Just before I'd left New York, a friend gave me two books about "third-culture kids," highly mobile children who spend at least part of their childhood living in a country other than their parents'. Their first culture is the one from their parents' home country, the second is the culture they're currently living in, and the third is what they define as their personal culture, which may be a mix of the two. The books explored how these children face challenges because they have to create their own unique sense of "home," which is that third culture. As a result, they may not feel a strong sense of belonging anywhere, but are likely to be multilingual and multicultural.

I was offended by what I interpreted as an insinuation that I was damaging my kids—that they were going to spend their tender years without mooring, with no sense of identity. I wanted to raise them with a sense of being grounded in their American identity, with the kind of cultural adaptability that had been so formative in my own life, but I also wanted them to feel that they belonged. My goal was for them to be globally competent Americans, able to think about how their actions and choices have consequences for other people around the world and our environment. But now I wondered what identity they were going to pick up in Hong Kong. Being in an international school anywhere represents a buffer from the local culture.

Adding to my concerns, the kind of excessive living I was worried about back in Manhattan was much more amplified in Hong Kong. We attended a two-year-old's birthday party that felt more like a wedding with a cocktail reception, sit-down meal, speeches, and a professionally produced *This Is Your Life* film of the child's two apparently very long years of life. Students were chauffeur-driven to preschool. Some of the kids' helpers came to school and spoon-fed them their lunches, even in the upper elementary school grades. If they wanted *anything*, they got it. Expat families in Hong Kong were more spoiled than New York City ones.

I wasn't far removed from all that, though I wish I could say otherwise. Before we moved to Hong Kong, I was still getting my bearings as a new mom, juggling two kids under two in the urban jungle. Given Alex's demanding work schedule, which called him away for business travel frequently, the days were a blur of diaper changes, feedings, and balancing kids' nap schedules, which left me little time for myself. Most days I felt lucky if I took a shower! Then here I was in the plush land of helpers, where going without help was social suicide. It was ridiculously tempting.

We hired two helpers (a Filipino woman and, later, her niece) and a driver. In this environment, you never have to change a baby's diaper. You can take five-hour lunches. You never have to do a load of laundry, ever. I was surrounded by other women who spent their long lunch hours complaining about the help. I was new to motherhood, and this cushy lifestyle was in contrast to my having had extremely limited help with two little ones while in New York. Here, in Hong Kong, I was taking advantage of the chance to experience motherhood lite.

When I look back on those years in Hong Kong, I was deeply conflicted by the whole concept of "the help." These were often married people who were leaving behind spouses and children for two years or more so they could earn money. I had been so privileged to never have to consider functioning while missing my family. Were we wrong for taking advantage of their plight? Or was it good we were helping them out of poverty? I felt uncomfortable with the idea of someone else taking care of my kids whenever I pleased, yet I got swept up in it anyway.

I started taking tennis lessons and became good at it—because I practiced for two hours every day while the kids were napping or in school or cared for by the helpers. It was all so easy that we decided to have a third baby, a girl we named Victoria. I'm not sure we would have gone for number three if I had to do all the heavy lifting myself.

Before too long, I started to grow weary of life in paradise.

The friendliness of our neighbors soon became stifling. Everyone knew everyone else's business in the building. When I went down to check the mail, someone would stop me and say, "I hear Alex is in Singapore today!" or "I saw you playing tennis this morning." Although it was well intentioned, it began to feel invasive and gossipy. It didn't help that our building's walls seemed paper-thin and I could hear surrounding neighbors' toilets flushing and every incorrect note a child played while practicing the piano. I was accustomed to the privacy of New York, where no one bothers you unless you seek out conversation. Why had I decided on being surrounded by other expats? The answer is that I didn't know any better at the time.

I insisted that we find our own space outside an expat complex. The real estate agent thought we were crazy. Why would anyone want to give up the creature comforts we had? But within six months, we had moved out and rented a house in a beautiful, leafy, heavily Chinese neighborhood.

I was amazed to see that the houses all around us had armed guards—or, at a minimum, seven or so watchdogs. "The only problem with living in a house here is the burglaries. You have to get a dog. They don't break into houses with dogs," my expat friend Catherine said.

We went to the pound and rescued tick-covered Hanna, our wonderful German shepherd mix, whom we nursed back to health. But she did little to ease my mind about burglars. With Alex often gone for work, my paranoia about break-ins grew, and within a few weeks we asked our driver, Danny, to move in. Danny was a warm-hearted, funny man who loved our kids, and they loved him back. He taught the kids to ride bikes, and he was my go-to guy whenever I heard a noise. ("Danny! I think there's a burglar on the roof!" "Miss, there's no burglar on the roof." "Danny! Will you go check anyway?" He always climbed up, with my tennis racket in hand, to indulge me.)

Six Types of Parental Involvement in Education

One of the pivotal voices in education that has influenced me the most is Joyce Epstein, a professor of education and sociology at Johns Hopkins University. It was a thrill to meet her in person in April 2018 at the annual meeting of the American Educational Research Association. Her work has been the bedrock for all education researchers who study parent involvement in schools and communities.

Her often-cited Framework of Six Types of Involvement from 1992 offers strategies for parents to productively engage in their children's education. While the framework offers ideas for teachers as well as students, these are the six ideas specifically for parents:

1. **Parenting:** Creating a home environment that is conducive to children's learning. This includes participating in parent education programs targeting specific skills or knowledge, such as nutrition or technology, but also refers to ways that parents model pursuing their own continuing education, such as participation in GED programs or university courses.

2. **Communicating:** Effective communication between parents and their kid's school via phone, email, or in person, such as parent-teacher conferences, documents on school policies, and student report cards.

3. **Volunteering:** Parent participation at the school. Volunteer opportunities typically include being class parent, joining field trips, or offering other forms of classroom support, often related to student literacy. This can deepen the relationship between parent, teacher, and student.

4. **Learning at home:** The umbrella for all the activities at home directed toward student learning. Unlike parenting, these activities have an explicit focus on learning, such as keeping on top of homework and other assignments, academic goal setting, and when or how to use technology at home for academic purposes.

5. **Decision-making:** Collaborating with other parents in the PTA, attending local school board meetings, or participating in local or national advocacy groups. This involvement is directed toward systemic action at the school or district level.

6. **Collaborating with community:** Drawing on resources outside the home or school. These activities can include enrichment programs at local community centers, universities, or tutoring centers, for example. This involvement also refers to ways that parents are active in their community and help their children stay active as well through volunteering.

Around the time of our move in January, we decided to change direction in our great Hong Kong education experiment. Tutor Time was a good school, but it didn't offer an immersive experience. James's classmates were all English-speaking expats and half the classroom instruction was in English. I'd hired a tutor, Miss Mei, to come to the house three times a week for an hour to supplement James's Mandarin lessons, and she was terrific—but it still wasn't enough. I knew he was primed to learn anything, and I didn't want to waste this singular opportunity to put him in an environment where he would speak, read, and write Mandarin consistently and learn about the culture.

So, hats in hands, we were back at The Prison. This time we were begging them to let James into their preschool. It was a public magnet school, which meant that it was open to children of all backgrounds living in any part of the city. It was a popular school because of its focus on Mandarin. It required applications and interviews, just like the popular New York City magnet schools did.

When we visited the school, we were told we had missed the application deadline for the following year, and there were no remaining spots. Mandarin had suddenly become so popular that this once-struggling school had become a hot ticket. "Please, give him a chance," Alex asked in Mandarin.

For the next three afternoons, we dressed well and politely camped out in front of the admissions office. When someone peeked out, we'd ask, "Any updates?" or "Is there a chance we can be seen today?" Whenever they said they were busy, we'd just say, "No problem. We'll wait," or "We'll come back tomorrow."

Sitting there for three afternoons in a row meant they were going to have to deal with us one way or another: either kick us out or give James a shot. I was banking on the latter, and eventually I was right.

We had an interview time for that weekend, and a team of four teachers and the head of admissions all gathered to interview James, to find out if he was special enough to warrant this opportunity. I had to think fast about something that would make him stand out.

"Ask him about the bus routes! Ask him how to get anywhere you want to go."

James had memorized two hundred pages of Hong Kong bus routes.

"How do you get from Central to Causeway Bay?" a teacher asked.

"Peak or off-peak?" James said. "And regular bus or mini-bus? Express or local?" He did this all in Mandarin, so Alex translated for me.

I sat back and watched as my three-year-old son showed the adults in the room exactly what I hoped he would. In just a few moments, he made it clear that he was inquisitive and a sharp study. Several teachers gathered around to watch this little spectacle. I hoped they wouldn't be able to resist him. Eventually they saw us to the door and said, "Thank you. We'll let you know."

James has absolutely no recollection of the event.

I was still biting my nails when I described the day's events to a fellow New Yorker friend in Hong Kong who'd also sent her daughter to Tutor Time.

"Are you crazy?" she asked.

I heard that a lot. The more polite way of saying it was, "You're so brave," but they really meant the same thing. Few people could understand why I'd want to drop my child off at a bare-bones local school when I had the option of a cozy international school with our previous neighbors. I couldn't explain it at the time, but I knew this was the better fit for our family. I didn't want to spend years living in Hong Kong and know nothing about the local culture, including its schools. I still wasn't sure about the whole third-culture concept, but I knew that this experience would be a true piece of James's identity as he grew up. He'd be able to say that he lived and studied with the locals in Hong Kong rather than "visiting" with the other international kids.

Opening the mail from the school was nearly as exciting as my college admissions process. He'd gotten in. I was so relieved.

Scoping Out a New School

Insist on observing a class because a school's mission is just lip-service until you see it in action. Watch the interactions between teachers and students. Speak to current families there to get the real scoop. They are often the greatest resource because they know the climate and classroom teachers. Most important, children are the reflections of their parents, so the parents are the best indicator of the values and culture of the school.

Here are some questions to ask teachers, administrators, and parents:

- What are the teachers' backgrounds, and where were they educated and certified to teach?
- What is the teacher and administrator tenure policy and turnover? What is the average annual teacher turnover rate?
- How long have the members of the school's and district's leadership team been in place?
- How many days per month are children taught by a substitute teacher?
- How many students are in a class and per teacher?
- What is the daily routine or schedule?
- What is the curriculum, by subject, and how often does it change, and why?
- What are the behavioral and academic expectations of each child at each grade level?
- What electives are offered, who teaches them, and how often do they meet?
- Is there a second language or language immersion program?
- What resources are allocated to teacher professional development?
- What kind of discipline is expected of the children?
- How will your child be encouraged to be an individual there, and how will her identity be respected?
- Are there any supports or interventions when individual or groups of students are pulled out for more focused academic or other work? How is this organized?

- Are there options to accommodate your child's specific learning needs (more advanced classes, tutoring, English as a second language, time with the teacher after class)?
- Do children sit at desks or tables, or in another formation? Why?
- Is there homework? If so, what is the homework policy?
- How will the teacher track your child's development and communicate it to you?
- Are there extended hours before and after school? Are there school-sponsored activities before or after school?
- What is the school's mission statement, and how is it implemented? How are the values and mission of the school reflected on the walls of the classroom?
- What ongoing schools do most children attend when they leave this particular school? What is the support offered to students and families to place them at these schools?
- How is the school accredited and with what organization(s)?
- What is the spending per pupil, and how does it compare to that of the district? (The Every Student Succeeds Act in the United States requires schools to make this information available.)
- What is the breakdown of the school's funding, and how is spending prioritized? What are the budget shortfalls?
- What are the expectations of parent involvement?
- How does the school communicate with families?
- Who greets the child at the school's front gate or door?
- How do the students get to and from school?
- How much exposure to technology is there, and how is it employed? Why?
- What are the families' demographics and backgrounds?
- What recent challenges or areas of growth has the school faced?
- What are the stated and unstated fees associated with enrollment?
- Look at the ways the school invites (or doesn't) members of the community into its halls.
- Do the school's activities reflect the diversity of your local community?

What I ultimately learned from our beloved Prison (which was actually named Kiangsu & Chekiang Primary School, nicknamed Suzhe) was this: as long as the building is not likely to crumble into a heap of asbestos and lead paint in a strong wind, the building doesn't matter. I quickly got over my prejudice about what schools *should* look like. The best places are not necessarily the fanciest ones. There are thousands of nicer-looking schools out there, but at this no-frills place, my son *loved* learning.

However, it took time for me to get over my preconceived notions. I not only had to let go of the entitlement mentality I'd grown up with but also the entitlements I still had. It was a process.

Classes were taught in Mandarin, and the instruction was consistently challenging, with an established curriculum that had weathered many years. Tsoi Laoshi (*laoshi* is an honorific term meaning "teacher" and is part of every teacher's title in China—just like we call doctors "Dr. So-and-So") was young and vivacious and always had a smile on her face, but she was fierce when she was focused. It was terrifying to hand over my firstborn son to a stranger in a different culture who spoke a language I couldn't speak, despite my Mandarin lessons.

But I quickly learned I could trust Tsoi Laoshi to nurture and educate my son just the way I hoped. She came to know his strengths and weaknesses and took time to understand our family and James's home life. She was someone I'd want as an emergency contact for the rest of our lives. She came to feel like a trusted aunt, like part of the family.

Every day, James came home with homework, even though he was only four years old. At first I balked at the idea, but he was excited to do it. It was easy homework, but it was still structure and practice. He copied numbers and Chinese and English letters a few times every day. He had math assignments too. I have since come to appreciate the importance of early exposure to math for children, not just literacy,[2] and I think this is something that's far too often overlooked and undervalued in US preschools. At this age, the math exposure was mostly about counting and learning to trace and recognize numbers.

The immersive education made a major difference for James's Mandarin. He was picking up the second language beautifully and in fact was chosen to represent the school in the Hong Kong National Poetry Competition. Every day, a performance teacher pulled him from his class for fifteen or twenty minutes to practice reciting his poem about blowing bubbles and their movements with choreography—for *months*. This was our introduction to what it meant to teach to mastery. James recited his poem so many times, I can still utter every word, though I didn't speak a lick of Mandarin at the time.

All that effort paid off: he won the competition, even as a nonnative speaker. I was thrilled, but more important, *he* was thrilled. He was honored to represent his school and have performed up to his teacher's expectations. He couldn't wait to tell her.

His success is a reflection of his teacher's dedication to him, I thought happily.

Every month the school invited the parents in for a celebration for all the kids who had a birthday that month. When I saw how the teacher lavished attention on all the kids, I realized that she loved all the kids, not just mine. She was made to be a teacher.

Because James's education was now in Mandarin instead of English, I took up the mantle of his English-language education. While he was learning to read Mandarin at school, I taught him to read in English with story-driven Letterland Phonics and signed him up for a weekly English phonics class with a nearby Australian mom. I was hoping that these lessons and the English we spoke at home would keep him on pace with his grade back home.

Any worry I had about whether James's excitement about school was strictly tied to Tsoi Laoshi dissipated with time. James continued to love Suzhe, though he had different teachers the following two years. It was an excellent school with dedicated and caring teachers at every step. Charles joined as soon as he turned two, and both kids thrived there—though I got a lot of disciplinary calls for Charles that I never did for James.

"He refuses to sit down for story time," his teacher told me. "Instead he pushes his chair around the room."

"Charles, you have to sit down when the teacher is reading," I told him.

"But Mama ... it is not funny. The story is *not* funny."

I turned away to hide my chuckles. Charles was the rebel, a bit chubby, and sometimes cheeky, but mostly accurate. The teacher was never going to win this one. And Charles happily continued to attend school every day, skipping up the hill, through the school's ominous entryway and to his classroom.

After two years at Suzhe, we needed to decide where to send James for elementary school. Alex and I went on the perfunctory international school tours where the language of instruction was English and Mandarin was an optional second language. Ultimately we decided to keep James at Suzhe for first grade, where he could continue with his Mandarin with a more socioeconomically diverse and local student body. I would continue to supplement his English learning at home.

Meanwhile, back in the United States, preschool education researchers were publishing studies about how children's brains are primed to learn in the early years, particularly in areas such as language acquisition. Not only are babies and toddlers taking in massive amounts of information about their mother tongue, but they're also easily able to take on a second language concurrently.

We get it backward in the United States: most schools don't offer a foreign language until middle school, but by then, the optimal window for language development is closed. Of course, you can learn another language at any age, but it's less labor intensive to learn one as a child. Research shows clearly that we should teach second languages starting in preschool.[3]

The Benefits of Bilingualism

In 2018, Great Britain's *Independent* reported, "Princess Charlotte Is Already Bilingual at Age Two." The comments were a mix of people admiring how bright the young princess is and many readers reflecting on feelings of inferiority. While I'm positive that Princess Charlotte *is* lovely and bright, I'm sure it helps that she has a Spanish-speaking nanny. It's quite natural for a child that young to pick up whatever language or languages are spoken regularly.

There are important benefits to learning a second language at an early age. Research from the University of Washington's Institute for Learning and Brain Sciences shows that it improves several areas of cognition, especially related to executive functioning, such as switching attention, flexible thinking (cognitive flexibility), and updating information in working memory.[4] In seniors, it's even protective against the effects of Alzheimer's disease.[5]

Yet in the United States, many people do not learn a second language, with the important exception of the 25 percent or so of the population who hear a language other than English at home.[6] This is a stark contrast with Europe, for example, where 54 percent of people speak at least two languages.[7] Twenty-five percent of Europeans speak at least three languages. In some places, such as Luxembourg, the Netherlands, and Singapore, the number of bilingual people reaches close to 100 percent.

Many kids in the United States grow up believing that English is the only language they need to know because so many people around the world learn it. That's a shame, because bilingualism not only fosters empathy and understanding for people from other cultures internationally, but also even within our own borders, to name but one benefit. And in a nation as diverse as the United States, I would call this a necessary life skill.

If you want to raise bilingual kids even if you're not bilingual yourself, I have a few suggestions. One is to take advantage of our easy access to culture in other languages. For example, there are play groups and classes for babies (in tumbling, music, and art, for example) offered in foreign languages. A second idea is to hire a babysitter who speaks a foreign language and ask that person to speak only her native tongue. A third method is to watch TV in that foreign language to gain familiarity with the sounds and culture associated with it. For example, there are many popular Japanese cartoon series, *anime*, in Japanese that your kids can watch. You can add subtitles so you're picking up a few words yourself.

During our time in Hong Kong, I made some very close expat friends, and I will forever appreciate the way they took me under their wings to help me navigate the city when we moved there. But I also loved hanging out with the local families I met through the school, and I felt that we got a true feeling for the local community in this way. One family ran a fruit stand at a local market; one father was a mailman. What we shared were mutually high aspirations for our children's education. Parents were very welcoming, inviting us to cookouts and parties. One time we gathered at a local beach for a barbecue. The kids had a blast, and no one in sight was wearing Chanel. There were still some helpers even in this environment because they were affordable, but only a few families were overtly wealthy.

Despite our grounding with local families, we were still living a spoiled lifestyle. Danny's wife, Virgie, had come to join us, replacing our former helpers, and my life was much easier than it would have been back home. I felt pangs of conscience about the kind of role model I was. What was I teaching my children, living with one foot in my real values and one foot in the posh expat life? After all, my mom had raised me to do my own laundry, cook, and hold part-time jobs in place of an allowance since I was a teenager. Over the years, I had scooped ice cream at Ben & Jerry's, sliced and served bagels starting at the crack of dawn, waitressed at a local Japanese restaurant, and stuffed envelopes and worked in a mailroom. The kids were thriving among our chosen community of expats and nice local families. But this still didn't feel sustainable in the long term; it didn't feel like real life.

This can't go on forever, I thought.

*　　*　　*

Unfortunately, a tragedy hastened my next decision. One weekend in July 2010, Danny was in a nearby public park playing a heated game of pickup basketball on his day off when a local Hong Kong man suddenly punched him in the face. It was a punch that landed in just the wrong spot. A quarter of Danny's skull was removed because of brain swelling, and he would forever be in a vegetative state. Witnesses had seen the attack, but no one knew what the motive was. Was it racial? What was said before that punch? We would never find out, though investigators and newspapers speculated. Doctors advised Virgie to let him go, but she wouldn't. Ever since, she has dedicated her life to taking care of him, and we've continued to help fund their children's education. Danny wasn't just Danny to us; he was and will always be Uncle Danny.

Nothing was the same after that. Hong Kong became a painful place.

What are we doing here, anyway? I wondered, and finally broached the subject with Alex.

"I'm ready to move," I said.

Finally.

"How about Shanghai?" he asked.

Investment banks were always looking for employees to go to mainland China, but few people wanted to give up their cushy Hong Kong lives for the challenges in a developing country. For us, though, it seemed like an interesting new adventure. Once Virgie was set up to return to the Philippines with Danny, we contacted a Shanghai relocation agent and set the wheels in motion.

Within six weeks we were packed up and leaving Hong Kong. New adventures awaited. I had no idea what I was in for—a good thing. If I had known, I don't think I ever would have gotten on that plane.

SHANGHAI

2010–2012

James: 6 to 8 years old

Charles: 4 to 6 years old

Victoria: 16 months to 2 years old

CHAPTER 3

Mission: Impossible

Welcome to Shanghai

Alex had lived in Shanghai for a term during college, but I had visited only once before our decision to move. Because of that, my vision of the place was a little . . . overly optimistic. I imagined taking aimless walks on sinuous cobblestone streets, strolling past ancient temples and carts of steaming dumplings. I knew it was modernizing at a great pace, and I was excited to see what kind of hybrid awaited us. Although it was less than three hours away by plane, it was a world away from Hong Kong's subtropical, comparably seasonless, predictable routines and glamour. Shanghai was also another world away from its own rich cultural past.

The air was gritty—I could taste the smog the moment I stepped out of the airport—and everything looked dirty and gray. This place ripe with culture and former beauty was falling apart from the overly rapid growth of an old city. The breakneck speed of expansion led to rampant poor quality and shortcuts as buildings were erected overnight. It was different from when Alex had been there a decade earlier. Now, romanticism and nostalgia were slipping away daily, pushed aside by skyscrapers and shopping malls, and new housing and chic industrial spaces built on the footprints of former factories.

Ironically, Shanghai reminded me a lot of the Japan I remembered from my youth, which was making rapid transformations as it built up economic momentum in the 1980s. Seemingly overnight, Japan went from being an underdeveloped country to one with state-of-the-art education, technology, and infrastructure. The Japan of the 1970s transformed from a country with smokers and loogie hackers on every corner to orderly lines of well-dressed and respectful pedestrians today.

Twenty-four million inhabitants made Shanghai the world's most populous city in the world's most populous nation (China's population is currently at 1.4 billion) and one of the fastest developing. Since 2006, Shanghai has tripled its gross domestic product. International brands, from food chains to luxury retailers, have been moving in at every opportunity. The world's largest Starbucks, with over four hundred employees, opened in Shanghai in 2017. The landscape is literally changing daily as new buildings pop up where entire city sections were razed. Real estate prices continue to soar as the city gets taller and more spread out. While I was excited for the opportunity to be a part of the greatest economic growth of my lifetime—what I fantasized as being able to enjoy the riches from the gold rush—I didn't comprehend that such growth meant that *nothing* stayed the same. It was wholly destabilizing.

The economic growth doesn't mean that Shanghai is just a city for wealthy people. While the number of millionaires across China is growing at an impressive rate, there is still staggering income inequality. Migrants move from the countryside to Shanghai to work for rich people; it is truly a city of the haves and the have-nots. And this time I was determined we would not live among the "haves" or expats.

Our friend in Hong Kong threw us a farewell party, during which my friend Sandra pulled me aside and practically shook me: "Are you out of your mind? To leave *this* for Shanghai?" But I knew it was time for us to pursue something more meaningful and less materialistic. We made the conscious decision to strip down our lifestyle in Shanghai and not accept expat compound housing, though we were embarking on what expats deemed a "hardship post" in a developing country. And some of these compounds resembled Stepford, with multiple grocery stores, a gym, pool, playgrounds, theaters, basketball courts, and the like and an international school across the street.

Instead, we chose a home that had the bones and potential to be beautiful on the inside but was previously a Communist tenement without any amenities. There were enough exposed cables intertwined and zigzagging between the buildings that they could have ignited the entire city block. *It'll be like a family detox*, I thought.

It was a little more "detoxy" than I had expected.

The day after I signed the lease, I returned to the apartment with our real estate agent. For the first time, I opened the kitchen cabinets—and found cockroaches munching away at whatever gelatinous residue was ensconced in the wood. Black mold filled the refrigerator.

The real estate agent just shrugged. "This is China, and it's an old house."

I began making lists of all the things that would need to be repaired. In the meantime, I told myself, *I'm a New Yorker. I'm tough. I can handle anything.*

But could I?

Please let that be my imagination, I thought as I saw what appeared to be a large rodent scampering past the kitchen cabinets. But, alas, it was a rat.

There were lots of rats, along with other assorted critters and bugs. We did our best to seal up the place and keep all our food tucked away. Still, every morning we saw fresh evidence that we'd had unwanted visitors.

Toto, I don't think we're in Hong Kong anymore.

At dinner, we'd watch termites come through the walls, and I'd call the exterminator, who showed up with the backpacked gang straight out of *Ghostbusters*. Our walls would be pumped so full of chemicals that they were sweating.

We are going to die, I thought.

I had no idea what toxic brew was being sprayed all over our home to keep the bug population down. I just didn't know of any other option. I hoped we wouldn't live there long enough for the chemicals to build up in our systems—that is, if the smog outside didn't get us first. I had already started training myself to take shallow breaths outside, which was more self-delusion than anything; maybe the cancer wouldn't get me if I didn't breathe it all the way into my lungs. Inside, we installed hospital-grade air purifiers in every room in our home.

We didn't have reliable hot water, so we often filled the tub with pots of water heated on the stove to bathe, and I installed water filters in the hopes of staving off whatever might kill us in there too. This made the already low water pressure result in trickles running from faucets and showerheads. I never knew what to expect next—like the time Shanghai's food authorities had to investigate reports about pork that glowed blue in the dark and determined it was infected with phosphorescent bacteria.[1] And there were reports that giant watermelons and cabbages would literally explode because they had been pumped full of growth accelerator to make them more appealing to customers. Most produce in Shanghai was enormous.

"How much for the plums?" I had James ask for me at a stand.

After a few words exchanged, he translated back to me: They weren't plums. They were cherries!

Most of the time I learned that I just needed to keep a sense of humor about these things or I'd drive myself crazy with worry. But not everything could be easily brushed off.

Shortly after we moved, a fire broke out in a nearby high-rise building that was full of older pensioners. The subcontracted and unlicensed workers had used flammable construction materials on a building that had no sprinklers. The fire department showed up, but the single accessible fire hydrant would allow their hoses to reach only as far as the fifth floor out of twenty-eight floors, so they could only watch as people jumped to their deaths. Finally, after several hours, the firefighters climbed to the top of nearby buildings and extinguished it from there.

Hundreds of people must have died in that fire due to a lack of safety measures and infrastructure regulations, but the government covered it up and minimized it—corruption was rife, and they had the megaphone to dominate the media. We heard only what the government wanted us to hear, so we had to interpret all reported news with a massive grain of salt. It was often propaganda. And those who spoke against the government could be imprisoned or killed. This was in sharp contrast to our constitutionally protected right to free speech in the United States.

I realized how unsafe and exposed we were and how spoiled I had been previously in a country with building codes and reliable emergency services. Here, I felt completely helpless. It was another necessary humbling—an undoing of years of unappreciated privilege.

Even the mundane chore of shopping was a wholly different experience from home. Unlike shopping at a Best Buy or Costco in the United States, labeled prices in Shanghai were guidelines to begin to negotiate the price at the understood 30 to 50 percent below asking. At first, I was uncomfortable negotiating prices in a store, especially because I had to have James do the haggling for me, but I got used to it. People viewed you as stupid if you paid full price for anything.

One particularly memorable shopping trip took us nine hours to buy ten items at the electronics superstore Gome. Once you picked out what you wanted and found out if it was in stock, you would go to a back room to pay cash. Finally, you would pick up your item and move to the next department. It was better than taking our chances at all the small shops with potentially counterfeit merchandise that would pop up one day and disappear the next. Because we were the biggest spenders of the day, James received a prize on our way out: a children's ice shaver machine, the Chinese version of the Snoopy Sno-Cone Machine. It was little more than a cord attached to a plastic-handled serrated knife. It felt like the makings of a Chinese version of *The Texas Chainsaw Massacre*.

Another reason it took us so long to get through our shopping was that no one seemed to enter a line from the back. It was one of the many ways decorum fell by the wayside in Shanghai. You got into line as close to the front as you could; otherwise, you were a chump. People pushed and shoved, regardless of who they hurt. (One personal low point for me was shoving aside an elderly woman who cut in front of me in a public restroom because I just couldn't hold it anymore. It was truly every woman for herself.) It took me some time to understand that many of these people literally had to fight for food at some point in their lives; they knew poverty in ways I never would, and many of them had learned to look out for their own for survival.

When we first moved to Shanghai, I arrived with a single focus in mind: for the kids to be immersed in the language and culture of the place where they were living and not have an isolated expat experience. I had a gut feeling that the local Shanghai schools were good academically even if they were bare-bones. I felt that at this young age my kids' Mandarin would be solidified.

Unlike in Hong Kong, I knew we would not look at any international schools, even though our relocation agent tried to talk me out of my plans multiple times.

"You realize we're a Communist country?" the agent said, clearly wondering how ignorant I was.

"Of course," I said, though I wanted to scream. "We're moving to Shanghai for the local schools. They've been learning Mandarin in their preschool."

"But are you sure you don't want to see the American school?"

"I'm sure."

"You just see it first? It's very nice. The local schools are . . . not so nice."

"Yes. I am serious. I am sure." She was persistent, but I did not yield.

After knocking on the doors of about ten public schools when we arrived, we secured a space for James at Luwan District School #2. Technically we weren't Shanghai residents, and because the school year was beginning in two days, most schools were not open to the idea of kinda illegally (it was somewhat of a gray zone back then) letting us register a foreign child who might not be able to handle the academic rigor and could require too much attention.

I was more nervous about Charles, my little Tigger, who could be challenging for the more rigid instructors. Okay, that's generous: this kid got into "energetic" trouble all the time. He was an adorable bundle of stitches and knocked-out teeth, and I worried that the Chinese preschools would watch him dash around the playground and decide he was too much.

We showed up at Zhong Fu Hui preschool, the only preschool the relocation agent had recommended. Four-year-old Charles swung through the jungle gyms around the playground while six-year-old James sat with full attention and spoke to the head of admissions in Mandarin in an office adjacent to the play yard. I waited with much trepidation, hoping no one was noticing Charles leaping off the equipment with all the grace of a flying monkey. Then the admissions director came out to say that Charles could start next week.

What?

Oh, no, I thought. *She thinks James is Charles.*

But no—they decided that James was so poised and intelligent that his little brother must be fine too, and I wasn't about to correct them.

James has never let Charles forget that fact. "I'm the one who got you into preschool," he says.

Both James's and Charles's schools were arguably among the top schools in Shanghai. James's school, a model school that other schools in the district modeled their curricula after, was decorated with placards all over the entrance to prove it. I also got the sense from the administration that everyone there actually cared about James. There was a tangible warmth when they held his shoulders when speaking to him. For all these reasons, I pushed hard for this school, even after they said they were full to capacity. And while Charles was among a handful of non-Chinese students at his school, James was the only foreigner, or *laowai*.

If I thought The Prison was bad at first look, I hadn't seen anything yet.

From the outside, James's school was located in a charming setting. The school was more than one hundred years old and housed in a painted gray brick building with white fenestration. It was located along winding and historically affluent Fuxing Lu, a tree-lined street in what was the city's French Concession area during the nineteenth century. Only some of the neighborhood's original European-influenced architecture, including that of the school, had survived Communism. Every morning, James passed through a twelve-foot-tall wrought-iron gate to reach the five-story building that educated over a thousand first through fifth graders.

Inside, James's school was a different story. Whereas the Hong Kong school was austere and bare-bones, James's new school could be deemed dangerous by Western standards, and at least unhygienic by others. It had all the physical charm of the psychiatric institution in *One Flew Over the Cuckoo's Nest*: fluorescent lighting, beige linoleum flooring, white walls with no decoration, and classrooms stuffed from edge-to-edge with wood-top desks that wobbled on metal legs. There was a wall-to-wall blackboard at the front of the classroom and no artwork anywhere. When it was wet outside, which was often in Shanghai, the linoleum floors felt as slick as an ice rink. Luwan #2 had an ever-present and damp smell of urine and bleach.

Although I had no idea of this when I signed him up, the boys' and girls' bathrooms had no doors or regularly running plumbing; they were tiled rooms with a single sunken trough that was flushed with water at the end of the day. Boys could stand over it while girls had to squat. I'd later come to find out from James that many children chose to hold it in for the entire school day because they could not bear the stench.

It felt . . . well . . . *gross*. Yet I would come to understand it. Many of the public toilets in the Japan of my youth were a sunken basin over which one needed to squat.

Education spending in the United States often goes toward things that *look* good: buildings with polished floors, shiny lockers, a new football stadium, an auditorium with comfortable seating, new exercise equipment. We spend it on technology, buses, playgrounds. While these are important elements of a typical US school campus, we should take a cue from the schools in China and Japan. The highest priority should be investing in areas that directly inform academics: teacher recruiting and training, salaries, ongoing professional development, support for those learning English as a second language, and resources for students with special needs.

In Shanghai, I never saw a budget breakdown and did not need to for a simple reason: it was very clear where the money was going. It wasn't going into building maintenance, technology, heavy and shiny textbooks, or sports equipment; it was going toward teachers.

Unlike in the United States, all primary school teachers in China are subject specific, so James had a homeroom teacher and different teachers for math, Chinese, English, and his other classes. (The Chinese, English, and math teachers received higher salaries than the other teachers.) This made a lot of sense to me, since we all have our strengths and weaknesses and these teachers could continually invest in a specific area of expertise and pass it on to their students.

I tried to get comfortable with our new expat life, but many times I worried that we'd made a very bad decision by moving to Shanghai. The city seemed to lack a sense of compassion. Some of the news reports were particularly horrific. A driver hit a two-year-old girl playing in a parking garage near her parents' fruit stand. Rather than stop to help her, he ran her over again to be sure she was dead because he didn't want to be responsible for paying her medical bills. Passersby didn't stop to help either; no one wanted to get involved. The YouTube video of the incident received millions of hits within days.

Seeing the lack of compassion carried out to its extreme actually made me feel more empathetic. Those around me were literally and figuratively far hungrier than I would ever understand. It made the kids tougher.

When the boys were old enough, I sent them to the corner kiosk to buy items for our household. Sometimes sellers would take advantage and the boys would come home with black bananas, half-eaten containers of ice cream, and the like.

"Go back there and demand a refund," I would tell six-year-old James. And though he was nervous at first, he gained the confidence to speak up for himself.

One day James convinced me to look at the site of the building fire in person. Before that, it had been easy to stay disconnected from the story. Even while the building burned a few blocks from us, the gray smoke intermingled with the usual haze of pollution and didn't look much out of the ordinary. But after we saw it in person, I felt haunted by the sight of its blackened skeletal frame of concrete, acknowledging for the first time that real people had burned to death, suffocated, and leaped to their deaths there. I couldn't get the image of the inferno out of my mind.

A few months in, I found it was getting harder and harder to get out of bed. Each day I was afraid to go into the kitchen because when I turned on the lights, I was going to have to face the truth: odds were fair that the contents of our cabinets would be strewn across the floor because the rats had gotten into them. Again.

Every time I opened the front door of our home, I was assaulted with the stench of the upstairs bathroom, which smelled like a thousand porta potties on a summer day, though no one knew why. The hardwood floors were splintering. I spent half my days waiting for contractors to fix any one of the laundry list of things that had gone horribly wrong. Internet service was throttled by the government, so it could take days to download my favorite American shows to get a taste of home, like *Grey's Anatomy*; *House, MD*; or even my guilty pleasure: *The Real World*. I couldn't find my way around or communicate. Few people had smartphones, and there was no GPS.

Through all this, I had already gone through five live-in *ayis*, or helpers, who were paid the average $600 per month salary. The first left because she felt she could not care for three children (most parents had one child), the second because she was suffering from health problems, and the third because she had little patience and resorted to hitting my children. Although I was taking Mandarin lessons, I experienced firsthand the challenges of learning a new language in my late thirties. When I went to the mommy-and-me playgroup with eighteen-month-old Victoria, I sat in a confused haze as the teacher spoke to the other mothers and they reacted appropriately. I never knew when I was supposed to smile or laugh at something she'd said, so I mostly just sat there with what appears in photos to be a permanent grin covering up confused concentration. I stayed quiet and became an expert mimic. I didn't want to have a negative impact on Victoria's experience with my own personal language and cultural handicap in any way.

Then came an unexpected introduction.

"Hi, I'm Jianing," a young Chinese mother said in unaccented English as Victoria made her way through a maze.

"Johnny?"

"No, Jianing."

"Joh-nny," I repeated, more slowly.

"Jianing," she persevered and only a bit louder.

"Johnny!" I repeated.

"Oh, forget it," she conceded with a smile. I felt like I had insulted her, but she was nonplussed. Eventually I learned how to say the name correctly (Jah'-ning), but she never made me feel bad for how long it took.

"Are you new?" she asked. "Where are you from?"

I was relieved. Nobody had made an effort to speak with me during the previous few gatherings. It made me realize how much I needed some adult connection here and how much I longed for a friend.

"My husband and I are from New York. We moved here from Hong Kong last month."

"But you look Asian. Are you Hong Kong Chinese?" she asked me, not in the politically correct way I was used to. I knew my appearance, with Asian blood, could be confusing.

"No, I'm half-Japanese. Where are you from?"

"I'm from Shanghai," she replied. I was excited. It felt like I was meeting a born-and-bred New Yorker in New York City—a rarity. With China's immense population and Shanghai as its largest city, I had yet to meet anyone from Shanghai.

Jianing had lots of beautiful freckles on her porcelain skin. Her round face was framed by jet-black bangs and shoulder-length hair. Even the hush-toned way she spoke demanded quiet and respect; her voice was delicate compared to the brash-sounding Chinese I had been hearing. I can't tell you how she got this way, but in a country where speaking loudly over each other is the norm, she had somehow figured out that everyone around you silences themselves if you speak quietly and only when you have something to say. She had attended a teaching university to learn to teach English to elementary school students; hence her excellent speech. I later learned that she had been the top student in her class every year since first grade.

When the bell rang for gathering time, Victoria and I followed Jianing and her daughter, Yiyi. I wasn't sure we were welcome, but I wasn't sure we weren't either. I was like a puppy seeking approval from its mother. Jianing and Yiyi sat in the group circle and made space for Victoria and me. I was grateful. While we sang, Jianing stared at me. I felt embarrassed because I was just imitating sounds, not forming words. Afterward, I followed her to the lunch that was served in the playgroup dining area, and we shared a table. I copied the way she ate and how she fed her daughter. She didn't say much—as was her way—while I blathered on nervously. I felt like the new kid at school who's presented with the possibility of having a new friend. In this way, I probably wasn't so different from my kids, only more aware of my desire.

To my deep gratitude, from that point forward, Jianing always made space for us and translated anything the teacher said, even during long presentations. I appreciated that so much. I lived in fear of replicating my own early childhood with my mother, where I missed half of my kindergarten field day because my mother couldn't read the English notices. The whole time we were in China, I made sure to enlist the help of nearby adults (neighbors, teachers, tutors) to translate all school communications for me.

From this casual first encounter, Jianing felt like my guardian angel. Eventually I took to calling her Little Buddha because of her wise, calm ways. As an only child, she welcomed me as her "sister." The bond with her sustained me through many difficult moments in Shanghai.

Being around Jianing was a relief from the stress I felt at home, where every day was a battle with my own psyche, trying to convince myself it was right to be in Shanghai, despite all the tough living. All the stress and anxiety of daily life were compounded by arguments with my husband over my inability to speak and read the language. He grew tired of translating for me.

More and more, I worried we had made the wrong decision to move here. "Hong Kong is Asia for beginners," my new Shanghai neighbor and friend Mary had told me. "Shanghai is the real deal."

Was it *too* real? I was slipping steadfastly into a depression, though I tried hard to hold it together for the kids. I found it harder and harder to get out of bed in the morning, until one day, I just couldn't. Hanna, the protective guard dog we adopted in Hong Kong, always knew when I was down—she came and licked my foot sticking out the side of the bed.

I called Jianing and left a message to let her know I wouldn't be at the playgroup with Victoria that day. She called me right back to find out why. It was our first phone conversation and left me feeling better—a fellow human cared that I couldn't get out of bed. Jianing came to my rescue and became my light in a dark time. From that day on, she called every day to ask how I was doing, and she'd often drop by to check in on me.

If my children had not been happy here, I'm sure I would have tried to leave, but even as I sank into a hole, I saw them thriving. They wanted to go to school every day. They were excited about what they were learning. I didn't always understand the lessons, but I allowed the rhythm of my children's daily schedule to help me manage my feelings of having no control.

Each day I took James to his school's front gate, then walked Charles to his classroom. Twice a week, I took Victoria to her playgroup. I felt so good about how they were doing academically that it almost counteracted how much I was falling apart inside.

Almost.

CHAPTER 4

Star Trek:
The Next Generation

Education as a National Value

James and I hopped into the car after I picked him up from school one afternoon toward the end of second grade.

He turned to me, beaming, and announced, "I joined a club today!"

"Oh really? What kind of club?" I replied.

"Well, it's this special club that you join before you start third grade." And he started singing in Mandarin:

We are the heirs of Communism
Along the glorious path of the forbearers of the Revolution
We love the motherland and the people
"Young Pioneer Members" is our proud name
Ever be prepared to contribute
To completely destroy the enemy
For our ideal, we courageously advance.

I had no idea what he was saying because we had not covered this particular vocabulary in my Mandarin for Beginners course, but he was so happy that I felt happy too. I even asked him to sing it again so I could take a video. Only when I, proud Mama Bear, sent it to my new dear sister, Jianing, did she explain what he was reciting. James had just pledged his support to the "club" of the Communist Party. And he was so proud to do so!

Until this point, James had worn a green bow around his neck every day, which represented his having been a "Young Seedling" of the Communist Party. On that day, the children all retired their green bows and received red scarves as a promotion to becoming Young Patriots.

I may have been a bit concerned, but I kind of thought it was cool he was thriving in such a unique, immersive experience in a public school. The nation that was giving him this opportunity was asking for some gratitude in return. It wasn't a bad concept, regardless of the politics and my own childhood US history lessons on how Communists were the enemy. And at the time, it felt harmless.

Probably more than anything else, I gravitated toward appreciating that James was being taught about his place in the world. He was in China. He was expected to pay tribute to the nation. One can call it indoctrination into nationalism, but he was a part of something bigger than himself. This contrasted with my experience growing up. I pledged allegiance to the flag while attending a public kindergarten and first grade in Connecticut, but that was it until summer camp. In the United States, a requirement to recite the pledge varies not only from school to school but sometimes even from classroom to classroom. In hindsight, I wished we had a more unified practice of being patriotic in my childhood and honoring what it means to live in a free and democratic nation.

In sharp contrast to the downsides of Shanghai, education was *everything* here. In China, they truly believe education is the great equalizer: everyone can succeed if they work hard enough and all children deserve high-quality schooling.

Education was Deng Xiaoping's major initiative. Deng succeeded Chairman Mao Zedong, the founder of the People's Republic of China who led from 1949 through 1976. Deng, who ruled from 1978 to 1989, believed that the Cultural Revolution, Mao's effort to purge the nation of capitalism and its ties to history to further the communist agenda, had produced "an entire generation of mental cripples" because youth had been recruited to the military when they should have been getting an education. Determined to right this wrong, he repeatedly touted education as the way to economic prosperity and took major steps toward education reform. He also instituted China's one-child policy in 1979, which meant that parents pinned all their hopes on one child. They were likely to do anything—spend anything and sacrifice anything to ensure their child's success in school—that they believed would translate to their whole family's secure financial future. "The future" was something people thought about all the time. Deng promoted the belief that education was a national priority, meant to serve the public good.

Luwan #2, where James was enrolled, had six classes per grade with up to thirty-five students per class, each taught by a single teacher. That worried me a bit. My Western upbringing had drilled into my mind that this was *too many students.* Class size is such a constant topic in American schools. "The smaller the better" is the usual motto, and almost half of all states have mandated caps or incentivized reduced class sizes. How could everyone get individual attention in a class of thirty-five?

The truth is that there is some evidence that class size matters, but it seems to matter far more in the United States than in Shanghai. The STAR (Student Teacher Achievement Ratio) project, the most methodically sound study on class size, done in the 1980s, was a four-year experiment across seventy-nine Tennessee schools to find out if reducing class sizes would have any significant impact. The researchers found that students from kindergarten through third grade benefited from class sizes of seventeen or fewer students, showing better scores in reading and math.[1] The effect on minority students was about double that of other students.

It seems to make logical sense that smaller class sizes are beneficial: teachers can provide more individual support this way if anyone's falling behind, and there's less likelihood of behavioral problems when a teacher can keep a closer eye on all the students. The trade-off, though, may not always be worth it. A smaller class size means a need for more teachers (at a time when there are already teacher short-ages in many rural areas) and less money for professional training and overall resources in budgets that are already stretched thin. Ultimately it can lead to the recruitment, hiring, and retention of less-qualified teachers.

And yet it was clear from the start that the Shanghai schools were far ahead of their American counterparts despite the larger class sizes.

How? I wondered.

I was about to get an education on what student-centered teaching really means.

James's homeroom teacher, Tan Laoshi (Teacher Tan), was also his English teacher. The literal translation of 老 (lao) 师 (shi) is "old, experienced, wise" "teacher, model, master." Tan Laoshi looked about fifteen years old, with a high-pitched voice to match. She was usually flushed, as if she had just run a marathon, and at just under five feet tall, she was only a tad taller than James. Tan Laoshi had just finished her final year at Normal University in Shanghai, a teachers' college. She had never left China, didn't have a passport, and spoke nearly per-fect colloquial English. Instead of saying "aiya," as Chinese people may say after dropping a pencil, she would say, "Oopsy-daisy." It was both charming and a testament to her dedication to perfecting her English language skills despite having never set foot in an English-speaking country.

In China, the education system and its citizenry are oriented toward the global prize. It starts with an education system that seeds national pride and sentiment. China was the phoenix rising from the ashes, and the global picture was synonymous with the greatest social mobility.

The nation's commitment to education comes straight from the top, President Xi Jinping, so I have no doubt they will get there, and soon, just as China has already come so far in such a short time. In his second-term, three-and-a-half-hour inaugural address on October

18, 2017, President Xi mentioned education a whopping twenty-nine times.[2] Without any term limits to his presidency in a single-party nation without elections, and with his thirty-year plan that runs through 2035,[3] it almost feels like China's educational growth has no bounds.

English is considered the third main subject after language arts and mathematics. The same students who couldn't speak a word of English when James was in first grade, which is when Shanghai students start learning English, were rather fluent by the time they finished primary school in sixth grade. And these are public school students. It was both inspiring and intimidating.

Tan Laoshi's dedication to mastering English reflected the mentality I encountered with many other people in China who were committed to fluency in English for themselves or, more likely, their children. English-language learning is a multibillion-dollar business in China.

I loved Tan Laoshi not only for her commitment to education but also her care for her students. There are a great many things about Chinese families that are different from American families, but one of the key differences is in the way they express affection—or, rather, *don't* express affection. Most of them don't say "I love you" or hug or kiss, especially not in public. It's so culturally foreign that several YouTube videos went viral in 2016 and 2017 showing American-born Chinese college students calling home and saying, "I love you" to their parents (many for the first time), to show viewers what the reactions would be. Rather than saying "I love you" back, the parents were mostly baffled and responded in various ways—for example, "What's going on?," "Is something wrong?," and "Are you drunk?"

It must have been quite a spectacle when I gave James a hug and kiss every day at the gate of his school. Tan Laoshi took to hugging James good-bye at pickups, maybe because she was copying me and had seen this demonstrative behavior from Western films. I never saw her touch any other students.

How Do You Model Your
Family's Commitment to Education?

There's a simple way to tell what you're modeling for your kids: track your time.

How much time do you spend each week taking your kids to soccer practice? Working at the office? Working from home? How much time on reading? Television? Cooking together? Chores? Video games? Socializing with friends? Going out to eat? Visiting the library? Exercising?

It can be eye-opening to write it all down and chart how you're spending your time as a family and individually. If you're complaining that Johnny doesn't understand his math work but you're taking him to karate four times a week, then you're teaching him that karate is more important than studying math until he understands it.

Note, too, the quality of the time you spend as a family. What are the conversations about, and how can you raise the discourse? How much time is spent on screens (both the adults and kids) and how much on substantive personal interactions?

Rarely did I see other mothers or fathers at school because most parents worked to support a multigenerational family of seven: an only child, both sets of parents, and themselves. At pickup, I would be among a sea of grandparents, all at least a half-foot, if not a full foot, shorter than my 5 foot 8 inches, who had come to pick up their grandchildren. Some still sported the iconic tunic-length Mao jacket, a remnant military uniform from the reign of Chairman Mao Zedong. The jacket was a constant reminder to me of China's recent chaotic past, when up to 75 million Chinese were starved or purged by Mao's policies. Eventually I worked up the nerve to ask people about their views on Mao. Unlike the prevailing Western view that he was an authoritarian killer, many Chinese people consider him to be a great unifier of different peoples over expansive geography who created a world superpower.

Once the front gates were opened for pickup, it was a mad rush to catch a glimpse of the final moments of class in session. It felt a bit like Walmart opening its doors on Black Friday. Once I reached James's classroom on the first floor, I loved peering through the rear window to see him sitting in the back row. After a while, I learned that those who need the most academic attention sit in the front, while those who received the highest exam scores sat in the back.

I always waved and smiled, and he sneaked a bigger smile back. While in Hong Kong, young students at international schools were learning how to read and write on tablets and were listening to their iPhones on the buses to and from school. At our kids' schools in Shanghai, the emphasis was on pencil-to-paper writing, daily arithmetic quizzes, and drills. Every day James came home with graphite all over his sleeves and the side of his right hand from writing all day long. I quickly came to regret having bought him a yellow winter coat; it kept him warm, but it was stained with pencil lead almost immediately. It was a comforting sight for its academic implications, but it required a nightly regimen of aggressive, skin-chafing scrubbing.

When the teacher gave the final good-bye to the class each day, James would gather his backpack and coat and speed-walk through the aisles to make his way to the front door. For the first few weeks of school, six-year-old girls a full head shorter than James would form a train behind him, pushing to get close. They would raise their hands up to the top of his head and stroke his hair, as if petting a dog. James, already the absent-minded-professor type at such a young age, didn't swat away the hands as I might have, but just kept walking to meet me at the front of the classroom. I assumed the girls thought James was handsome, but I later realized they had never touched non-jet-black, fine hair. James's golden hair was a novelty.

James was thriving, and soon performing at the top of the class. He enjoyed the challenging curriculum and his fellow students. We were off to a terrific academic start.

*   *   *

Charles also loved his new preschool (and Victoria would later join him there). Zhong Fu Hui was a public school like James's, but it felt flush with cash by comparison. In China, compulsory education does not begin until first grade, the first year of elementary school, so there were far fewer pre-school options. Spots at those that were considered very good were highly sought after. Parents would do anything for admission, and the elites gravitated to this one. The building was well maintained and decorated with student artwork. Some moms I'd see at pickup were toting coveted and pricey Hermès Birkin bags, either real ones or very good knockoffs.

There was no official office of admissions: apparently you either knew someone or needn't bother applying. I later surmised that there was a second category of admissions: cute foreign children to use in school marketing materials. There were a couple of blue-eyed, blond Western children who stood out in the sea of dark hair and eyes. Al-though he had brown hair, four-year-old Charles with his pink-framed John Lennon glasses fit the foreigner bill just fine. When we walked down the street, passersby would point to Charles as if he was a celeb-rity, saying, "Ha-li Poa-ta!" ("Harry Potter!").

Zhong Fu Hui had a grass courtyard surrounded by a U-shaped three-story yellow building that housed the school's four hundred students. There was a lush, green grassy field, a playground, and a running track within that U. The classrooms all received ample sunlight. The parents were educated and had economic means, there was a constantly evalu-ated curriculum of study and play, and the school offered weekly pro-fessional development to its teachers. Preschool here was a four-year program starting at age two, with a one-year feeder "mommy-and-me" playgroup starting at age one, which I had attended with Victoria.

Once children began school in Shanghai, the school took full re-sponsibility for their well-being. For example, before classes began, Charles had to wash his hands at an outdoor sink and attend a daily health inspection by one of the three nurses on duty to receive a color-coded pass before being admitted. There were three colors: red meant the child was fine, yellow meant maybe a little cold or cough (but okay to be in class), and blue meant too sick to be in class. A child who had a fever or other illness was cared for at the school infirmary.

This felt completely foreign to me at first. In the United States, if your kid is sick, you are told to keep him at home, and if he gets sick during school, you need to come and get him. Here, there was no expectation that an adult family member would stay home all day with a sick child because most parents worked. That said, families who had the means did keep their sick children home. Everything was changing in China during its rapid economic growth; I was experiencing the country for the first time in the midst of this transformation, even as I was learning about what made it tick.

Preschoolers get sick all the time, of course, and Charles tended to spike super-high fevers in the range of 106 degrees Fahrenheit. I sent him to school in March 2011 knowing he was a little under the weather, and they gave him the cold-and-cough type of pass for a few days. He had a fever on and off, which I was treating with Tylenol. But one afternoon when I picked him up, things got scary: When we got home, he collapsed on his bed and wouldn't rouse. His forehead was burning up.

I hailed a taxi to the emergency room of the local public children's hospital, where I saw limp-bodied children in the arms of parents strewn along the hospital's narrow, potholed driveway, sitting alongside corrugated tin-roofed kiosks that offered tchotchkes and toys. They all seemed desperate for help, maybe because the hospital had turned them away or they couldn't afford the meager expense of treatment. Many were migrants from outside Shanghai, like our ayis.

Please let this be a sterile needle, I thought as they drew sample after sample. This was nothing like a US hospital, and the standards were not the same. The floors were worn, the walls were cracked, and the chairs were chipped.

I found out that I could pay just a few dollars extra for VIP treatment, which meant a nicer room and things like faster access to X-rays, and I took it.

An hour later, a doctor came to talk to me with a medical book outstretched in her hand to help us communicate. She pointed to an entry in English:

"Leukemia."

I couldn't catch my breath. It felt like all the blood left my body. Tears streamed. It was just Charles and me, and I couldn't communicate with anyone.

I held his body on that hospital bench, numb, and rocked him back and forth in what felt like an eternal hell. I took pictures of his charts on my smartphone to send to a pediatrician in the United States once Charles had a bed in the intensive care unit. I needed a second opinion. *My baby boy cannot have cancer*, I thought.

The next forty-eight hours were such a blur that most of it has been completely wiped from my memory—from the shock, I think. I just remember that my mother was suddenly by my side with a suitcase full of Charles's favorite candies and snacks from the United States.

I do remember that what woke me from my self-imposed stupor was when our US-based pediatrician came up with an alternate diagnosis based on the blood test results. I shared our doctor's assessment with an English-speaking doctor at the hospital, and he went off to review his medical textbooks. The following day he said, "Mrs. Clavel, your doctor is right. It's not leukemia." The words I'd been praying for. "It's Epstein-Barr."

I'd never felt relief quite like that. For two days I had been terrified that my son was going to die, and now I was being told that he had a virus that would probably be dormant in two weeks. In the United States, doctors would no doubt have told me to just take him home and have him rest, but here, they insisted on keeping him in the hospital, putting him on three different and continuous IVs and monitoring him with X-rays every other day. I had to trust my child's care to a place that had just severely misdiagnosed him, and it was difficult. I moved into the hospital with him and barely slept. I reported back to our US pediatrician daily. Alex was away on business, so I enlisted family to help. My mother had flown to Shanghai within twenty-four hours of the leukemia misdiagnosis and thought she was coming to say good-bye to her grandson.

Jianing showed up at the hospital with homemade food every day for two weeks, showing me that I had indeed made a true friend. But what happened next surprised me: Charles's teacher showed up, and then several classmates and their parents. These were people I barely recognized and couldn't communicate with, and yet here they were, coming to the hospital to cheer Charles up.

It was a side of Shanghai I'd not been a part of before; it was community.

I had been so caught up in my own survival that I didn't realize Charles was making a life for himself at school. School *is* a community unto itself, and I hadn't appreciated the bonds among the students, teachers, administrators, and parents that transcended the classroom. It was heartwarming to me, and an experience I'll never forget. In the worst moments of my life, when I was scared and alone, *people showed up.*

As soon as Charles was coherent again, I began working on reading with him in the hospital. It was in those weeks that he learned to read in English. I feared that he had been too hyperactive to care about books before, but now that I had a captive audience attached to IV poles, he didn't have much choice. We did the Bob Books for reading skills together for hours on end. They're little square books in boxed sets that teach sight reading and phonics skills, and we went through the first five boxed sets in that room. By the time Charles left that hospital room, he was healthy again—and an emergent reader. Little did I know then that he would become a prolific reader; you can't tear him away from any page on almost any topic now.

One of the things that surprised me most about Chinese schools is how competitive they are, even at a very early and impressionable age. Toward the end of Charles's three-year preschool, I started considering elementary school options for him for the following year when he would begin first grade. His teacher recommended a private school (private schools in China are much cheaper than in the United States and more accessible), so at 9:00 a.m. on a Sunday morning we found ourselves in a room filled with hundreds of families. A teacher called out children's names one by one.

"Ke Lang?" She called out Charles's Chinese name.

"I love you, sweetie. Now go on," I whispered, so as not to draw more attention to my foreignness, and gave him a big squeeze.

Over the next three hours the room thinned out considerably as children were returned to their parents.

Finally, Charles and a couple dozen other children walked in. Charles was grinning with his pink John Lennon glasses and no front teeth (he hadn't had them for several years after he fell on them at age three). "That was fun, Mama!" he said.

Then the principal announced, "Congratulations! For those of you remaining, your child has been accepted to the World Foreign Language School."

What I had witnessed was a human filtering system, a real-life survival of the fittest—*Survivor* for kids. The prize: admission to the school. Assessment results are not kept confidential to save children's feelings. Academics, like nearly everything in Chinese culture, are unapologetically competitive.

Despite this acceptance and after some thought, I decided to send Charles to school with James at Luwan #2. I knew that James was thriving in that environment, and I also liked the idea of keeping the kids in public school together.

Children in China are expected to know roughly five hundred characters before they started elementary school. Because I didn't speak Mandarin at home I had hired a lovely tutor named Zhang Laoshi (who charged thirty dollars per hour), who came to study with the boys after school twice a week so that they had the academic language support from home that I could not give them.

Charles was selected to be the male master of ceremonies for his preschool graduation ceremony, which resembled the opening ceremony of the 2008 Beijing Olympics in its professionalism, ingenuity, choreography, rehearsal time, and overall length. He also won the most prizes on the school's first sports day. Six-year-old Charles was learning how to win and was loving it. And, frankly, he didn't know any better.

China values competition in almost every aspect you can imagine: they have contests about knowledge of the law and reading traditional Chinese poetry. Winning a contest is thought to be a win *for your city or nation*—to serve China and act as a good citizen by winning awards. Education news out of China is filled with academic competition results.

So it looked as if I would have two children pledge their allegiance to the Communist Party in return for a world-class education.

Fair trade.

Family Values:
What Is the Purpose of Education?

We all want our kids to love school and enjoy learning. So what do you do when your kid doesn't, or you're faced with the dreaded "I don't want to go to school. Why do I have to go?"?

"To learn!" is not a good enough answer, so think about this ahead of time. If you want your children to appreciate their education, make sure they know why it's important to *you, them, and even the greater society*. Consider this in relation to your own family's education values. Also, there is much more beyond the straight academics: making friends, learning how to operate in society, learning teamwork, overcoming conflict and mistakes, and embracing challenges to expand your capabilities in a sheltered place to prepare for a successful launch into adulthood.

Find ways to bring up your values in conversation even before your kids start school. These conversations can help set them up for a more meaningful experience even during their preschool years. Think about having a family mission statement and posting it in a highly trafficked area of your home.

Consider these questions. There are no wrong answers!

- What is the purpose of education?
- How do you define *learning*?
- Why do your kids think they go to school?
- How do you discuss education with your children?
- What educational goals do you have in your family?
- How often do you discuss education and school in your family and individually with each child?
- How do you stay in touch with the educational performance of your children?
- How might your values be different from those of your neighbors?
- What resources are available to you to support your educational values?
- Does your extended family support your educational values?
- How are your educational values similar to or dissimilar from those of your parents?
- Do your children appreciate their education?

CHAPTER 5

Get Smart

The Meaning of Mastery

E very afternoon I picked up James at 3:35 from his first-grade class-room. On one particular day, he didn't come out. As usual, the classroom was crammed with grandparents charged with picking up the kids and getting an update from the teacher. This day, I couldn't edge my way in, so I remained outside and peered through the corner of the classroom window. *What was delaying him?*

All his classmates filed out like eager ducks in a row, save for two or three others. Then the classroom door slammed closed like that of a jail cell when an inmate has just discovered his new home. I couldn't ask anyone what was going on because of my limited Mandarin. I just stood there and waited in the dank hallway that smelled like a combi-nation of some gratuitously employed chemical cleaning agents trying to mask the odors of an outhouse.

Finally, the last of the other kids exited the classroom and went home with their grandparents. Through the sliver of the classroom's front door, I sneaked hand signals over to James—a big hands-in-the-air for "What's going on?" and a point to my watch for "It's getting late!" He was seated at a desk in the middle of the room. He looked embarrassed, waved me away, and then pretended not to notice me. After a few glances toward the teacher, he ran over to the door, opened it a crack, and quickly told me, "I have to stay and work with math teacher." Then he rushed back.

Math? But that was his strongest subject. *He was being detained for that?* The teacher hadn't looked up once to acknowledge that I was waiting. She was keeping him, and I was just an inconsequential wall-flower.

Twenty minutes passed.

I watched James walk up to the teacher's desk, where she looked over his work and shook her head. She made some marks on his page and said a few words to him. Then I watched him trudge back to his desk and write, write, write some more. Thirty minutes passed.

I'm going to be late picking up Charles and Victoria.

My anxiety grew. I had no way of communicating with their pre-school to explain to them that my older son was being held hostage by his teacher, so I was not going to make it by 4:15. I felt helpless. It was just a handful of months into the school year in our new host country, and I didn't know the proper customs and protocols yet.

Then I saw James cry.

I felt my adrenaline go into overdrive. The teacher made no move to comfort him or even talk to him. She just kept looking ahead flatly, letting him struggle. I unraveled. I was his mother; I was supposed to be there for him, to look out for him, to stand up for him. How long was this supposed to go on with *no* communication? How long would she sit, oblivious to my crying son? He was still my baby, my six-year-old, in a foreign country, in a school of *my* choosing. I'd made an irreversible gamble on this school and I was terrified of any damage I may have caused.

It took everything I had not to burst into that classroom and yell, "What are you doing to my son?" But fear held me back. Because we weren't permanent residents of Shanghai, James did not attend legally, so I felt like a wrong move on my part could get him thrown out of this school. This bare and freezing school.

What have I done?

The longer I stood outside that classroom, the more I questioned the sacrifices we were making by having him at this school. The kids wore their winter coats all day because there was no heat in the building. There was only a concrete courtyard with a solitary basketball hoop where there could have been a playground. I thought it would be good for James to see what it was like to strip schooling down to its bare essentials: to learn in a place without material privilege that prioritized academics above all else and to develop the grit that would take him far later in life. Was that the right choice?

It was as opposite as imaginable from life at a Manhattan private school. At this school, it didn't matter where you came from or who your parents were; some of the brightest kids in his class were dealing with the worst poverty at home. I wanted him to know that we were all equals, especially when it came to the opportunity to learn.

But watching my son laboring over math equations at his desk, tears flowing down his cheeks, I felt helpless and angry. What gave anyone the right to treat him this way when he'd never so much as spoken out of turn?

Finally, after an hour, I couldn't wait any longer. Shaking with emotion, I knocked on the classroom door until James came and opened it for me. I said as calmly as I could to the teacher, "He has to go now," and I pointed to my watch. She didn't say anything, but she didn't stop me from taking James by the hand and walking out with him.

We rushed out to where the driver was waiting for us. (You don't drive in Shanghai unless you are a local, think you're a local, or are insane. People drive on the sidewalks. They drive forty miles an hour through red lights. It's like an entire city of stunt drivers playing a game of chicken with one another and pedestrians. People *did* get killed, but I was amazed it didn't happen more often.) We were in the middle of rush-hour traffic in winter with a driver whose breath could kill small animals, in a 1980s-style Buick (yes, a Buick!) minivan with windows that didn't open. I couldn't shake my anger and anxiety.

"How could she do that?" I asked James. "What was going on in there?"

He looked so ashamed. He prided himself on his academic achievement.

"I didn't get a 95 on my quiz, so I had to stay after until I got it all right," he explained.

Each math class started with timed drills: a math warm-up to get the brain ready and set the tone. They had to write down the answers to one hundred problems in five minutes before the next lesson started. A passing grade was 95 or above.

Let me repeat that: *Anything below a 95 was considered failing.*

It was an entirely different mindset from the United States, where the pass/fail line is usually significantly lower, at 65, and even at that, kids can fail several tests and still pass a class, or fail more than one subject and still move to the next grade. Here, kids had to master the subject *every day*, or they couldn't move on.

"There are two kids in my class who stay after every day, and sometimes some other kids too," he said nonchalantly.

I barely slept that night, planning what I would say the next day. I felt guilty I had put my son in this situation, with no control over how he was treated.

Because the math teacher didn't speak English, I couldn't express myself to her. But I could speak with Teacher Tan, so that's what I did.

"Tan Laoshi," I said, "can I speak with you about something that happened yesterday?"

"Oh, yes," she said, blushing bright red as she did every time she spoke with me.

I explained how hard the math teacher had been on James.

It was clear that Teacher Tan had already conferred with the math teacher about the previous day's happenings. "It was not punishment, just meant to help him learn," she explained. "She wants to help him learn all he can. I think she is just of a different generation."

It was funny—the math teacher was in her late thirties, maybe early forties, but in China, that was an "older generation." The homeroom teacher looked like a middle schooler, but I knew she was about twenty-three. Because of China's rapidly changing economy, teachers who were separated by even five years had very different educational, professional, and personal backgrounds, and therefore different styles of teaching. Some of the older teachers even used corporal punishment, whereas younger ones rarely did, if ever.

I learned that teachers often kept kids after school as long as it took to master the day's lesson. That occasionally meant right through dinner. Teachers provided dinner on nights when students were still in their classrooms beyond the customary mealtime.

The Teaching Profession in China

Over the past twenty years, requirements for teaching have become stricter, and teachers in Shanghai are expected to have high-level certifications. All teaching candidates in China must pass a national written exam and interview, which certifies them to teach preschool, elementary school, secondary school, or vocational school. Every five years they must reapply for their certificate, proving they've met stringent requirements. Among those requirements are a minimum of 360 hours of professional development, an ethics evaluation, psychological and health tests, and an annual assessment of their teaching. Those who teach in the major cities are expected to be the best of the best.

Teaching is a revered career choice in China; it commands much more admiration than it does in the United States. There's even a national holiday on September 10: Teachers' Day. The profession offers a steady salary and good benefits, so even though it's not the best-paying job around, it's still attractive to many people.

Teachers in Shanghai spend less than 50 percent of their work hours in the classroom—about twelve hours per week at the secondary level and fifteen at the primary level.[1] The rest of the time is spent on collaboration and professional development—which can mean sitting in on other teachers' classes, taking courses, meeting with other teachers to discuss best practices, visiting other schools, helping to create school-based lesson plans, and knowledge and skills training.

Teachers in Shanghai have the potential to receive incentive pay. Seventy percent of a teacher's salary is base pay, and up to 30 percent comes from bonuses that depend on the principal's assessment of the teacher and students' performances.[2] In the United States, it would be unfair to tie a teacher's pay to the grades of the students she happens to get each year given the diverse starting points of students.

Parents allowed this in part because of China's one-child policy. When you have only one child, you have only one chance for the next generation to lift your family, which could include two sets of grandparents, one set of parents, the child, and his or her future family, out of poverty. Whatever the teacher says, goes.

I often caught myself staring when a teacher reported on one of her student's wrongdoings. I would watch the triangulated aftermath unfurl in real time: the teacher would speak to the grandparent, the grandparent would point a rapidly shaking finger at the child, and the child would bow her head with puppy-dog eyes seeking forgiveness. In the United States, there can be an almost reflexive distrust of teachers, whereas in China, parents recognize that a teacher's sole motivation is to make sure each child learns to the best of his or her potential.

I left school that day feeling conflicted. I didn't like that James had been reduced to tears, and I didn't like how I had no control or voice when my child was being kept after school. But I did come to respect the reasoning behind it. I came to understand that the kinds of drills James did every day at the start of class provided the teacher with invaluable information about his daily learning progress. The teacher was constantly assessing for mastery.

* * *

In James's school in Shanghai, I learned that "No Child Left Behind" is a reality, not just a slogan. Every child repeats the lesson until he or she fully understands it. In the United States, I often hear people say, "Well, my kid is just bad at math," or "She doesn't have the math gene," and that sets the precedent. Parents who reinforce this message are doing their children a disservice.

Students benefit from high expectations and high standards. Failure should not be an option. There was no "bad at math" at Luwan #2. Nobody got through school being "bad" at anything; it was seen as a matter of mindset and persistence, until every student mastered the material.

What I didn't know at the time was that James wasn't crying because of what the teacher did. He saw no problem staying after to receive extra help. There was no stigma associated with being kept after class; lots of kids stayed after class, and eventually everyone understood the lesson.

He was crying because of me. He knew I was waiting there and that I was upset because we were going to be late. That's what made him feel ashamed. And, boy, did that cause me to reflect with shame.

What's punishment in the United States—staying after school—isn't a punishment in a mastery-focused education system like Shanghai's. Clearly I too had a lot to learn, especially with regard to how students interpret mastery.

The teacher's lack of emotion wasn't a lack of caring; James's tears were simply a reflection of his perseverance. It was me, seeing it through a Western lens, who had it all backward. He *liked* his math teacher. Heck, he would even say her dedication to him cultivated his love of math because she made sure he mastered all of its foundational principles. And fast-forward a handful of years when James and Charles returned to the United States: both placed two grade levels ahead in math class. It's a *huge* point of pride for them.

Of course, mastery was possible for James only because every teacher was willing to stay after school as long as it took until each student "got it." That's tremendous dedication.

Extending Your Skills at Home

One of the key aspects of mastery is that children should be able to apply what they've learned in school in situations outside the classroom. You can give them opportunities to build on their studies in everyday ways:

- **Games and crafts:** Practice spelling and vocabulary with Scrabble and Boggle, spatial relations with puzzles and drawings, math skills with card games, and engineering skills with building blocks, for example.
- **Measurements:** Measure and weigh items around the house employing both the standard US and metric systems of measurement so your kids have the ability to visually estimate. Make it a scavenger hunt.
- **Baking:** Select and follow a recipe, including creating a shopping list, going to the market, getting organized, and setting timers. Experiment.
- **Directions:** Discuss directions when you drive or take public transportation. Practice right, left, north, south, east, and west. Discuss distances, and employ math and formulas like speed and velocity.
- **Nature hikes:** Teach your kids to use a compass, and to identify flora and fauna. Ask them questions they may have addressed in school: Why are trees important? What is photosynthesis? Compose a haiku, limerick, or music verse about what you observe.
- **Grocery shopping:** Ask them to figure out percentages (How much is 25 percent off?), fractions (How much does half a pound of Swiss cheese cost?), and subtraction (If we have $10 and this costs $7.50, how much change will we get?). You'll see many ways to practice math skills when you look for them.
- **Look it up:** Conduct research with your children. Recent work has shown that curious children can ask up to seventy-three questions per day. So when you are asked a challenging question like "Mama, why is the sky blue?" search for the answer with your child. First, theorize with your child and discuss why the sky is blue. Go to the library and scour

its physical resources. Then go online and review the links offered by Google and seek reliable resources. Links to NASA and *Scientific American* are likely more accurate than an unknown individual's blog. Compare the Wikipedia research to these other sources, and review how this information was downloaded, when, and by whom.

- **Money:** Examine it. Who and what is on the dollar bill? What does the Latin wording on the penny mean? What building is on the nickel? Where was a particular bill minted and in what year?

- **Nutrition:** Read through and discuss the nutritional information on your packaged foods. Research various vitamins and minerals. Calculate the nutritional information for multiple serving sizes of items based on the package or information on the Internet. For example, if you eat two servings of rice, how much of your suggested daily amount of iron is included?

Any worries I had about James being "just a number" or that the school cared only about my child's academics were quickly dispelled when I got his first report card. It was a forty-six-page bound book titled "Shanghai Municipality Student Record Book." The top of every page was about the academics in each class (his grades, whether his handwriting was neat, areas for improvement, and so on), and the bottom of every page was about his social skills.

The report card required three separate evaluations in each subject: from the teachers, the parents, and the student's own self-evaluation. Specific categories of assessment included:

- Asking questions when you don't understand
- Completing and correcting homework on time
- Ability to make mock-ups and experiments
- Respecting the teacher
- Willingness to study with partners and listen to others' advice

- Taking care of public property/no scribbling
- Participation in cultural activities in and out of class

I was amused by James's math teacher's comment: "Even though you come from a foreign country, you have a mathematical brain and are responsive. I like you so much!"

The Chinese teacher suggested that he needed to practice his calligraphy, and he dutifully wrote back, "Teacher Zhao, I will try my best to make my writing better." In the parents' section, my primary comment was, "I am extremely happy with the education he is receiving here. Thank you for all your dedication to James." I would have written more, but this rudimentary Mandarin was about as much as I could eke out.

It wasn't just the report cards that illustrated how the teachers' knowledge of my kids surpassed my own at times. A few years after we moved from Shanghai and were living in Tokyo, I learned that James is color-blind. It came as a complete surprise to me, especially because I had always spent so much time with him. I felt terribly guilty about it. *Had he suffered through all his years of learning? How could I not have known?* That said, all his Chinese textbooks were basically made of newsprint paper with black lettering. But what was even more surprising was the response of Tan Laoshi, James's Luwan #2 homeroom teacher for two years. (We used to return to Shanghai two to three times per year to visit our friends and for the kids to attend a Mandarin-language school to keep up their Mandarin.) She was utterly unfazed—she'd known it all along, and also knew it hadn't held him back in any way.

Then it happened. The heavy clouds lumbering over Shanghai parted, and the Organisation for Economic Co-operation and Development (OECD) gods spoke to me: "You did good. The kids will be all right."

The PISA (Programme for International Student Assessment) scores were released in late 2010. Only when they stirred international debate and made global headlines did I learn what they were. Suddenly there was *proof* that Shanghai's education system produced the top academic performers in the world.

PISA is a test of fifteen-year-olds around the world to find out which countries are leading the way academically. It debuted in 2000 with thirty-two participating countries and occurs every three years. Most participating countries are members of OECD, and therefore among the world's largest economic powers. By 2015, over half a million fifteen-year-olds in seventy-two countries and economies took the two-hour test on a wide variety of skills: science, mathematics, reading, problem solving, and financial literacy.[3]

Shanghai first participated in PISA in 2009, and the scores were released just after our arrival in late 2010. By then, thirty-four OECD countries and forty-one partner countries and economies were participating. Shanghai was separated out from other Chinese cities because of its separate economy and because China is too massive to administer such an exam nationwide.

The results? Shanghai blew *everyone* away, annihilating its competition and conquering every subject. Shanghai ranked *three* full grade levels above the average score overall.

I examined those results, and suddenly all my sacrifices felt justified. When friends back home told me I was crazy to live in Shanghai, I no longer felt the need to defend my actions; the proof was in Shanghai's pudding. Shanghai was top in math, reading, and science, with average scores of 600, 556, and 575, respectively, in 2009. Compared to the students in the OECD countries who took the test, US students were *below* average in math (487) and barely average in reading (500) *and* science (502). It was a much-needed sign for me that our Asia experiment wasn't off the rails after all.

After learning about Shanghai's astounding PISA scores and reflecting on my kids' experiences in school in China, it got me thinking about the concept of mastery. In fact, I became preoccupied with it. What did it mean to master a subject?

Mastery is a buzzword in the education community, but in the United States, it seems to mean that students have learned what a specific teacher expects them to know—which might be far different from what the neighboring teacher may expect. So what *is* mastery?

Mastery is about being able to apply the information to other contexts and real-life situations, or to provide insights that go beyond simple recitation of what the teacher or book said. It's about depth and commitment. In 2017, when Charles attended a California public middle school and received straight A's but hadn't done much homework or pushed himself, I felt such grading was doing him an absolute disservice. Students have to earn an A. They are not entitled to one for showing up and regurgitating what they already know.

Grades are one indicator, but they're not always reliable. In the United States, a letter or numerical grade may not represent how well a student understands and can apply the material. Part of that grade may be class participation, effort, attendance, behavior, homework completion, neatness, and extra credit. And multiple-choice exams can be a guessing game that may not require students to actually know the content.

In the process of researching this book, it also became very clear to me that our education system filters reality, creating the impression that everyone is exceptional and that most can achieve perfection. This has changed a lot since I was a student. A's are more achievable, extra credit helps inflate poor grades, and children (and their parents) feel that they don't have to settle for a subpar or even less than excellent score. If an A is more easily attainable, what happens to the motivation to work hard? And with these lowered learning expectations and sometimes countless opportunities to retake exams or resubmit projects, I would argue that this has the counterintuitive and deleterious effect of teaching our kids that life is an easy A.

During the Clemson versus Alabama 2019 NCAA football final, a friend's nine-year-old daughter exclaimed, "Why doesn't he get another chance?" when the Alabama kicker missed a field goal. In real life, you usually get one shot.

There is a push in the United States to drop letter grades altogether in elementary and middle school. Today, parents and kids are more likely to see competency-based grading; that is, instead of seeing a report card filled with letters A to F or numerical averages, there's a scale of 1 to 3 or 1 to 4 representing "below grade-level standards," "approaching grade-level standards," "meets grade-level standards," or "exceeds grade-level standards." But that standard is usually set by the classroom teacher, often without alignment with fellow teachers in the same school in the same grade in the district as a whole, as well as those above and below. This means that most teachers don't know what was taught to their incoming students the previous year or how to prepare students for material they'll need to learn in coming years, especially when the next grade is in a different building.

In my experiences with my kids, teachers can teach widely different content within a grade level over the course of one year, let alone thirteen years (K–12). This leads to accumulated *holes, holes, holes.*

I often wonder if this is a reworking of the same wheel. When I was growing up, my report cards until high school were "excellent," "very good," "good," "fair," and "poor." To me, the biggest difference is that back then, "excellent" or "A" or "exceeding expectations" meant the kid was exceptional, and everyone knew it. I knew I deserved an A in my classes because I had worked my butt off. But that's just it: I had to work for it. And when I got an easy A, I lost respect for the expertise and competence of the teacher. More often than not, I hadn't even learned that much because I didn't fight for or earn that knowledge. That's when it sticks.

It's not easy to teach to or assess for mastery. Often it's easier to base grades on a simpler factor: compliance. Did the student turn in her homework on time? Did she memorize the ten things the teacher told her to memorize for the test? Did she come to class on time and take notes? This is all good behavior, but it does not indicate mastery.

Grades and other forms of assessment are important, but so is reaching your own educational goals. One way to think of goal setting is in terms of the typology developed by Manu Kapur, professor and chair of learning sciences and higher education at ETH Zurich in Switzerland, who based his system on success, failure, and learning. According to Kapur, both learning successes and failures can be productive or unproductive. Passing a test a student crammed for overnight, for example, could be considered an unproductive success because the learner may ultimately retain very little of what she studied. Inversely, failure can be very productive if the outcome is that learners retain material over the long term. Productive success results in "both improved performance on problem solving and sustainable learning."[4]

China has well-defined expectations about what needs to be learned at each grade level. Schooling in China is compulsory for only nine years, starting at age six: six years of primary school and three years of junior high. Only the top 60 percent of students in Shanghai go on to an academic senior high school (which starts at tenth grade), so early schooling is a very big deal. It's a pyramid, and everyone is working their way to the top.

In Shanghai, as in China as a whole, test scores are of immense importance. The main way students get respect in China is through these scores. The top student in each district is a celebrity, and these kids are often interviewed in the newspapers.

There aren't as many standardized tests as in the United States, and because the Chinese tests have few, if any, multiple-choice questions, the exams more accurately depict what students have learned throughout the year. They carry a great deal of weight, and there are definite consequences for those who don't do well on the high school entrance exam, the *zhongkao*, or college entrance exam, the *gaokao*. The education system is purely meritocratic; connections, athletic abilities, recommendations, and legacy do not open any doors. In China, students who don't do well on the zhongkao are tracked into a nonacademic high school, and those who score low on the gaokao are accepted only to the country's lesser universities.

Each year starting in grade 6, students take district-wide exams until the final "big" exam, the zhongkao. The exam covers Chinese, English, math, science, history, and physical education. Students take two practice exams, then the final one in June or July. This exam is the main determining factor in whether students go on to a vocational, technical, or general (academic) senior high school of their choice. Senior high schools may also have entrance exams of their own. At the end of high school, there's the *gaokao*, for which the entire city practically shuts down.

The vocational and technical high schools lead to middle- or lower-income-earning jobs. It should be noted, though, that there are lower unemployment rates in China for people who graduate from vocational and technical schools compared to academic high schools; it's easier to find a job, but they're lower paying.[5]

The outcome of doing poorly on these exams is not the same as receiving low scores on US college admissions exams like the SAT or ACT. Some US colleges don't require SAT or ACT scores anymore. Moreover, students can take them multiple times and submit only the best section scores of the bunch and superscore, which means totaling the combination of the highest verbal and math scores to present the student's best overall score.

We don't administer tests that reliably measure mastery of a well-defined subject matter. For example, research has shown that spaced repetition leads to longer-term retention of material when compared to "massed practice" (cramming).[6] So while cramming is adequate for preparing for many multiple-choice tests, knowledge acquired under these conditions is unlikely to stick.

Educators and parents in Shanghai did not seem to limit their expectations of students by socioeconomic background, parental levels of educational achievement, or any notion that some kids cannot master the content. Children there grow up with a growth mindset—the belief that their intelligence and abilities are the result of effort, so they can change and grow over time.

Does Mindset Affect Academic Performance?

In 2017, the Brookings Institution set out to study how much a student's own growth mindset could affect learning outcomes in the United States.[7] To find out, they asked 125,000 fourth through seventh graders to rate the following statements as "Not at all true," "A little true," "Somewhat true," "Mostly true," or "Completely true":

1. My intelligence is something that I can't change very much.
2. Challenging myself won't make me any smarter.
3. There are some things I am not capable of learning.
4. If I am not naturally smart in a subject, I will never do well in it.

Students were categorized as having stronger growth mindsets or fixed mindsets (believing their intelligence was mostly unchangeable) based on their responses. The researchers found that students from lower socioeconomic brackets were more likely to have fixed mindsets and that students with greater growth mindsets had higher scores in math and English language arts.

That doesn't mean the mindset caused the higher grades, so the researchers did some further digging. They went back to a year earlier in each student's records to make matches to ensure fair comparisons—that everyone was at the same starting line and showing the same abilities. Then they measured actual changes in scores over the following year. They wrote, "That is, we compare students with the same demographic characteristics, the same test scores in the current year and in a previous year, the same responses to the surveys for other social-emotional measures collected by the district, and within the same school and grade, to see whether students who look the same on all of these measures but have a stronger growth mindset learn more over the course of the following year. We find that they do."

Sometimes, however, mastery is a challenge for parents too. I saw this in the case of a fifth-grade math lesson when I visited a well-reputed Los Angeles public charter school. Seventy-nine percent of the school's students receive free and reduced-price lunch at the school, a commonly used indicator of a school with a high percentage of families living in poverty, according to the federal poverty line.

The teacher was giving a lesson on division, following the California Common Core State Standards. The teacher wrote a 1 on the white-board and circled it. She proceeded to show the students long division. She then wrote a 2 and circled it. She then showed the students how to complete the same equation with the short division method. Then came the monkey wrench: she wrote a 3 and circled it.

"Students," she said, "we have reviewed this several times already. What is another way to solve this problem?"

What?

I furiously flipped the page in my black-and-white old-school composition notebook and scurried to catch up by copying over the first and second methodologies. I quickly copied the third way. Then she said, "Okay. Now, who can walk me through the fourth way?" My mind was blown. At the age of forty-four, I was being taught not just *two* new ways to do division but *three!* Yes, there were *five* different division methodologies. I suddenly understood why so many parents were complaining that they could no longer help their elementary school children with their math homework and why they were seeing the Common Core as the enemy.

Jordan Haarsma, a recent Stanford graduate and senior education consultant in Silicon Valley, sympathized when I mentioned the "bad at math" mentality to him. "It just drives me crazy because I get middle school students who tell me they're bad in math. And it all starts because they are tested on things like having to know these five different ways of adding fractions, and when they only master one or two ways—the ways we had to learn—they get a 40 percent on the test. Students should be knowledgeable about these other ways and some students may need to use these other ways, but that's where it should end."

If a student can reliably solve a problem, is it really necessary to hold the child accountable to the multiple other ways to solve that same problem? Or should those ways be saved for those who have trouble with the original concept?

During the Chinese New Year school break, we visited my mother in Connecticut. Since we had a month off, I decided to enroll James in a US school for three weeks to make sure his English was up to speed. Only one school, a private one, agreed to take him for such a short time. They sent a full-sized yellow school bus to get him each day; he was the sole passenger. That was a thrill for James, who'd never been on a real school bus before, let alone one that made him feel like a king.

The teacher and assistant (and, frankly, I) were a bit unsure about how this first grader would fit into the classroom midyear, especially having never attended school in English or in the United States.

On the first day, the head teacher covered the blackboard with arithmetic problems and asked the class, "Can anybody get us started and tell us what to do here?"

James raised his hand sideways, ruler-straight through the tips of his fingers with a 90-degree bend at the elbow, because that's how you do it in China.

"Yes, James?" He stood up, pushed his chair in, faced the board, and *boom!* Off to the races.

"Five. Fifteen. Twenty-two. Is that a six or an eight? Six? Then the answer is twelve. Seventeen. Nine . . ." Rapid-fire, he rattled off numbers.

The room fell silent because no one knew what was going on. He was reciting the answers to *all* the problems on the board, one after another, because that's what he did in China—speed drills. The Connecticut students on a sleepy, snowy, picturesque New England morning straight from a Norman Rockwell picture minus the onesie fleece PJs were just getting started on learning addition and subtraction, and James was stone-cold proficient. He shocked them awake.

His new teacher called me immediately for an after-school parent-teacher conference. Yes, I was terribly nervous.

According to his teacher's account, the students and teachers were gobsmacked as James motored through dozens of problems verbally. "Didn't the administration say that this new student had never been to school in the United States before?" He wasn't the genius his new Connecticut teachers had imagined. *All* his Shanghai classmates could do this within the first handful of months of first grade. In this respect, it seemed to be a lightbulb moment for the teacher who did not know a six-year-old could do this from classroom instruction alone.

If we wonder why the United States falls behind in math, one place to look is the classroom wall. While many early elementary school classrooms have plenty of "A is for Apple" letters, weather charts, motivational slogan posters, and student art on the walls, there's very little numeracy. Go and check it out in your child's classroom. How many numbers or number lines do you see in the room versus how many letters or complete alphabets?

One principal at a nationally awarded Blue Ribbon elementary school in Silicon Valley (capital of the world for science, technology, engineering, and math, no less) told me that research shows that children just cannot grasp challenging math concepts in elementary school; students can't be expected to learn math as easily as words because words are everywhere and numbers are not; and we just don't use numbers as often as words. *Justifications, straight from the top!*

* * *

The fact that Shanghai students were ranked several grade levels above the OECD average on the PISA exam comes as no surprise to Chinese students who've seen what education in the rest of the world is like, including our system.

Xi Yi Vivian, a Beijing native now working in Silicon Valley, attended boarding school in Beijing during elementary and junior high school because her parents were diplomats who traveled often. The expectations at her school were just like those in Shanghai, and she did drills until it was second nature.

When Xi was in high school, her parents moved to the United States, so she attended ninth and tenth grades at a public school in Massachusetts, our highest-ranking state for education. She described math class in this way: "As long as you stay awake, you can do the homework." Homework, she was surprised to learn, was just a repetition of what they'd learned in class that day. In China, kids take the day's concepts and apply them to different types of equations and problems out of class. For example, she says, "In class you would learn $A + B = C$, and then for homework you struggle to figure out $D - E = ?$"

Although she had to work hard to learn English, she barely worked at all in math because it was all ground she'd already covered. She spent eleventh and twelfth grades at Phillips Exeter Academy, arguably the best boarding school in the country, where math was still more of the same—not a challenge. From there, she went on to double-major in math and economics at MIT. "Only when I got to MIT was math at the same level of rigor that I'd experienced in China in junior high school," she says.

Math *can* be MIT level so early in Shanghai because teachers are not afraid to push memorization, challenging homework, and discipline. Parents in the United States often have negative associations with these techniques.

* * *

Flash cards, speed drills, repeating what the teacher just said: these *work* for learning foundational basics. Americans rail against repetition by calling it "boring" and "mind-numbing." It's not the be-all and end-all, but rote memorization is unfairly criticized, in my opinion, and the research backs me up.

In a 2016 article in *Scientific American Mind*, Jo Boaler (Stanford University) and Pablo Zoido (Inter-American Development Bank) argue that "American schools routinely present mathematics procedurally, as sets of steps to memorize and apply." They tie these shortcomings in the typical US mathematics curriculum to the country's midlevel standing in the PISA test. Math in the United States is not taught as an inquiry-based subject but is instead mechanically presented as a series of steps or procedures. In order to address this shortcoming in US math instruction, Boaler and Zoido created Youcubed, a foundation that builds students' "number sense—essentially a feel for numbers, with the agility to use them flexibly and creatively."[8]

In addition to copious drills, Chinese students are also directed to develop deeper understandings of the concepts they memorize. Teaching math through a flexible conceptual approach seems to be part of the Chinese success story. The research of David Kember, professor of curriculum methods and pedagogy at the University of Tasmania, shows that Chinese students aren't in fact doing pure rote memorization; instead, the approach is a hybrid.[9] The students are able to apply mathematical concepts beyond the examples they work with directly in their classroom drills. While this may appear as rote memorization to outsiders, Kember describes this as an intermediate approach that bridges more superficial learning with an attempt at deeper learning. Once kids have the basics down, they extend their knowledge to ever-more complex problems that require them to actively *apply* concepts. These broader problem-solving skills are reflected in their PISA scores.

Parents in the United States often ask me if Asian kids are just naturally smarter. No, I don't think they are. Those who thrive usually work harder under the watchful eyes of parents and teachers who expect more. In Shanghai, I learned that successful students have an entire team to support them—their nuclear and school families. And, remember, each doting and watchful grandparent had only one grandchild. The cultural context around education and learning supports excellence. No excuses.

Forming Your Support Network

A support network is key for your child to thrive in school. This is something I saw clearly in both China and Japan. Here are some ways to create a strong support network to foster your kids' education:

- Get involved in online parent and education-specific affinity groups. Just be careful to filter through the good advice and the not-so-great advice.
- Place ads in local papers and circulars, on bulletin boards in shops, and at the library. If you are looking for, say, a Japanese tutor, post in a Japanese market or circular.
- Ask your local librarians if they notice tutors coming in to study with students, and ask for their names and contact information.
- Walk up to teachers or coaches you come across and ask them if they tutor! You can find them in libraries, schools, parks, and coffee shops where they may be working with students.
- Post on college job boards and career centers, and call colleges' offices of financial aid for introductions.
- Find professors on sabbatical, retirees, high school students, college students, people between jobs, entrepreneurs looking to make money, recent immigrants, and recent stay-at-home moms. Many people don't even know that they are seeking a job.
- Ask your school and your kids' teachers who want to make money outside school.
- Inquire at your community center or church.

- Use online tutoring apps like Wyzant.com to find tutors. Comparison-shop because the first tutor or class may not be a fit for your child, and it can turn her off the subject matter if the relationship continues. You may need to get different tutors for different children and different subjects. Not all kids are the same, and they may require different styles and levels.
- Equip yourself with knowledge on the Common Core and your state's Common Core State Standard. All content is categorized by grade and subject area. It's readily available on both the federal and your state's Department of Education's websites. If your state uses another set of standards, ask your classroom teacher or school administration for the name(s) and links. All of this information is public and readily accessible.
- Observe your children as if they are an ethnography experiment, and pick up on anything they may be curious about. Then give them information on it.
- Pool your resources with like-minded parents and create an after-school homework or class with a teacher you found together.
- Research, contact, and observe after-school programs and tutoring centers.
- Ask other parents. Ask the moms or dads of the children doing well in school.

When we got back to Shanghai, I peeked in on one of James's after-school speech classes, where fifty six-year-olds sat quietly in rows of seats for an hour each week. I had no idea what the teacher was saying; all I could see was a horde of mesmerized little children keeping still.

The teacher paced back and forth in front of them with a head-piece microphone that blasted at a volume meant for an outdoor pep rally, not a double-sized classroom. Every now and then, she'd smack down a long rectangular metal bar the size of a chopstick on her desk—

BANG!—to emphasize a point. The children's eyes widened. Who knew there was a way to get fifty first graders to stay still and listen?

No one will regret having learned multiplication tables in third grade, but they will regret it down the line if they can't pass upper-level math because they didn't get the fundamentals down. Children gain self-efficacy and build self-discipline by learning these skills early. Then they can confidently move on to higher levels without worrying about mistakes on the first step of the equation or losing focus because they have to think through everything. In India, children memorize the multiplication tables up to 20!

The insistence on mastery is the reason first graders in Shanghai are able to learn the beginnings of algebra, which really just means that letters can be substituted for numbers so it's a little more abstract in thinking. In contrast, the Common Core standards for math in the United States don't list algebra until high school.[10] When you see mastery in action, you realize how little credit we sometimes give our youngest learners. They're capable of so much.

The insistence on mastery spills into every aspect of students' lives in Shanghai. Like my mother did for me, I hired a piano teacher to give my children lessons. The teacher was telling them that they would need to practice. To entice the kids, I said, "Kids, you only need to practice for fifteen minutes every day." It was a bargain compared to the hours I had to practice. The teacher stood there in silence for a moment, then walked out and never came back. I had apparently just broken a sacred code. Oops.

The differences between the educational expectations in the United States and Shanghai were apparent from the start. At Charles's preschool in Shanghai, every week the students would spend time in what I came to call "The Brain Room." Classical music played in the background, and there were cabinets filled with hundreds of drawers holding puzzles, magnifying glasses, flip charts, paper, and flash cards.

Each child progressed independently from one level to the next, and when someone was done, he would raise his hand and tell the teacher. If the teacher agreed, the child would clean up neatly and move on to the next drawer. The exercises resembled those required on the Educational Records Bureau exam, an intelligence assessment used for entrance to some independent elementary and specialized public schools in the United States.

Watching the kids work through those drawers during an open house was thrilling; they were filled with excitement about their activities and worked through each one in absolute silence—all eighty-five of them. I thought it was a wonderful way to teach children from a young age about being self-directed learners, as well as being responsible for organizing their own things.

Charles was thriving, and both he and James were popular among their peers because they were among the top students. Charles's beloved teacher even asked him to sign artwork that he had given her because she said she knew he was going to be famous one day. In the United States, smart kids are labeled "nerds" while athletes are often revered. In Shanghai, the smarter you are, the cooler you are.

Beyond the actual academics—the math, reading, and science they learned—the extraordinary discipline and self-control my kids were introduced to in Shanghai (and later Tokyo) is part of what set their education apart from the US system. It's not easy to get a room full of young kids to sit still and focus for any length of time, but discipline and self-control are qualities that will benefit them throughout their lives.

Research conducted by Angela Duckworth and Martin Seligman, both at the University of Pennsylvania, demonstrated that the best predictor of final grades is not IQ but self-discipline.[11] Using various measures to determine eighth graders' level of self-discipline, they checked in with students at the beginning and end of the school year. Duckworth and Seligman found that self-discipline scores had more than twice the impact as IQ on their final grades, attendance, hours spent on homework, time starting homework, and time watching television.

Students should have more opportunities to learn self-control and discipline both at school and at home.

How do you help cultivate self-control and discipline at home? It's important not to step in every time your kids say they're bored. It's not your job to entertain and say yes to them all the time. It's okay for them to be bored sometimes and to find productive uses of their time on their own. Their ability to find intrinsic value in learning (learning for learning's sake) will get them far in life. If they are motivated only by their parents' dictates or grades, they may flag when those external motivators are removed.

It's great when learning can be fun, but knowledge is the reward and gift that keeps on giving. We underestimate our kids if we think we have to pander to them or entertain them in order for them to learn anything. Another way to think about it is that "school is the work of a child," as the saying goes in Japan.

This isn't to say that kids should sit and do math drills all day. We all need breaks to increase oxygen flow to the brain, improve our concentration, speed up our metabolism, and stay productive. However, Chinese educators may say that physical activity needs to stay on the playground, not in the classroom.

Both recess and physical activity are important. According to the US Centers for Disease Control and Prevention, children aged six to seventeen should have at least one hour of physical activity a day.[12] Standing up to stretch or move between classes is a simple way to introduce a few minutes of activity. Children's brains naturally lose focus after sitting still for hours; a "brain break" for a few minutes can help to refresh them so that they can take in new information.

We all need brain breaks at regular intervals. Research shows that the brain is not idle during times of rest and daydreaming. Maybe right before bed, you replay the day's events in your mind—things you wish you'd said differently, things you saw, people you met. In restful states, we process. We absorb lessons and integrate them into our memories.

During those ten- or fifteen-minute breaks between lessons, students have a chance to effortlessly process and absorb the lesson they've just learned instead of jumping right into a new topic without closing out the previous one. Without breaks, the brain gets overloaded.

Breaks are something highly ranked Finland does well. In most first-through twelfth-grade classrooms there, each subject lasts forty-five minutes, followed by a fifteen-minute break where students can go outside and see their friends and teachers can meet up in the teachers' lounge. Students go outside in any kind of weather, soaking in some vitamin D and fresh air, socializing, and exercising. Shanghai follows a similar pattern: thirty-five to forty minutes of class followed by a ten-minute break.

A typical schedule in Shanghai includes scheduled exercise time every day, as well as five minutes for eye exercises set to music with a prerecorded voice giving instructions. The eye exercises are like acupressure-based massages to relieve pressure around the eyes; they are thought to improve eyesight and focus, especially after long periods of reading. (Find instructions, including a video, at www.eye-exercises -for-good-vision.com/chinese-eye-exercises.html.)

The length of the school day is about the same for elementary school students in Shanghai and the United States (six to seven hours per day on average). However, a typical fourth grader in the United States might be expected to sit in class from 8:00 a.m. until lunch at noon, which is four hours without a break for movement. After recess, they might have a gym class where they can get physical activity, but probably only twice a week. On other days they might walk to art or music class. But much of the time, elementary school students sit in one classroom all day with one teacher, and breaks are at the discretion of the teacher. In many schools, recess and gym are both indoors on all but the sunniest, warmest days.

In spite of my feeling that James's school was getting it all right, when I asked his principal if she was proud of Shanghai being ranked number one on the PISA scores, her response was, "What?! Look at this school. We don't have enough art or music. And we don't have enough physical activity. We have to do so much better." While the principal valued Shanghai's academic outcomes, she also wanted many more opportunities for her students to be healthy, artistic, and creative. For example, music education has been tied to facility for foreign language learning, perhaps because of their shared focus on verbal skills by cultivating listening skills, as well as the intensive, scaffolded training required in both areas.[13]

Thriving in Elementary School

- Make sure that your child is mastering the fundamentals of reading, writing, and arithmetic. Read with her, read to her, discuss the story; watch how she writes and what she writes about; review math with her in everyday contexts like when you go to the grocery store or are counting trees walking down the street. Since I was my children's English teacher, I had my kids write essays and stories and read books as part of the daily routine, even over holidays.

- Keep a copy of a book like those in E. D. Hirsch Jr.'s series that are grade specific to learn what content should be covered.

- Have an area of your home where you keep daily and weekly schedules, school handbooks, school notices, daily family messages, and so forth.

- Decorate your home with educational posters (for example, a world map, presidents of the United States, multiplication tables, the alphabet, planets).

- Understand the classroom's homework and technology-use policy, and support it at home.

- Review your school's policies with your children so they are aware of the rules they must follow and behaviors expected of them.

- Support your school's disciplinary policy, unless you are certain it has been unfairly imposed on your child.

- Have close communication with all of your child's teachers, and make them aware that you are on the same team and that you would like them to tell you about any academic or behavioral changes they may notice (good and bad) in your child.

- Get to know what the teachers do not cover. For example, if they believe that smartphones are the future and children do not have to know their multiplication tables, then you need to teach them at home. If you want your children to learn cursive but this is not taught at school, you must teach it yourself. If your teacher does not assign challenging reading, you must do so and discuss complex themes with your child.

- Gauge your children's attitudes on learning, and encourage a growth mindset. What do they think they are good and not so good at, and why? What are the positive and negative associations they have with specific skills and content? Must learning be fun? Is it okay to make mistakes? What are the rewards of learning? What are some strategies to get through the mud?

- Check local colleges, learning centers, community centers, and libraries for supplementary classes (math, reading and writing, chess, puzzles, choir, coding, painting, drama) that are offered after school or on weekends.

- Explore content-specific tutoring options, and be sure you hire the right person, not just the first one you find. This is an influential relationship: what a student learns in a single hour once per week may be the equivalent of one week of in-school learning on that subject. Tutoring is not just for kids who are struggling in school; it's also to get deeper knowledge than what's taught in class and to nourish their curiosities.

- Get to know your child's curiosities and cultivate them with books, subscriptions to magazines and newspapers, lectures, and trips. Observe them keenly to suss these out.

- Add an educational component to family vacations: visit local museums, or use trips as an opportunity to explore local history and create a dynamic history lesson out of the experience.

- Create a family "brain room" area with activities: games, arts and crafts, models, sketch pads, origami, puzzles, stencils, journals, and more.

- Prioritize tech-free family time so your kids develop social skills.
- During family time, prioritize talking through the things you've each learned that day so you can grow from each other and offer expanded information about the subjects that excite them. Create bonding memories through learning and growth.
- Know your own strengths and weaknesses. Know what you can offer your child and what needs to be outsourced.

James and Charles were very happy in school in Shanghai, and they couldn't wait to learn more. They didn't suffer because of the memorization-heavy, disciplined, test-heavy atmosphere. They liked being challenged and thrived on the sense of academic competition.

The students who scored highest on tests in each class were awarded stripes. In second grade, James was ranked second in his class, so he received two stripes. He proudly pinned his three-square-inch white plastic badge with two thick green stripes onto the top of his sleeve every day, labeling him a leader in the school. He couldn't wait to get to third grade because he was sure he could be the top student in his class, with three stripes, and so he worked even harder.

I was so proud to watch true meritocracy in action and to see my children engaged in learning in ways I had never been as a child. It was a pleasure witnessing their growth.

CHAPTER 6

The A-Team

China Tops the Global Scene

I made the cheerleading team!" squealed Olivia, one of the highly competitive Chinese students I advised about the US university admissions process.

"You did what?" I asked incredulously.

"And not even JV. But the varsity team! Var-si-ty! Me. Varsity. Letterman jacket, here I come. *Woo-hoo!*"

"Olivia, will you still have enough time to study?" I edged in.

"I'm in America! Land of *Bring It On* and *The Blind Side*," both iconic high school cheerleading and football films, respectively. "That's where all the popular kids are, and you know that I'm shy. I want to meet people. It's like dancing. I *love* dancing."

When Olivia decided to make her way to the United States as an exchange student in her junior year of high school, she headed to Orlando, Florida, to stay with a South African family in a tribal-style bungalow with an assortment of dogs and a cat.

I knew Olivia would do well at her prep school, and she did. She was on the headmaster's list, joined the Key Club, won the Orange County Quiz Bowl, placed in the Florida Science Olympiad, and earned the highest grades in her advanced-placement biology class. She was one of those Chinese students headed for excellence.

Now my star mentee was shaking her pom-poms all over Florida while also working on an independent research project about the neurocognitive restrictions of cochlear implant recipients' rehabilitation.

"How many Chinese applicants can say they know the toe touch, pike, herkie, hurdler, and the tuck?" she asked. I could hear her trademark grin through the phone.

Olivia was a standout student academically and artistically; she loved painting and had been taught by her father. Her parents were artsy adventurers who got married in a jazz bar. "Basically, they were like the Beat generation people, but the anachronistic Chinese version," she explains.

"How did you get the name Olivia?" I asked. Her Chinese name, Yi Wang, wasn't close.

"My mom drove by a store that said 'Olivia's Pool Supplies' and thought it sounded nice," she said.

Olivia is living the dream of many Chinese high schoolers. She had no problem making a life for herself in the United States. She received multiple acceptances to excellent colleges. She ended up at the Wharton School at the University of Pennsylvania, where she again joined the cheerleading team, much to my amusement.

She was a newly minted adult, doing all the things a typical American college student does, including getting tattoos (!) and loving it, but she was still pulling off a near-perfect grade point average and spending her summers working a marquee job as an analyst for Goldman Sachs. She's fashionable, bubbly, joyful, up for anything, and frighteningly smart. She sent me one of her first college papers, and it held up to something I could have written in my master's program. I couldn't help but admire her.

When I asked her if she planned to return to China after graduation, she responded, "Why wouldn't I go back? I want to go home." When I speak with the students I mentored who are now in college, they *all* plan to return to China.

*   *   *

Returning to China is an interesting development in the country's study-abroad story. Whereas the goal used to be for students to study overseas to find jobs and move to the United States or Europe, now the students' goals have significantly shifted in tandem with the country's economic outlook. Whereas in 2011, 55 percent returned to China, in 2016 nearly 80 percent did.[1]

The high rate of students returning to China reflects two major developments. One is that receiving a work visa in the United States is a more challenging prospect than ever before. Much of the foreign-born talent that studies in the United States is unable to stay to work once they graduate. The other major factor is that China's economic growth has led to a rising standard of living in the country as a whole. While 88.3 percent of Chinese people lived in extreme poverty in 1981 (the equivalent of surviving on less than $1.90 per day today), the number dropped to 1.9 percent by 2013.[2]

There are now opportunities for the country's growing group of professionals to find meaningful and challenging work in China itself. It used to be that big Chinese businesses would import many of their executives from overseas, but now that is shifting. Students like Olivia know they can rise to the top in China by bringing their American studies and experiences home.

Not surprisingly, the daughter of Chinese President Xi Jinping chose to return to China when she graduated from Harvard in 2014.[3] Xi Mingze studied under a pseudonym so as not to attract attention. President Xi never lived outside China, but the next generation has different expectations.

Students like Mingze and Olivia offer perhaps the greatest hope for developing more intercultural understanding between the United States and China. Their firsthand experiences with US culture and norms indicate great potential for collaborations between US and Chinese citizens on all levels, from personal relationships to research and corporate partnerships, and even improved diplomatic relationships between the two nations.

* * *

After the 2010 PISA scores were released, I grew fascinated by the public outcry in the United States, which I followed by reading the op-ed pages of the *Wall Street Journal* and *New York Times*. Criticisms abounded, charging that China rigged the test-taking to include the best students or that China's top high school students tested well but were not participatory, independent, or critical thinkers.

Then President Barack Obama offered this comment: "Our generation's Sputnik moment is back," referencing when the Soviet Union beat the United States by launching the first satellite into orbit in 1957. "As it stands right now, America is in danger of falling behind."[4] Was this the swift kick in the pants the United States needed to redouble its commitment to education? That was when I knew that I couldn't watch from the sidelines and needed to be a part of the action.

As I worked through my master's program in global and international education while living in Shanghai, I set out to work with Shanghai's high-achieving adolescent population—the ones who were stunning the world with their PISA scores. More specifically, I wanted to understand the *why*s, *how*s, and *who*s of the highly aspirational and increasing number of Chinese students who were applying to US universities. Following international student flows became a pastime for me, maybe even an obsession. Perhaps I could predict future global economic trends and powerhouses through this study.

For many Chinese students like Olivia whom I met during this process, attending a US university was the holy grail—an unattainable dream just a generation ago. Deng Xiaoping had opened up China in the 1980s after Mao Zedong's three decades of Communist rule and his purging of the intellectuals during the Cultural Revolution (1966–1976). Suddenly Chinese students who aimed to study abroad did not have to take the grueling multiday, subject-specific college entrance (*gaokao*) exam, the single factor that determined college placement. Instead, these students focused on prepping for the SAT or ACT.

Back in New York and in Hong Kong, I had been an admissions interviewer for my alma mater, Dartmouth, so I understood a bit about
the admissions process at US universities. I was tasked with digging
deeper with these applicants about their volunteer work and extracurriculars, for instance. We interviewers didn't participate at all in
whether the students we spoke with were ultimately accepted; we just
provided more information to the decision makers. What I most enjoyed was getting to know this generation of leaders; I learned a great
deal from how they foresaw the future, which informed my own parenting.

That experience and my master's program both fueled my desire
to help students in Shanghai who aimed to go to college in the United
States. These students usually didn't understand the soft factors, like
teacher recommendations and community involvement, that top US
colleges prioritize beyond the hard numbers reflected in GPAs and test
scores.

"Give me your top students," I said. Ironically, it wasn't as lucrative
having top students as my clients because I could work with only a
handful of them every year. The competitive US colleges to which they
were applying often have unique and numerous essay questions rather
than a single boilerplate personal statement, so I had to spend more
time with each student for the same flat rate. But I wanted to find the
most ambitious students and learn what made them tick. I began this
work with the preconceived notion that they all needed help with their
critical thinking skills.

At the time, the most frequent criticism of Asian students in the
US university admissions process was that they were not sociable, creative, or independent thinkers, so the students and I would work on everything from interview skills to what to emphasize (or de-emphasize)
on their admission essays. I assigned them readings that American
high schoolers would know, and I encouraged them to think critically
about the material and answer questions that were opinion based
rather than fact based. I asked lots of "why" questions about their own

lives: Why did they care about the causes they did? Why did they want to follow the career path they were considering? Why did they want to go to the United States?

On the surface, these students were like many others who apply to Ivy League colleges: top students who got as close to perfect on their SATs as possible. Almost all of them were determined to attend a "top twenty" school. Only two of China's universities, Tsinghua University and Peking University, crack the top thirty universities in the world, but seven of the world's top eleven universities are located in the United States.[5] In comparison, Japan's highest-ranking university, the University of Tokyo, comes in at number forty-six in the global rankings.[6]

How does our country do this? How do we go from such middle-of-the-road rankings in our primary and secondary schools to being an unquestionable leader in higher education?

One answer is that we pull the best talent from all over the world in terms of professors, researchers, and students. Tenured faculty often garner significant prestige and opportunities for growth and innovation; we attract the best of the best to these havens of intellectualism, just as we should be doing on the lower levels. Once mandatory education is over, our US university–educated scholars earn Nobel Prizes, cure diseases, and invent world-changing technology.

As a result of our universities' amazing standing in the world, the United States receives 19 percent of international university students worldwide, more than any other member country of the Organisation for Economic Co-operation and Development.[7]

Chinese students do the most to take advantage of these resources. Some Chinese students spend just a semester abroad, but for many, the goal is to receive their entire college education in the United States or Europe.

In 2016, 544,500 students left China to study abroad, an astronomical increase over the 179,800 students studying abroad just eight years earlier. In 2017–18, Chinese students were the largest group of international students studying in the United States, at 33.2 percent, or over

363,000 students. Indian students were the next-biggest group, at 17.9 percent of the total, or over 196,000 students. California received the most international university students. New York State followed close behind with over 121,000.[8] Eight percent of all students in the University of California system (over 270,000 students) were from China in 2017.[9]

Chinese families who can afford to send their children overseas are willing and eager to do so, and they don't all wait for college. Between 2013 and 2016, Chinese students increased their share of high school students in the United States by 48 percent; as of 2017, they made up 42 percent of all international secondary students in the country.[10] Many believe it gives them a leg up on college admissions, and it saves the students from wasting time on gaokao prep back home. Mirroring their picks for higher education, Chinese students' top destinations in the United States for high school are California and New York.

According to an article in *Forbes* magazine published in November 2017, Chinese students contribute about $11.4 billion to the US economy through tuition fees and other expenses.[11] This is *big* business for the US economy.

It's worth noting that this situation is changing today as US immigration policy becomes more restrictive. Top students from around the world are being shut out of US universities and are looking elsewhere for an excellent university education in English. The number of international students in Canada grew 41 percent between 2015 and 2017 alone.[12]

Right now, the US higher education system is playing a formative role in the development of social and financial capital among Chinese citizens. While they are studying in our universities, we should aim to entice them to stay and contribute to the US economy. We also need to encourage US-born students to liaise with and foster lifelong relationships with individuals from this economic powerhouse.

According to the World Bank, the United States has the biggest economy in the world, at $20.4 trillion. China follows in second place at $14 trillion, and Japan ranks third at $5.1 trillion.[13]

Our students have much to learn from their Chinese classmates' study habits, intercultural competence, and ability to master a second language.

Can We Test for Global Competence?

In 2018, the OECD's PISA test added a section on global competence. The OECD defines *global competence* as follows:

> Global Competence has clear, practical outcomes. The globally competent person brings his/her knowledge, understanding, skills, attitudes, and values together in order to work with others to solve globally-relevant problems and to improve the collective well-being of current and future generations. Young people who develop Global Competence are better equipped to build more just, peaceful, inclusive and sustainable societies through what they decide and what they do.[14]

Veronica Boix Mansilla, principal investigator of Project Zero at Harvard, was part of the research team that developed the test with the OECD. Boix Mansilla explains the test's significance this way: "What makes the new OECD PISA framework exciting, in my view, is not only its clear potential to help us gauge how 15-year-olds today think about pressing issues of local, global, and intercultural significance, but also its power to inform educational practice in every region of the world."[15]

Although professors at Harvard were instrumental in the international collaboration that produced the global competence test, as of this writing, the United States has decided not to administer this section to US students.[16]

Once I had many success stories with getting my clients into top schools like the University of Chicago, Duke, and Columbia, some of my American friends asked me to coach their children too. "I can't," I told them. I knew I couldn't do the same no-holds-barred critiques on work by American students without having them get defensive.

Getting in the door to top American universities was more competitive for Chinese students than for Americans. I had to push hard with my students because they needed to gain admission solely based on merit—not donor connections, legacy, or athletics. They needed to prove they deserved a spot. I had no problem saying, "Start over" when they showed me their essay. This led to numerous psychotherapy-like sessions on why they joined a particular club and the most transformative experiences of their lives, reading classic novels and discussing how to integrate them into their essays, and interview prep to help them speak about themselves with eloquence and confidence. These students completely overrode my preconceived notion that Chinese students lack critical thinking skills. They just needed to be prodded.

In Shanghai, I conducted an information session with a group of about twenty rising seniors. All but one had spent their junior year abroad in US high schools. While I value the academic skills that come from this global view of the world, I also admire the compassion and empathy that these students demonstrated. One student's story has particularly stuck with me. He attended St. Ann's, an elite K–12 private school in Brooklyn whose notable alumni include contemporary artist Jean-Michel Basquiat, fashion designer Zac Posen, and actress Lena Dunham. He had worked at an AIDS clinic and was asking about how to access microloans to establish a similar program in Kenya. He wanted to put his knowledge to use for the benefit of others, not just personal benefit.

Others followed a more individualistic path. One student attended Phillips Exeter Academy and wanted to study finance at NYU's Stern School of Business. Another attended a private school in Florida and, though a junior, graduated as the valedictorian having taken all AP courses.

Other mentees knew more about other cultures than many of my adult peers back in New York, despite the latter living in a "melting pot." I was surprised to learn that sometimes when I would mention our family move from Hong Kong to Shanghai, many American acquaintances did not know any difference between the two Asian cities; one even asked me if my children would still be attending the same schools. My Chinese mentees paid attention to international news and history, not just what they might need to know for a social studies test but because they understood that global trends and concerns affect all of us. This particular aspect of their personal stories and ambitions resonated strongly with me. I respected my mentees for the scope of their goals, and their drive to travel outside their comfort zone to make their goals reality. My mentees have gone on to the University of Chicago, Columbia, Yale, Duke, UC Berkeley, the University of Michigan, and other competitive schools. A University of Chicago student who had never studied at a US high school yet spent every summer in high school in a US college program was fluent at the college level in both Japanese and English; he won China's national Japanese speech competition as a high school senior. Olivia is finishing her senior year at the University of Pennsylvania, where she's on track to graduate with high honors.

On the dark side of the college advising business, my employer asked me many times to write the application essays for my mentees, a directive that came from the families that hired us. I was never willing to do that, and I found the request (and, to be honest, it was often more of a demand) maddening. My students would earn their spots, or not, based on their merits and willingness to work for it. All my students have earned every bit of their success. I pushed back against the growing sense in China that the nation's elite and wealthy class can buy their way to success. One family would throw a fit if I didn't respond to their son's applications with a full set of notes within twelve hours, regardless of whether it was day or night. One time, when I was pressured to work with a less-than-stellar student, his father demanded that I get him into MIT even though he was a straight C and D student.

I eventually ended up quitting this job because of this subset of clients. It turns out that students who grow up with a sense of entitlement are not enjoyable to work with anywhere in the world.

These globe-trotting students from Shanghai are in stark contrast to their US counterparts. Many Americans never even leave the country—only 42 percent have a passport.[17] Only about 11 percent of US college students go abroad at any point during their undergraduate studies, and 64 percent go for eight weeks or less.[18]

Study abroad is far more common in other countries. In fact, between 2005 and 2012, study abroad around the world grew by 50 percent (from 3 to 4.5 million), which includes US students.[19] It has increasingly become a way for students to demonstrate language proficiency and intercultural experience, as well as to cultivate an international network, all of which can lead to internships and jobs in other countries. The OECD also lists high-status credentials, knowledge of business methods in other countries, and a competitive edge for applying for jobs as benefits of studying abroad.[20] Our personal experience speaks to the job opportunities and benefits that studying abroad can afford; Alex was offered his positions in Asia because he learned Mandarin and lived in China many years before we moved there as a family. According to the 2018 Open Doors report, almost a third of US students who study abroad choose three European destinations: the United Kingdom (12 percent), Italy (10.6 percent), and Spain (9.4 percent). Only 3.6 percent of US international students go to China.[21] This may partially be explained by the fact that many middle and high schools offer only European languages, so students have their earliest opportunity to study a European language rather than Mandarin or Korean, for example. Other languages are often learned at home or through outside classes.

The most recent survey of US students learning a foreign language in college shows an enrollment drop of over 9 percent between 2013 and 2016, with a decline of over 15 percent between 2009 and 2016. Spanish remains the top language studied in college, with the next most popular language, French, at less than one-quarter of the enrollment.[22]

Study abroad is mostly a pursuit of better-off Caucasian students whose parents can pay the large price tags; 70.8 percent of US international students are white.[23] This is yet another way the prosperity cycle continues for the elites: studying abroad often gives those students an advantage in their career search.

In Shanghai, children begin learning English in first grade as a precursor to the idea of studying abroad. But Charles's preschool teacher thought it was so important to expose her students early that she wrote English words next to the Chinese characters around the room. She'd have the morning greeter say, "Hello. How are you?" instead of speaking Mandarin. But one day, through the help of another mom, the teacher explained to me that there would be no English in the classroom for the next week because outside observers from the Municipal Department of Education were visiting, and it was against the rules to teach English to such young children. She and the principal had thought learning English was so important that they had broken the official protocol.

When we moved to Shanghai, none of James's classmates could communicate with me in English; when we visited four years later, they all could. Their worlds had opened up. Learning a second language early gives children a clue that other perspectives and cultures exist and matter. James's classmates also enjoyed not having to read Chinese subtitles when watching big movie blockbusters like *Star Wars*.

In other cultures, it's the norm to study world history and to follow international news. In the United States, we enjoy our position as a superpower, knowing that our television shows, music, movies, and food get distributed all over the world. (I watched James Bond movies in Tokyo and ate KFC in Osaka when I was growing up.) Perhaps we see and hear too little in return, particularly from non-English sources; we believe we're the most important nation.

This is one area where I always felt different from my peers growing up. Because I'm bicultural, I grew up with strong connections outside my country of birth. I've always seen this as a personal asset, something that has allowed me to adapt to new situations and expectations relatively easily thanks to having more of a global worldview.

Although I grew up traveling internationally and was raised by an immigrant mother, I didn't *truly* understand what globalization was about. I thought globalization was about the fact that the Anchorage airport had an udon kiosk where I ate dinner during layovers from JFK Airport in New York City to Narita Airport in Tokyo; I didn't realize it's about the fact that we're all interconnected and interdependent, so we should help each other survive, prosper, and live in peace. But once I began to understand this, that's what I needed my children to learn.

You don't have to grow up bicultural to adopt this mindset. The world we're living in continues to become more global. Politically, our country faces issues that are global in scope, which require us to collaborate with our counterparts in every corner of the world. Such challenges (and opportunities) include climate change, global health epidemics, food security, refugee crises, and energy.

Both in the classroom and at home, we need to discuss current events within and outside our borders. We may think we're shielding our children from troubling events, but how will they develop empathy for refugees without understanding why people flee their home country? How will they understand the value of our democracy without learning about dictatorships around the world? We need to do a better job raising children who hear other perspectives, examine them critically, and offer educated responses for the betterment of us all.

"Morgan Stanley wants us in Tokyo," Alex said.

It came out of nowhere. It had been two years since we moved to Shanghai in the fall of 2010, and I finally had my easy out—and I was shocked to realize I didn't want to take it. So much had changed for me, and for us, since we'd moved there; I felt like a different person from the one who had been so depressed she could barely get out of bed.

Shanghai had toughened me up, helped me to figure out which battles to fight for my kids, and helped to crystallize the direction I wanted my own life to take. I had started my master's in international comparative education there and worked as a college consultant. I read anything and everything on education, and although I couldn't stand working with the students who expected to buy their way into the best colleges, I *loved* working with the hard-core dedicated students. I was inspired by meeting families willing to sacrifice nearly anything for a great education for their kids: mortgage their house, sell their cars, devote all their waking time to it. I loved being in a place where kids' faces were not buried in tablets and smartphones, especially in school.

I loved so much about Shanghai by then, and I felt crestfallen to leave the kids' schools and Jianing behind. When we announced that we were leaving, Jianing and her kids came by every day, and several of the kids' teachers cried. *Cried.* They gave everything to my children. Despite the fact we were headed to my childhood playground, where I could speak the language and much of my family lived, Shanghai had become a symbol of growth to me. For the first time, I liked who I was as a parent and felt that I was coming into my own identity as a mother. I cherished the gains my children had made in school. They were happy—dancing in our living room and running wild through our beat-up lane with the neighborhood children. James was most upset about the fact that he would not become the tip-top three-stripe leader in his third-grade class, which he had been vying for since two-stripe second grade.

We were packed up and gone in four weeks. I bawled my eyes out on the way to the airport in Shanghai. I hid my heavy breath and tears from my children, staring out at the dilapidated homes under the expressway, deeply inhaling the smog that had once been my undoing.

Global Thinking Starts at Home

Given all the benefits for children of becoming more globally minded, you may want to encourage this way of thinking in your own home. Here are some ways to do that:

- Display a calendar of local cultural events and festivals, and plan family outings to explore these different cultures.
- Go to museums and check out their permanent collections to learn about the globally inspired resources in your own backyard.
- Encourage school international fairs to be about language, culture, and history, not just food. Enlist students and not just parents to contribute. And discuss the history of the foods. Many children may not know that pasta originated in China, for instance.
- Make getting a passport a family event. Travel as widely as possible, outside the United States if you can. For those of us in the northern states, Canada is a drive away. Montreal is fully bilingual (English and French) and like Europe in many ways. Mexico is also an option. Alternatively, Puerto Rico, a US territory, uses the US dollar, but Spanish is the dominant language.
- If you aren't able to organize trips outside the United States, take advantage of the diversity in your own neighborhood. Start shopping at a local ethnic grocery store as a part of your monthly routine and take the kids. If this is not possible, explore a recipe from another country once a week or once a month. Order foreign ingredients from an online grocer.
- Study the flags of other countries, listen to their national anthems, and learn about their histories.
- Encourage your kids to read nonfiction and historical fiction about cultures outside their own.
- Look for diversity in your own backyard. Get to know your neighbor who may have a different cultural background than your family has.

- Explore stories from the international section of the newspaper, and have your kids read *National Geographic Kids* or similar publications that can help them learn about kids in other cultures.
- Make a global-minded TV news show *your* family's show and commit to watching and chatting about it. I am a huge fan of Fareed Zakaria's *Global Public Square* (*GPS*) on CNN.
- Check out how your favorite US TV shows, films, and their stars are faring around the world and discuss why.
- Give your kids opportunities to learn another language before middle or high school if possible. You may be able to work online with affordable tutors who live in the country with the target language. For example, even after we left China, my children were tutored by Mandarin teachers based in Shanghai twice a week online for a handful of years. I believe the live interaction with a trained teacher is more effective than an online app. (See the Benefits of Bilingualism box on pages 38–39.)
- Learn about dual-language or immersion programs in your district, and try to secure a spot.
- Watch foreign subtitled films with your family. Read translated novels, or Japanese manga. Listen to the global top 50 pop songs on the charts, not just the US top 50.
- Watch a nonsubtitled foreign TV show and discuss your observations; you can find them easily on Netflix, for example. Narrate what you think is happening. Watch the clothing, sets, and actors' mannerisms. What are some stereotypes you may be applying or tearing down? Afterward, conduct some research on what the show was actually about.
- Put the largest world map you can find on the wall by your dining table or a highly trafficked area of your home. This signifies its importance as a family value and piques your kids' curiosity each time they walk by it. Memorize it with your kids by making it a game.
- Study and discuss the history, demographics, and geography of other nations.

- Get to know and host international students in your community. Look for organizations that are accredited through the Council on Standards for International Educational Travel. AFS Intercultural Programs offers opportunities to host international students, as well as support for sending your high school student abroad to study.
- Encourage your school and district to host international students and to send its own students overseas.
- Learn about and enjoy the hobbies and sports of other countries—for example, Japanese origami paper folding; card games; Chinese mah-jong; the Ethiopian *eskista* dance that is performed almost entirely by the shoulders; France's *la marelle ronde*, a spiral-shaped hopscotch game using one foot; India's national game, pachisi, which is also popular in Turkey; Iranian backgammon; Nigerian hand-clapping games; and South Africa's mancala.
- Learn about the unique holidays of other countries, like Sham el-Nessim, which marks the beginning of spring in Egypt; National Day in China, which celebrates the 1949 founding of the People's Republic of China; Bonn Om Touk in Cambodia, which marks the end of its rainy season; or the five-day-long Diwali festival of lights that illuminates homes and temples throughout India with candles and oil lamps.

TOKYO

2012–2016

James: 8 to 12 years old

Charles: 6 to 10 years old

Victoria: 3 to 7 years old

CHAPTER 7

Growing Pains

Coming "Home" to Japan?

O ur real estate agent met us at the front door of our new home to give us our keys and walk us through the place.

"Oh, kids, look, we can put some plants out on the—"

Crash!

"... terrace."

Charles was so excited that he ran straight through the screen door onto our terrace, Superman style.

"I am so, so sorry," I said, bowing my head, adapting to the expected mannerisms of the Japanese culture. "Do you have the number for a handyman?" I asked. I suspected we might need it.

Although all three of my kids were running through the house like reality TV stars checking out their new home at the start of a season, I was also excited for the countless opportunities that would await us in Japan. Until then, I had been trying to ignore what I considered to be my parenting shortcoming: my children did not fully understand my heritage, and therefore their own, in contrast to how dutifully my mother made my Japanese heritage fundamental to my identity. Until this time, my children looked in the mirror and couldn't really understand the significance of their Asian features.

Though I was nervous about yet another adventure and all the unknowns, I was comforted by the familiarity that awaited me in Tokyo.

So I rallied the troops, ready to set sail and push forth again. I had cooked lots of Japanese food at home, and we visited Japan to see family frequently during our two years in Shanghai. Our new Tokyo home would be thirty minutes away from my aunt's by subway. James was obsessed with baseball, and it's a national pastime in Japan.

Although my kids had been hearing me speak Japanese with family and Japanese friends their entire lives, they didn't speak the language themselves. Japanese is a difficult language that takes laser focus to learn, and I'd never taught it to my children because, frankly, I didn't have the bandwidth. Now with James's and Charles's knowledge of Chinese characters as a base, though, at least the written language would be easier to pick up because 70 to 80 percent of kanji characters have the same meaning in both languages. They didn't seem nervous about this because they had built a pretty strong can-do mindset, having already mastered both Mandarin and English. They had the confidence that they could do it again with Japanese.

I was excited for my children to get in touch with their Japanese roots, but I also felt confident about this move for their education. I had attended school in Japan during the summer of my later elementary school years, so I knew it ran a tight academic ship. Japan ranked high with its 2009 PISA scores: eighth in reading, ninth in math, and fifth in science (these standings have improved since then; Japan ranked eighth in reading, fifth in math, and second in science in the 2015 PISA).

Japan's PISA scores reflect the priority it places on education as a nation, with an ongoing assessment of the needs of the country and its citizens. For example, Japan's 2013 national education plan recognizes that it is facing unique challenges because of the confluence of a low national birthrate, an aging population, and globalization. The world is growing increasingly competitive and interconnected. In response, its Ministry of Education, Culture, Sports, Science, and Technology (MEXT) outlined updated policy directions for education: (1) promoting higher competencies in academic and social emotional achievement, career readiness, and independence; (2) developing global human resources, such as increasing the number of research universities and improving English language skills; (3) eliminating inequities and improving universal support systems; and (4) supporting collaboration between schools and communities.[1]

As in China, school isn't compulsory until grade 1 in Japan, so everything before that consists of day care, private school, or limited public school (sometimes chosen through a lottery). In some areas of Japan, just as in New York City at the time, schools hand out only a limited number of applications, and you have to wait in line in person. We looked into a few private kindergartens for Victoria because no public kindergartens for three-year-olds were in our vicinity and there were no openings at local day cares.

In Tokyo we went through a preschool application process that was stunningly competitive and ritualistic. We completed a meticulously handwritten (about five-point-size type, if I had to venture a guess) application with no fewer than one hundred questions! These questions, which seemed at times highly invasive from a Western vantage point, included whether Victoria was breast-fed and for how long, her physical and emotional development to date, her age when she first walked and spoke, her character, her favorite books and toys, places she plays, whether she is a picky eater, her toilet habits (specifically her frequency and control of #1 and #2), her sleep habits, and whether she is right- or left-handed. We posed for a grim family photo wearing navy blue suits (we looked like we were at a funeral) and practiced our honorific Japanese for a sixty-minute formal interview with the headmaster about our values and academic beliefs, again donning all navy (even the umbrella and our indoor slippers were navy, and Victoria sported a white handkerchief with her name in embroidery).

Navy clothing is a mostly unspoken rule of dress code formality in Japan, and you break it at your own peril. As a general rule, Japanese adults don't appreciate "creative individuality" when decorum is called for. Wearing the right clothes and behaving in the right fashion means you're showing respect. When I spent time in Japan in my youth, I learned quickly that you don't want to be "different" there. Despite all the politeness, you can easily feel like an outsider.

From the Japanese side of my family, I was raised to be extremely conscientious of my surroundings and the unspoken expectations of me within that environment. There are many unspoken rules in Japan. And that's the thing: I'm sure I broke these unwritten rules many, many times, but because they are so subtle, I wouldn't have known it. In Japan, a common phrase is *kuuki wo yomu*, "to read the air," to describe being able to pick up on the subtle clues about what's socially acceptable or not in a given situation.

I have heard the Japanese described as "inscrutable" by numerous foreigners transacting business there. I would venture to say that's simply because these international businesspeople can't "read the air." For example, when Japanese people bow their heads, it's an act of deference to acknowledge one's place within a particular context. I sometimes worry that those who do not understand this practice may think Japanese people appear subservient.

Respect for elders is an important value in Japanese culture, one that I wish was more widely practiced in the United States. Living as a multigenerational family (rather than the smaller nuclear family) is common in Japan. In Tokyo, my mother's younger sister, who was like my surrogate mom growing up, lived with us off and on, making an invaluable contribution to our immersive Japanese experience.

At the first preschool interview, three-year-old Victoria was scheduled for a full two-hour observation session. Also, since we had just arrived in Japan, Victoria did not speak or understand a word of Japanese, so she needed to be coached on basic salutations like "good morning" and "good afternoon." She also had to learn prompts like, "Please go wash your hands . . . Stand in line . . . Pick a book you would like to read . . . What is your favorite food?" and the like.

Her Western father was incredulous that any of this was real. For the parent interview, he expected to mostly sit there quietly while I tried to give the right answers. I had prepared with a tutor daily for two months—yes, *daily for two months!*—while Victoria was also tutored for her observation session.

I had prepared answers to all the questions my tutor suggested they'd ask: What are the disciplinary policies in your house? What are your beliefs about education? What is your schedule? What kind of volunteering would you like to do?

I am a fluent Japanese speaker with the caveat that I speak household Japanese, so I was preparing the content of my answers with the tutor, but also learning how to include the correct honorifics to show respect to the interviewers. In Japanese, the words you speak are calibrated to the status of the person you're speaking with. There is even a nuanced difference between the actual words that men use versus women. I had to learn to speak the way an adult woman in Japan would speak to a senior-level boss or respected teacher.

After all those preparations, the headmaster decided to speak only English (unheard of during an interview) and direct questions only to Alex. (*Who knew she could speak English?!*) I tried to politely interrupt, but she made unbreaking eye contact with him—imagine *Jedi mind tricks*—and refused to listen to or even look at me. Alex turned absolutely chalky, broke out into a faucet-like cold sweat, and seemed to fall into a trance repeating, "We believe in her autonomy ... Autonomy ... She needs to have autonomy. You raise autonomous children." After all, I had spent weeks preparing, and he had arrived at the interview expecting to behave more like the plus-one. This whole scenario was made worse by three-year-old Victoria repeatedly piping in, "Do I get my lollipop now, Mama?" Yes, I had bribed her: it was 5:00 p.m., and she was tired and therefore uncooperative, but clearly the bribe was to no avail. The entire upper portion of my navy dress was soaked through with sweat, hidden only by its equally suffocating matching blazer.

Alex and I kept radio silence walking down the hill from that school until we reached an intersection where we could hail a cab. Then all hell broke loose. I imagine this must be *the* infamous street corner where all parents who just bombed their interviews argue. It would be a good spot to film a TV series titled *Parenting Disasters: School Interview Blowouts.*

When we arrived home, I kicked off the special-ordered, outright ugly two-inch-heel black leather pumps (in Japan, they don't carry my size 10 shoes in stores). I tore off my soggy, navy (woven and very intentionally *not* knit) Jun Ashida—an iconic Japanese designer—dress with matching blazer and went straight to bed. I didn't want Victoria to miss the opportunity to learn Japanese and her heritage culture starting at age three, when her brain would absorb anything. I had felt *so* prepared for this opportunity, yet we crashed and burned.

When we returned for the next phase in the application process, mothers were sitting at tables with their two- and three-year-old children in complete silence while the song "Under the Sea" was piped in quietly. You could hear an eraser fall. *Did this music put the comatose toddlers in some kind of trance?* Then the interviewer came to take Victoria with a handful of other tots. Immediately, Victoria started howling, reaching out to me as if she was being tortured because she'd never been alone with strangers before. After listening to her continued screams from the observation room out of my sight, *I* couldn't take it anymore.

"I'm so, so sorry, but I would like to take my daughter home now," I said to the administrators sitting at the dais table. "I would like to withdraw our application."

They looked at me as if I'd gone stark raving mad. This was one of the two top preschools in Tokyo, a feeder into Keio Primary School, which is a direct feeder into Keio University, the Japanese equivalent of Princeton University. A handful of the most competitive private universities in Japan can be traced back to preschools, so those aspiring to enroll their kids in specific universities often make their decisions about their kids' early schooling accordingly. You don't just give up a chance like this, but I did. This school's application process was a strong hint that it wasn't the right fit for us. We would keep looking.

We got through our next interview at Aiiku Youchien—*youchien* means "preschool" in Japanese—by learning from all the ills from our first go. The headmaster asked *me* all the questions from our playbook, including our household discipline policies, beliefs in education, and Victoria's character. I then said, "If there is anything I can do to offer support, I would be honored to be given the opportunity," mustering up the most honorific Japanese that could roll off my tongue. It was so formal I could have been speaking to the emperor of Japan. I practiced it so much that I can still say the phrase in my sleep. I wasn't just groveling; requisite due diligence had revealed this particular pre-K had a highly demanding mommy involvement policy.

Victoria was a model of good behavior through the child observation because mommies stayed in the room observing the kids. She couldn't speak the language yet, but this session was just about watching her play and interact with others. I wondered what qualities they were watching for: Friendliness? Curiosity? Sharing? Attentiveness? Regardless, I watched my joyful child and believed she must have been checking all the right boxes.

I give myself kudos too, because I managed to stay kneeling on the ground next to her silently, in *seiza* style, legs bent under me, for the full hour while all the other mothers stayed seated in a circle around the children. I may have left a better impression if I too had stayed seated, but Victoria wanted me closer. By the time I stood up, my legs had been frozen from a lack of circulation for a good fifty-nine of those sixty minutes. It's a miracle I somehow staggered out of the room in ill-fitting navy slippers without bracing for the back of a kiddie chair to prop me up.

We had each performed our best for the interview and observation. And, bingo! A week later, on a Saturday evening in November, we got the acceptance letter in the mail. I shrieked and bounced up and down like a hysterical jackpot winner in Vegas. I hugged Victoria with vigor, like I was squeezing the last life out of a tube of toothpaste. Then I dashed to the ATM in the dark to make the direct deposit for tuition—so that just in case it was a mistake, it would be harder for them to back out. We were finished; it was done. And, sure enough, the principal called the following Monday and asked to meet with me. I brought my aunt along in the event she needed to plead our case like an attorney for the defense with the most respectful Japanese.

"This is a very different culture and we need to make sure you can follow it," the principal said. "I have to tell you that the teachers were not in favor of accepting Victoria and your family. We've had a Western family here before and they were wonderful and very involved, but it was a lot of work for us to teach them. However, I like you and believe in you. Please make sure that Victoria understands the social norms here before she starts school."

I understood that what she meant was, "Get shaped up, or you will not be so welcome here. And, by the way, my reputation is on the line." While I was more than a tad intimidated, I felt reassured by how straightforward this headmaster was. And she was giving us a chance!

I enrolled Victoria in a local day care for children up to age three that had coincidentally just opened across the street. She would be immersed in the Japanese language and cultural practices before the school year started on April 1, 2013. In Japan, the academic calendar ends in early March and the new year begins just a few weeks after, making March a bustling time of activity: high school graduates leave for college, teachers transfer, schools ready themselves for the new students, and so on. James and Charles were now in second and first grade, respectively, so we were able to enroll them in the local public school without interviews.

The Hunt for the Right School for Your Child

- Scour groups on the Internet, and read all posts with a critical eye (meaning, take everything with a grain of salt). Then reach out to the posters and ask them questions.

- Make calls and send emails to the school and others associated with the school to get a feel for its community, academics, and leadership.
- Find current parents; they know best. When you meet one, ask for introductions to others, and keep doing this until you create a network of reliable sources. Past parents can be helpful for making introductions to current parents, but be aware that school cultures and teachers can change from year to year.
- Go to school information sessions, and find people there. But don't take one person's opinion as the whole truth. Canvass the others!
- Read the school's website for academic and curricular information, and gather all the information you can from it so that you can ask questions about it. However, you may find that schools do not practice what they preach; their websites are often marketing tools.
- Check out the campus on Google Maps, and walk around it if you can. Review how your child would get to and from school.
- Review the school's annual performance records, easily accessible online, mandated by the state.
- Review the school's demographics, also easily accessible online, to learn about its community.

I toured no fewer than twenty public schools in Tokyo before deciding where to live so the boys could attend a welcoming school that would offer support for non-Japanese speakers. Kogai Elementary School had a Japanese language program for nonnative speakers in which students get pulled out of class one period per day for individual Japanese instruction. Since the school was located in the midst of many foreign embassies, I felt the boys could learn Japanese and not be worried about adversely standing out.

I had attended Japanese public school in a neighboring area during summers growing up, so I was well aware of Japan's homogeneity and how those who are different can have a target on their backs for bullying. I was not going to allow my children to suffer from an identity crisis as a result of being perceived as foreigners. They were to be proud of their Japanese and American heritage, always.

I was thrilled that each child would be enrolling in a school where their individual personalities and needs would be welcome. All three would be socialized into Japanese language and culture, and James and Charles would be at a great school where they would build on all the academic gains they had made in Shanghai.

In Japan I continued to work on my master's degree. My comparative education work was gaining a new lens with a deep dive into the Japanese education system. I felt stronger and surer than ever before of my ability to bring my academic and personal insights together.

For my thesis project, I needed to conduct interviews with Japanese parents who had just returned from an overseas stint, so they had been educating their children abroad. The wait for my university's ethics approval felt interminable. There were numerous holdups because of translation issues. I had gotten so used to working at a furious pace on my master's research that the idle time was making me go a bit stir-crazy. So I wrote a few op-ed and personal essays about my experiences with my children in education and sent them to some newspapers. My article on the preschool admissions process in Tokyo was outright rejected by an editor at the *Japan Times*, but another editor there contacted me the following week to inquire about other story ideas. From there, I found myself writing regular feature pieces for the *Japan Times*. Eventually I had my own column, The Learning Curve, where I dug into all things education in Japan and greater Asia.

In addition to polishing up my research and writing skills, I was able to fill a niche there as an English-speaking education "expert" when media outlets like CBS and CNBC were looking to understand developments in Japan. While the number of Japanese people fluent in English is slowly growing, Japan in some ways is still isolated from the English-speaking world. This points toward Japan's inward focus, which sometimes leads to isolation in the global arena.

This work led me to a career as a freelance journalist and expert in education in Japan, though I also dabbled in gender and cross-cultural issues. *Who knew this is where life would take me?*

I felt grateful that the universe was responding positively to what I was so passionate about. I knew I had finally struck a chord when I received tons of both hate mail and letters of appreciation about a feature series I wrote on my thesis topic: children who return to Japan after an overseas sojourn (called *kikokushijo*). Upon their return to Japan, they were most often not culturally and socially accepted, though I felt that they should be Japan's global ambassadors. It was one of the paper's most read articles of the year.

Moving to Japan was a bit of a homecoming for me, but my Japanese identity had also caused me some conflict in my youth in both New York and Japan. I felt like an insider and an outsider simultaneously in both places. While I never doubted that the United States was my home, I also never felt like the other kids when I was growing up.

I was always wearing the latest kids' clothes from Japan, which made me stand out at school in the United States. I remember that in third grade my physical education teacher made me stop wearing my favorite Japanese Pink Lady teen idol sneakers because she said they weren't proper gym shoes. I felt torn between the two parts of my identity.

Returning to Japan as an adult with three kids of my own felt complicated and simple at the same time. After the struggles I faced in Shanghai, I felt more at ease in Japan. I knew how to speak the language, I could get around, and there was much less uncertainty.

But how would my American values fit in? How would I balance my Japanese and American identities as an adult in Japan? Answering these questions would end up posing unique challenges along the way.

CHAPTER 8

Mister Rogers' Neighborhood

*The Community Fosters the
Independent and Whole Child*

W hen Victoria was five and nearing the end of her final year of preschool, where she had been thriving for the past three years, she was invited to a school-sponsored sleepover with the other children in the class. The children and their teachers journeyed to a lodge in a national park and spent the night there without parents. Japanese children are afforded opportunities to become independent at an early age due to the thoughtful, nurturing, and protective support from adults and the larger community outside the home. In this case, the teachers, not the parents, were providing the support.

It was an end-of-preschool rite of passage, and Victoria could not wait. She'd made a lot of progress in those three years. She'd become a model Japanese citizen, reminiscent of how James thrived in the Chinese school culture at his primary school in Shanghai.

A couple of weeks after the sleepover, there was a mandatory parent meeting. (Opting out required a formal letter of explanation.) The teachers debriefed us with a PowerPoint slide show of photos from their adventure. Among the pictures were shots of our children picking up sticks outside and building fortresses, laying futons to get ready for sleep, and eating at long, low communal tables on bent knees.

Some of the most memorable photos were of same-sex communal

baths: children standing in a line covered in suds and helping each other wash off, with teachers in swimsuits standing by. Traditional family-style bathing at a bathhouse is common practice. It was innocent and natural, like siblings in a bathtub. I chuckled thinking about how US parents might react seeing these pictures and how I could understand the school principal's reluctance to admit Western families.

Japanese schools encourage children to work through their problems without adult intervention whenever possible. Starting in early childhood, kids have many opportunities for teamwork, sharing, taking care of one another, and working through disputes. At least in the younger years, classmates grow up more like siblings. Charles later wisely mused, "Mama, it's so much better in Japan. You make stronger friendships when you are kind of doing stuff on your own that you're not supposed to be doing. It's not good when your parents are watching everything you do."

Tokkatsu

In the Japanese context, *tokkatsu* (collaborative whole child education) is an explicit and integrated part of the Japanese curriculum, meant to foster every student's sense of personal and collective responsibility. World-renowned Japanese education scholar Ryoko Tsuneyoshi has examined the concept in depth.[1]

In all types of tokkatsu activities, students' autonomy is encouraged and emphasized. Students' cleaning responsibilities, for example, fall under tokkatsu. There are no custodians in Japanese schools, so children clean up their classrooms at the end of the day. They take turns sweeping and mopping, wiping down tables, and even cleaning toilets and sinks.

Cleaning *is* learning, albeit not in the academic sense. Chores are rotated, and each day one student is the classroom coordinator (*nichoku*). In the beginning, the teacher guides the students, but the goal is for the students to become more autonomous; they form small groups, divide up the work, and internalize the sense of social responsibility.

Students are also encouraged to organize class meetings and decide on topics or activities by themselves. "This fits the goal of cooperative autonomy, the encouragement of peer support allowing the teacher to step back."[2] Tokkatsu is a way of developing students' character, as well as serving as a form of classroom management for the teacher. The activities keep students engaged with the content and the implementation of class lessons.

When I picked Victoria up from Aiiku preschool one day during her first year, she trotted over to me with a proud smile on her face.

"I helped Mika-chan today!"

"Oh, that's great. What did you do?"

"She didn't make it to the bathroom in time, so I washed her undies for her."

Apparently Victoria washed and wrung the undies out in the kiddie bathroom sink, and then gave them to the teacher to hang to dry. This all took place without intervention from any teacher, though under her watchful eyes. Similarly, when we travel, I always take laundry detergent and the kids help: we do loads in the bathtub, ask for extra hangers, and sleep under drying clothing. It's like an assembly line with my three children. So Victoria's actions at the preschool offered the teacher a little bit too much insight into our home culture.

In Japan, there's less anxiety when children go off to school because they are expected to become independent prior to starting primary school. Children travel short distances to and from school on their own, starting in first grade. In Japan, unattended children walk around town and ride public transportation: buses, trains, and subways. Yes, six-year-olds are riding the subway by themselves in Tokyo, including switching lines and walking to and from stations and crossing streets. That's completely normal.

I knew that I had little to worry about with road safety, although the Tokyo metropolitan area is the most populous metro area in the world, with over 36 million inhabitants.[3] When we moved to Tokyo, I decided to try to get a local driver's license. I even took lessons to learn how to drive the "crank," a supernarrow 90-degree zigzag during which you cannot hit the curb.

I failed my driver's test on the first try—I had already been driving for twenty-three years!

I thought the test was over and ran through a final stop sign on my way to pulling over. Straight out of Alicia Silverstone's scene in *Clueless* in which her father praises his daughter for having talked her way into straight A's, I tried to sweet-talk the examiner. He shut me down within a millisecond. It turns out my New York instincts needed an immediate intervention and exorcising.

I was quickly learning the ways of my host and heritage country. I finally passed the exam a month later on my second try. This time, all ducks were in a row, with no fuss and following all instructions to a T. Nothing was going to get me a pass other than mastering the required maneuvers, reminiscent of my kids' educations in Shanghai.

During our time in Japan, I never saw anyone run a red light, except an absolutely flustered and late *me* trying to get to James's baseball practice on the outskirts of Tokyo. There were two rows of lights with greens and reds and arrows, and I couldn't quite figure out which light was mine. I promptly received a ticket and numerous points on my driver's license. Even when I spaced out during rush hour at a traffic light that had just turned green, not a single car behind me honked. Each person is expected to respect the rules and not bother anyone with needless noise pollution. And for the most part, they do.

During the first two weeks of elementary school, first graders are assigned walking routes, with a color-coded ribbon tied to their backpack to denote their route. Then teachers guide them home in groups after dismissal. The teacher expects the children to recognize their house and depart at the appropriate place. Kids learn where their classmates live too, so they can bring them assignments if they're sick. One time a boy was so focused on talking to Victoria during the entire route from school to our home that he passed his own home. "Rito-kun walked me all the way home and the teacher had to walk *him* all the way back to his home!" Victoria couldn't stop giggling when she recounted the story to me.

After the first couple of weeks, the kids can walk the route with their classmates or on their own. All first graders wear yellow hats and a large yellow cover over their boxy *randoseru* backpack flaps, so passers-by will know they are traveling on their own for the first time. The community keeps an extra-watchful eye on them.

Kids sometimes get lost and may need to approach a crossing guard or police officer for help. (Elderly people work as crossing guards at larger intersections, and in Tokyo, there are police booths every few blocks.) They might stop in at a convenience store or play with their friends. But somehow they all make it home.

It's a joy to see kids finding their own agency, exercising their curiosities and learning about the consequences of their choices on their own, without parents hovering or teachers lecturing. I've watched with amusement as a group of umbrella-carrying first graders at a busy crosswalk were so busy sloshing about that they missed numerous green lights. I've seen kids playing with dried-up worms and catching crawling pill bugs to proudly bring home to mom. When kids show up at home late from school after their adventures and miss the start of their piano lesson, they may get into trouble—but that's how kids learn responsibility.

Many Japanese parents now have GPS tracker cell phones nested in the backpacks as backups in case of emergency, but for decades, there was no tracking: kids just figured it out and parents didn't freak out because they knew that allowing their children to make mistakes and problem-solve on their own was a gift. The kids who now have cell phones usually have children's phones (*kodomo no keitai*), which offer a few key functions: a handful of preprogrammed numbers the child can call and receive calls from, a few automatic text messages like "I received your message," an emergency buzzer draw cord, and GPS. After a nominal initiation fee, kids' cell phones cost less than $8 a month. It's a great way to alleviate parents' concerns without giving kids pricey smartphones.

A long-running Japanese show, *My First Errand* (*Hajimete no Otsukai*), shows young children out on their first errands around town. It's a heartwarming show that encourages young children to learn how to read traffic signals, where to cross streets, how to pay for things, and how to safely navigate to and from home. The children carry *omamori*—Japanese amulets from shrines or temples meant to provide good luck and protection.

In one episode, a four-year-old girl is sent to take a diaper to her baby brother at his day care center. Her mother watches her walk down the block and return several times in tears with various reasons for why she can't make the trip. Mom gives her a pep talk, and the girl finally accomplishes her mission because she believes her brother will be sad if he has a dirty diaper. Meanwhile, the audience and a panel of commentators watch videos and a montage of pictures of the girl from birth through age four, and we celebrate with her mom that the girl has become more independent. The Japanese audience at home can feel nostalgia and pride along with the girl's mom, remembering their own experiences as children.

It's hard to let go of kids, especially at such a young age, but Japanese parents give their children more room to solve their own problems than we tend to do in the States. There is an unspoken commitment to the greater community, which allows children to be safer. In the United States, "free-range" parenting advocates often face a public backlash from parents who decry this technique as dangerous for children.

*   *   *

Because my Japanese mother grew up with the same ideas of independence as I witnessed in Tokyo, she brought me up in a similar way in New York City. By the fourth grade, I took public buses to and from school on my own. Some mornings I stood in the frigid cold trying to scarf down a prepackaged Entenmann's chocolate frosted doughnut while my eyes were thick with sleep and frost; other times I boarded the wrong bus. But plenty of other New York children were doing the same thing. That's rare now, though statistically, New York City is far safer than it was back then. The violent crime rate has steadily dropped since 1990.

I also flew internationally on my own from the age of six years old on to see my Japanese family. I had to spend several hours in a freezing airport in Anchorage, Alaska, during layovers, then fly to Tokyo, then to Osaka (my ancestral home, where my mother grew up). In Osaka, my grandmother would always be waiting for me at the bottom of the escalator at the airport, holding a bag full of my favorite Japanese treats. I likely hadn't eaten in twenty-four hours. Airplane food back then was really, really, really bad.

Most of the time things went off without a hitch. I wore a special badge to show that I was traveling alone, and a gate agent or a flight attendant was always looking out for me. One time, things did go wrong. The summer after seventh grade, my mother dropped me off curbside at JFK to take a People Express flight to a summer program in California. (People Express was a low-budget operation that existed for just six years; it was often nicknamed "People Distress.") My flight took off twelve hours after its scheduled departure, leaving me to sleep in the airport with twenty dollars.

I appreciate how navigating those times imbued me with a sense of fearlessness. And that's something I can give my own children: the chance to grow up independent too.

"They break an arm now or they break their heads later," I heard world-renowned Japanese architect Takaharu Tezuka say at a well-attended guest lecture I organized at an international school in Tokyo. The audience of largely Western parents audibly gasped.

In Tokyo I interviewed Tezuka for a feature for the *Japan Times* about the evolution of school design and purpose-built schools. Tezuka won international awards for his 2007 doughnut-shaped Fuji kindergarten that featured an expansive circular roof deck that preschoolers could zoom around endlessly like the *Looney Tunes* Road Runner.[4]

Fuji kindergarten was designed to give students the freedom for adventure and exploration. It contained easy access to tall trees for climbing and rails that allowed children to dangle their legs over the side. The deck had nets and other safety precautions, of course, but Tezuka understands the necessity of risk-taking for children as part of their growing process. Researchers from the University of Tokyo found that the school's students run an average of three miles per day because of the circular shape of the space.

I find his words a metaphor for so much of being a parent. While our instincts may be to fix situations so kids avoid pain, we shouldn't deprive them of valuable learning experiences that can guide them later in their lives.

In this respect, I view myself as a deliberate anti–helicopter parent.

Helicopter parenting is marked by an intensively hands-on approach to raising children. This parenting style, which has been researched extensively in Asian countries and the United States, has been critiqued for limiting children's abilities to solve problems for themselves and act autonomously in everyday situations. Research has demonstrated that choice is key to developing children's sense of motivation and gratification.[5] When parents make all the choices for their children, they deprive their kids of the opportunity to develop a strong sense of self. Later in life, many of these individuals rely on their parents for decision-making activities normally associated with adulthood.

Although I'm not a helicopter parent, I am sometimes torn about when and how to step in. In Tokyo, I did follow my kids on their way home from time to time, jumping into a doorway or behind a column if they turned around. During mommy confession lunches, I heard many Japanese parents admit to doing the same.

I found James's wanderings the most amusing. One day after school when he was in second grade, I spotted him walking into a Family Mart, a well-stocked convenience store that alternates seemingly every block of the Japanese urban landscape with a 7-Eleven, its competitor. (Not only are there 7-Elevens in Japan, but it's actually a Japanese-owned company.) *He doesn't have any money. He can't buy anything*, I thought.

Peering obtusely through its front glass sliding door, I saw that he was standing at the newspaper rack reading a newspaper. The paper was so cumbersome that he had pulled apart pages and sections that were never going to return to their proper folds again. The resulting heap resembled campfire kindling.

James was the sports enthusiast in the family as well as the statistics person. He memorized all the sports history facts and data he could— like the bus routes when he was in Hong Kong. At that moment, he was reading a newspaper devoted solely to his favorite pastime. I walked in.

"Hi, James," I said in an upbeat tone like I was his younger brother who just caught him with his hand in the cookie jar. He was so entrenched in his reading that he was doubly shocked to find me standing next to him and that he wasn't actually at the baseball game about which he was reading.

"Oh . . . hi, Mama," he said, looking like a deer in the headlights.

"I guess you decided not to come straight home after school like you're supposed to."

He nodded slowly, earnestly, resigned to the Big Heap of Trouble he was sure was coming his way. I could see the hamster wheel of explanations turning in his brain.

"This is the only *conbini* that has these sports newspapers," he said. "And I'm doing math when I read these statistics. And I'm reading in Japanese. And, please, Mama, don't be mad at me."

Truth be told, I wasn't mad at all. I was elated watching him explore his freedom because I knew he was safe. It was adorable. We were practicing the Japanese proverb "Send the adored child on journeys." *Kawaii ko ni wa tabi o saseyo.*

James sheepishly attempted to refold the newspaper and put it back on the rack. It looked exactly like you might expect. How many times had he done this, leaving avant-garde paper sculptures in his wake?

I went to the cashier to purchase the newspaper. He smiled and glanced at James with a familiarity that indicated this was old hat, and he wasn't at all annoyed about James's read-and-run habits. This young demographic is probably the lifeblood of such chain convenience shops; when kids start getting an allowance, this is where they spend it.

The end result was pretty great. Once I knew about James's interest, I started subscribing to three newspapers: the daily Japanese children's newspaper, *Asahi Elementary School Student Newspaper*; the *Japan Times*, the English-language daily; and the *New York Times*. Japan still has the world's largest physical newspaper circulation, with some offering both morning and afternoon editions. James woke up thirty minutes before breakfast every day to rush to the mailbox to gather the newspapers. Then he spread them all over the sofa and coffee table in our family room to devour. As he was not a big eater, this often seemed to be his main nourishment for the morning.

We all thrived under the expectations for children to be self-reliant. Both James (third grade) and Charles (second grade) were embarking on their own little adventures daily, gaining confidence navigating the good and the bad. In second grade, Charles fell off his bike on his way home from soccer practice and somehow figured out a way to repair a gear that had gone awry. To this day, mountain biking and engineering are two of his favorite pastimes because he gets to constantly rejigger his bike and test out the results.

In preschool, starting at three years old, Victoria was expected to pack her three schoolbags each day: one for her teacher-parent journal and change of clothes, one for her shoes (because there are indoor and outdoor shoes to change into and out of throughout the day), and one for her *obento*, or Japanese lunch box. Every day Victoria had to remember what to pack, and then she had to go through a routine of unpacking her belongings neatly in their assigned spaces at school.

The teacher specifically asked moms *not* to do it for them. If she forgot something at home, I was not supposed to bring it in for her. In contrast, when five-year-old Charles forgot to bring his swimsuit to summer camp in Connecticut, his camp expected me to drive over and bring one in for him, rejecting my suggestion to have him borrow one from a friend or use one from the lost and found. It never even occurred to me that they thought *I* was at fault for not packing the swimsuit because that was a mom's responsibility in the United States. I did not come in, and Charles did not swim that day.

Not only are children expected to take care of themselves, they are expected to take care of the greater community. Although there are no public rubbish bins on street corners, there is no problem with litter in Tokyo: everyone takes their trash home and separates it into numerous categories: burnables, nonburnables, paper, plastic, PET bottles, cans, Styrofoam, newspapers, cartons, unbroken glass, and batteries. Each type of trash is picked up a separate day of the week.

After Japan's winning opening match against Colombia in the 2018 World Cup, Japanese fans stayed after the game to clean up the stadium. Many had brought their own garbage bags from home. This is normal practice after sports events in Japan, but foreigners were so incredulous about it they filmed the cleanup efforts in multiple videos uploaded to YouTube, calling the Japanese the "best guests." A community mindset ingrained from early childhood is to not make trouble for others (*meiwaku o kakenai*). Be responsible for yourself while also helping the community.

The community mindset applies to lost belongings too. In the

United States, if you accidentally leave your wallet behind in a grocery cart, you might never see it again. In Japan, someone will return it or set it aside for you. When it's an item that can't be traced back to a person, it'll sit there until you retrieve it.

Our family visited a ski lodge for several days, and I was amused that a single glove was carefully displayed each morning on a stake along the path to the first chairlift. "Oh! That's *my* glove," Charles finally piped up.

I'm not sure how long they would have left it there, just waiting for its rightful owner to figure it out. But when my Japanese residence card (comparable in importance to a passport) fell out of my pocket when I went out for a run, I was confident it would turn up. Sure enough, someone mailed it back to me within the week.

There is one particular story that my children read in their textbook at school that strikes me as representative of the way Japanese schoolchildren learn that they are part of a greater whole. Caldecott Honor picture book *Swimmy* by Leo Lionni has been part of the second-grade curriculum in Japan since 1977, so parents today grew up reading this story as well and share this with their children.

Swimmy is a fast-swimming black fish living among red fish. All the fish are tiny and worried about swimming into areas where bigger fish are looking for food. Their fear paralyzes them and they don't go out to play and see the beautiful sea creatures that Swimmy does on his adventures. So he insists that they try a new plan: they'll all swim in a school shaped as a giant fish, with Swimmy acting as the eye. Working together, "each in his own place," they can outsmart the big fish and venture out without fear.

For me, this story teaches the importance of each person carrying out her individual responsibility for the good of all. Children learn that every person has a key role in achieving group goals. Swimmy uses his unique coloring for the benefit of the group so that everyone can swim safely.

This lesson is timeless.

* * *

Another common practice that ensures the smooth workings within the larger community is "rock, paper, scissors," what we in the United States may consider a childhood pastime. *Janken*, as it is called in Japan, is the default way decisions are made for something as inconsequential as who gets to ride in the front seat of the car to bigger concerns like who becomes the PTA president. It has also been employed for major financial decisions. And it can feel as if *all* decisions are made this way, so much so that there are dozens of varieties of this game that include everything from "curry rice janken" to incorporating it into song and dance. In 2005, the president of a Japanese electronics company couldn't decide which auction house should sell the company's art collection, valued at over $20 million. Christie's and Sotheby's were equally good, he thought, so he told them to play janken for the rights to sell the collection.[6]

The communitarian ethic in Japan is visible in every aspect of social life. You'll often hear Japanese moms say "*Gaman*" to their children. It means, loosely, "Be patient and have forbearance." It's a reminder to deal with difficult circumstances with poise. *Jiritsu* is a related term that indicates independence and self-reliance. These directives remind people to deal gracefully with problems without bothering others. They are central concepts to how Japanese society works.

Spend a day on the New York City subways and you'll witness the perfect opposite of this belief system. People clip their nails on the subway (Do they think it's going to biodegrade on the subway floor?), stay seated staring at their phones while an octogenarian or pregnant woman is standing, leave behind bags of half-eaten McDonald's for fellow passengers to deal with, and occupy multiple seats. It's common practice to put your personal wants and needs above that of the greater community, and you just won't see that in Japan. I wonder if it was always like this. Are we even teaching compassion and respect in schools? If so, are we modeling them in the greater community?

* * *

In Japan, this larger community ethos nurtures what we in the United States call whole child education. This trendy concept values children's physical and emotional needs, not just their academic ones. True whole child lessons both in and out of school can work only with whole community support, not just in the classroom, which is often the case in the United States. For example, if students are taught to be respectful to elders in a school lesson but then that behavior is not modeled for them in the larger community, let's say by offering their seat to an elderly person on a bus, the lesson can fall on deaf ears.

In Japan, respecting elders is modeled throughout the society. When kids walk out of those school doors, they see special seating for elders everywhere, taxi drivers taking their time helping people with wheelchairs, grandparents revered within the family. The difference is reflected not only in the overall culture but within the schools, and both seem to contribute to Japanese students' understanding that they are responsible for the good of the community.

When my grandmother passed away in 2015, the kids and I were a part of her funeral ceremony. It included sleeping with her body overnight, bathing and dressing her, touching her for her final farewell, and then packing her casket with freshly cut flowers and sending her body into the incinerator at the crematorium. Afterward we moved her remaining bones into an urn using elongated chopsticks. Her urn is kept in a dedicated shrine in my uncle's home. Every day, her favorite foods are placed at the shrine as a way of continuing to honor her spirit in the house. This intensely personal send-off is a show of reverence in Japan that she will forever be honored and thanked.

One of my favorite ways that the whole child education philosophy is practiced in Japan is the way nutrition lessons are baked into the larger curriculum.

James has never had a very strong appetite, but Charles and Victoria excitedly looked forward to their school lunches in Tokyo and discussed them every evening. They would pore over the monthly school lunch menu we posted on our refrigerator.

The menu not only lists the items to be served but also the ingredients and their calories. Meals included items like grilled mackerel with rice, seaweed salad with sesame dressing, miso soup, slices of melon, and stewed potatoes. On days when corn was served, students in grades 1 and 2 were asked to help husk. On or around holidays, celebratory traditional meals were prepared. And cuisines from all over the world, including India, Thailand, and France, were served, introducing the kids to a variety of cuisines at a young age. Victoria tried Polish food in her Tokyo elementary school in summer 2018 during Japan's World Cup soccer playoffs against Poland. Since then, she proudly references her love of Polish food.

One of the great things about the monthly menu was that it gave us an opportunity to discuss the foods with our kids and make sure we weren't preparing the same meals for dinner that the children had for lunch.

Japanese kids may not always want to try everything, but they do it anyway and are some of the least finicky eaters as a result of the cultural expectations. Aside from rare food allergies, menus are not based on what the kids "feel like" eating that day, and parents and schools don't cater to picky eaters. Children try everything and learn to appreciate what they're served. The same meal was rarely ever served twice in a single school year! In the United States, you can safely assume that your child will have the option of eating a burger, hot dog, or pizza and chips and a soda (!) every single school day.

On special tasting days, parents were invited to the school to sample the meals while the nutrition teacher explained the calories, health values, and local source of each ingredient. This reflects how the classroom teachers teach students about nutrition. Japan passed laws in 2005 and 2007 to promote nutritional education for children to encourage lifelong healthy eating habits. This has also led to an exponential increase in the number of school nutrition teachers, who now number in the thousands throughout Japan's schools.

The nutrition and health-related content and activities that are integrated into the school curriculum are known as *shokuiku*. Shokuiku incorporates nutrition, physical and mental health, being grateful for your food and those who produced it, and behaving respectfully at meals. Even basic table manners were covered in these lessons: how to sit up straight without fidgeting, hold the rice bowl, use chopsticks, and speak at acceptable volumes at the table. Home economics courses with information on nutrition are a standard part of the curriculum in elementary, middle, and high school.

Japan has the lowest rate of childhood obesity and highest rate of longevity in the developed world,[7] in part because lunchtime is seen as a learning opportunity to promote lifelong health. These lessons are integrated into school culture, so every child grows up knowledgeable about the importance of nutrition.

In addition to the focus on health and nutrition, lunchtime is a community event. The teacher supervises as students pull their desks together in clusters of four or five, and then students act as the cafeteria staff. The assigned lunch duty group for that week gets the food from the kitchen and serves their fellow students. In this way, the school saves money on staffing as well as teaching the kids responsibility and practical skills. The students are on an equal footing and take care of one another.

Before every meal, the students recite the same sentiments: "Thank you for the food. We appreciate it, and we will not waste any food here or at home." They don't waste food; they just don't. They're taught not to leave one grain of rice in their bowls, or it would be disrespectful to all the work that it took to grow it, harvest it, cook it, and get it to this point of eating it. And they don't overconsume. Often the children's lunchtime conversation itself focuses on the meal and its specific farm-to-table path.

What They Say Versus What They Do:
School Lunches in Japan Versus the United States

JAPAN

What They Say	What They Do
According to the Japanese Basic Law of Food and Nutrition Education, schools are to provide lifelong learning about healthy and sustainable diets.	A new position began in 2007: nutrition teachers are required to have licenses as both teachers and nutritionists. They develop school lunch menus and coordinate nutrition education, providing individual guidance as needed.
The Japanese School Lunch Act provides guidelines not only for nutritional values but food hygiene.	Children wash their hands before school meals, wear masks and hair covers when serving food, and brush their teeth after meals.
The Japanese School Lunch Act includes a goal to "enhance a sound understanding of food production, distribution, and consumption."	Whenever possible, food for school lunches is sourced locally from school gardens tended by students and nearby farms.

UNITED STATES

What They Say	What They Do
The US Department of Agriculture (USDA) required schools to add more fruits and vegetables to its meals starting in 2012.	In a large study of Boston middle schools, students discarded 19 percent of their entrées, 47 percent of their fruit, 25 percent of their milk, and 73 percent of their vegetables on average.[8]
In 2012, the USDA implemented new sodium guidelines so that schools would have to reduce sodium in meals incrementally and increasingly by three target dates in 2014, 2017, and 2022.[9] Over 70 percent of dietary sodium comes from packaged and prepared foods. The Food and Drug Administration's total recommended value is 2,300 mg or less per day.	That effort has gone so poorly that the first of three target guidelines from 2014 has yet to be reached: limiting sodium to just or less than 1,230 mg per lunch in elementary school, less than 1,360 in middle school, and less than 1,420 in high school—all more than half of the recommended daily intake for adults.[10]

What They Say	What They Do
According to USDA regulations, all grain products sold in schools must be at least 50 percent whole grain.	Schools can receive exemptions for a multitude of reasons—including if students or parents complain that they just don't like the whole grain products.[11]

There are nevertheless shortcomings of the community-based ethic in Japan, and there's a saying that fits this too. It's so commonly repeated in Japan it's a cliché: "The nail that sticks out gets hammered down." While it's a bit reductive, this saying hints at how Swimmy could otherwise easily have been an outcast in his community rather than a humble hero. And it speaks a lot of truth about my experience. My own experiences in summer school in Japan were painful because, being half-Japanese, I was an outsider. I was an outsider as a kid in New York too, but in a different way: in New York I was overlooked socially, whereas in Japan I was actively taunted.

When I arrived for school during the summer after fourth grade, many things about me stood out. I showed up ready to be the *best*—the best swimmer, the best recorder player in class—and that, combined with my somewhat fragmented Japanese and American background, made some of the kids want to cut me down to size.

After school one day, a group of boys chased me down the street. I didn't have the traditional Japanese *randoseru* backpack, just the purple JanSport I'd brought from New York. One of the boys yanked it off my back, threw out the contents, and stomped on an arts-and-crafts project I had worked on painstakingly for over a week. Then he tore out pages from the book I had just borrowed from the public library.

There are some social issues in Japan, such as bullying (a national average of 23.9 bullying instances per 1,000 students) of kids who are "different" and don't conform to Japanese ideals.[12] Almost 99 percent of the population in Japan is ethnically Japanese, and Japan doesn't have antidiscrimination laws to protect ethnic minorities such as the indigenous Ainu or Japanese citizens of Korean descent. Japan recently passed the first anti-hate-speech law in the country, but the law specifically excludes undocumented migrants.[13]

Even Japanese citizens who spend time abroad often find difficulties when they return to Japan. One student I interviewed for a piece in the *Japan Times*, Sotaro Irie, called his return to Japan the hardest time in his life: "I learned that in the US, if you have a different opinion, you say it—there is no right answer, so you do not have to be shy or embarrassed. And in Japan, there is a group opinion with one answer." Returnees often have to rediscover Japan's unique customs and expectations.[14]

My experiences of bullying made me especially protective of my children as I searched for schools for them in Tokyo. I worked hard with outside support to ensure that they would learn the language and culture quickly so they'd have an easier time fitting in.

While my negative experiences molded me, I also grew up understanding the value of the collective culture in Japan. Each individual is responsible for contributing to an overall sense of well-being in their community.

Japanese teachers are respected in the community at large for their role in shaping the future of the country. As I learned as a parent in the Japanese school system, that respect is hard earned—and much deserved.

CHAPTER 9

MacGyver

*The Problem-Solving Stuntman
in the Classroom: The Teacher*

Teachers in Japan go to amazing lengths to help children absorb a lesson. In one especially memorable scene, Charles's first-grade teachers came dressed in costumes to teach students about bodily functions. One teacher was dressed as poop—and on a parent observation day, no less! They sang "The Poop Song" (*"Unko no Uta"*), which is a bit like the *Everyone Poops* book (incidentally, written by a Japanese author), only in song format . . . and with costumes. Here's how it translates:

> *Your tummy feels refreshed*
> *Sei, poop poop puri puri puri*
> *Poop poop puri puri puri*
> *Every day your tummy goes grumble grumble grumble*
> *Every day your farts go poot poot poot*
> *It's your body's proof that you're alive*
> *Holding it in isn't good*

There were three decked-out teachers at the head of the classroom. Picture the poop emoji swirling with two arms and two legs sticking out of it. The teachers performed a choreographed dance full of twirls, fist pumps, and hip checks, with unbridled excitement about healthy digestion. The kids were dancing along. It was a truly interdisciplinary moment of science, health, and physical education. But there I was at the back of the class thinking, *Is this for real?* while looking to catch eye contact with a fellow parent who might be feeling equally as awkward as I did. No such luck.

To them, this was completely normal and much appreciated. Some parents were rocking out too! Although it was against the rules, I quickly took out my cell phone and took as covert a video as possible from the back corner where maybe nobody would notice.

Japanese kid culture is obsessed with poop. One of the most popular children's book series right now contains lessons on *kanji* (the Japanese writing system) where every example of how a kanji is used in a sentence contains a reference to poop.

This animated lesson is designed for the kids to learn about the four different kinds of poop. In this way, kids can learn what healthy poop looks like, so they can let their parents know if something is amiss. They learn to look for signs of dehydration and lack of fiber. They also learn from this song that they shouldn't try to hold it in or be embarrassed by bodily functions. They learn early on about looking after their own health.

In addition, students were required to keep a daily poop journal shared with their teacher and parents to include information such as the kind of poop they had each time, as well as more information on their health habits, such as their water consumption, their bedtime, and what they ate for breakfast. The journal included tips and guidelines for how to achieve the preferred "shiny poop," such as eating a healthy breakfast, drinking lots of water, and getting physical exercise.

The song and poop journal were part of a practical lesson I'm guessing those students are never going to forget, due in large part to the enthusiasm and dedication of the teachers. *I'm* sure not going to forget it. To this day, my kids still like to discuss what their poop reveals about their health. Much to my chagrin, this often happens at the family dinner table.

I loved the transparency of Japanese schools. A parent-teacher journal came home every day, where the teacher and I wrote notes back and forth about anything related to my children: homework questions, missed assignments, health, travel plans . . . *anything!*

In Japan, walking into my child's school didn't require an appointment, a check-in at the security desk, a badge, or a specific time slot. I could see for myself if Charles was paying attention in class or if Victoria's desk was organized. I watched what the teacher was doing to see what I could do at home to reinforce the lessons. I was never in the dark about what my children were learning; the lessons were easily accessible, and the teacher was always available to talk after class. And textbooks and the curriculum rarely change or change only intentionally and gradually as mandated by Japan's centralized Ministry of Education. It's a top-down effort, unlike the highly decentralized and local schooling system of the United States.

Parents must also sign off on a nightly reading log and grade the child in several categories after the child recites the daily language arts story. This shows the child that there's a single cohesive and cooperative union between school and home.

If anything was ever seriously wrong, I could expect a phone call promptly. When someone hit Charles during recess, I got a phone call the moment school was dismissed. The boy's mother called to apologize, then the teacher called to apologize, and it was all taken care of proactively, responsibly, and quickly.

Observation days for families are a common practice in Japanese public schools. At least two days per trimester, elementary schools in Tokyo encourage the parents and other supporting family members like grandparents to come into the classrooms and observe. Normally this occurs on Fridays and Saturdays (Japanese students are in school for half-days every other Saturday)—so that people who work during the week (mostly the fathers) can attend.

Observation days are not the norm in the city's international schools, however. I asked the principal of a Tokyo international school if his school ever had open observation days.

"Absolutely not," he replied. "No teacher would allow it. It's too disruptive."

To me, this is a wasted opportunity. Parents and teachers are partners and collaborators, not adversaries or strangers. It never occurred to me that a parent's interest in her child's education could be viewed as a disruption. In fact, there is nothing more important to a child's formal education than the successfully triangulated relationship of teacher-student-parent.

At both the preschool and elementary school that my kids attended, parents were invited to attend educational sessions led by our children's teachers about everything the kids were doing and what we were expected to do at home to help. At Victoria's Aiiku Youchien preschool, parents needed to write a formal letter if they were opting out of these sessions. By then, I figured I didn't have much to learn, especially for my *third* child and from a teacher in her twenties. But I was wrong.

Parent sessions were typically one to two hours long. They often started out in the auditorium with the entire group of parents and then moved into individual classrooms—or vice versa. Parents with more than one student in the school split their time.

At the beginning of each session, we formally introduced ourselves: standing up, stating our names and the name of our child in the class, and then mentioning any type of issue or concern that we might be having in the classroom or at home that related to school or the child's development. This was an icebreaking and bonding moment. In the early grades, we often broke into small groups to discuss a series of questions: How are you dealing with a child who doesn't go to sleep at night? How are you preparing your children for elementary school? What do you do about fussy eaters? Is your child particularly stubborn about something? How has your child changed in the past year? Then a spokesperson in the small group summarized the answers for the larger group of parents.

I was amazed by how open and honest parents were with their problems. It became clear that all this was possible because of the fundamental trust between the family and the school and the parents' respect for the teachers' expertise. In Japan, this sense of community was built into the school culture. I was surprised at how much mothers opened up in these sessions.

The preschool teachers demystified the developmental stages for us, explaining how three-year-olds are more self-focused and should be allowed to find activities that interest them; how four-year-olds need help learning how to make friends and cooperate; how five-year-olds should be given independence to problem-solve with other children without an adult rushing in. We never had to wonder why a teacher was acting (or not acting) in a certain way. They enthusiastically explained the intentionality behind it.

The elementary school teachers talked through the lesson plan, the atmosphere in class, and the students' achievements that trimester. They asked for cooperation in making sure children continued going to bed early and waking up early, even over vacations, to keep them on a schedule. They addressed social or educational challenges the class might be facing and advised us how to talk to our children about them at home. They encouraged us to make sure our children contributed appropriately to the chores at home. The teachers and mothers were partners, with the mothers handling everything behind the scenes.

I found myself taking notes at all the meetings, learning more and more about child development. It humbled me to realize that all the teachers, even the youngest ones, had so much to offer.

Contributing at Home at Any Age

Japanese parents believe that kids should start contributing to household chores as soon as they're capable. Here are examples of chores any child can do at different ages:

Ages 2 to 4

- Learn basic household chores through pretend and play.
- Organize toys.
- Sort trash and put it in the correct trash bins.
- Put dirty clothes in the laundry basket, sorting them by color.
- Water plants.
- Feed pets.
- Assist in easy meal prep: whisk, stir, knead, wash, and prepare veggies.

Ages 5 to 7

- Prepare their schoolbags.
- Tidy up their room: make their bed and wipe down their desk.
- Set the dinner table and return dirty dishes to the sink.
- Wash dishes.
- Learn how to use basic household appliances like the dishwasher, washing machine, and dryer.
- Share in the responsibilities of the daily household chores.
- Pick up mail from the mailbox.

Ages 8 and Up

- Take care of pets.
- Sweep, mop, and vacuum the floor.
- Learn the basics of cooking.
- Bathe by themselves.
- Use appropriate cleaning supplies.
- Clean bathrooms.

- Take care of younger siblings.
- Hang and fold laundry.
- Prepare easy meals.
- Run errands and go grocery shopping.

The same knowledge and care went into the curriculum in every grade. I came to appreciate how so many aspects of my child's learning were taken into account in the way lessons were planned. Japan's curriculum and education philosophies are based on proven, time-tested methods. Textbooks are written and approved by teachers, in contrast to those sold by corporations as in the United States. They figure out what works in their schools, and *everyone across the country does it.*

One particular example stands out. After dinner every night for a full month, James would read and reread, recite and re-recite the translated book *Frog and Toad Are Friends* (original by Arnold Lobel) for his Japanese language arts class, which was a chapter in his textbook. In the stories, Frog convinces his reluctant friend Toad to get out of his hibernation bed and out of his grumpy mood to enjoy the beautiful outdoors in spring. Then Toad takes care of Frog when he's sick, Frog helps Toad look for his missing button, and they go swimming together.

I must admit that I grew tired of listening to these stories, though I pretended to freshly enjoy them day after day as James did his homework on different aspects of the story. However, my visit to Kogai Elementary completely changed my mind about this seemingly tedious exercise.

It turns out there was nothing arbitrary about this story choice or the larger pedagogical practices behind it. Everything was intentional. The kids read it aloud and memorize it; they analyze the grammar, the vocabulary, and the moral of the story; they talk about their feelings about the meaning of the book; and they study the rhythm for recitation purposes. It's a carefully chosen text because of its applicability to various lessons. No propaganda was hidden in its pages (unless you find it subversive that frogs should be friends with toads). It's just a well-written and engaging story with positive messages about friendship. I watched these kids absolutely engage with the details: why quotation marks were used or weren't, why Toad is hiding under the covers. Hands shot up. Every child wanted to read aloud in class. They were waiting to find out what else this story could teach them.

I soon learned that every second grader does the same unit with this book, which meant I would get to listen to *Frog and Toad Are Friends* with all three of my kids! Three months of my life. No matter how bored by it I was, though, the kids never seemed to tire of it. The lessons were so enthralling for them that they squeezed every drop of learning out of that story. Like the Swimmy story, it imparts the values of friendship and community.

"Certainly in some places, social-emotional learning is baked into the curriculum," explained Stephanie M. Jones, professor of education at Harvard University, when we spoke after her presentation at the annual meeting of the Association for Supervision and Curriculum Development in 2018. She is spearheading research that pulls apart various curricula and nonschool programs and gauges their social-emotional learning based on five domains: cognitive, social, emotional, character, and mindset.[1] Developing these five domains in school curriculum goes hand in hand with helping kids to achieve academic success.

Over the years as I visited my kids' schools, I began to greatly appreciate the simplicity of the Japanese school system. Buildings were plain and, as in Shanghai, classroom sizes were large; their budget dollars were spent wisely. The schools were not responding to ever-changing "reform" initiatives. It was an efficient, transparent system that had stood the test of time.

In our second year, my editor at the *Japan Times* asked me to write an annual roundup on education in Japan for my Learning Curve column. "Just print last year's," I joked. "Nothing changes!"

In China as well, there was a steadfast nature to its educational plans. China's national education reform is every ten years, and due to the recent abolition of term limits, presidents may serve indefinitely. That, combined with one-party rule, means there's very little dissent and change within the government. It's easy for the president (who's been nicknamed in the media "the chairman of everything") to move his plans forward, and Xi has made it clear that he values education, particularly as a way out of poverty. "Don't let the kids lose at the starting line," he said when visiting a primary school.[2] (The flip side of this, of course, is that it could be very dangerous to have a president in power without term limits who *doesn't* value education.)

Both Japan and China are so different from the ever-changing mandates, regulations, and reforms in the United States, which sometimes means new curricula annually. A school might have a new social studies curriculum one year, new language arts the next, then math, and so on, and this cycle could then begin again. Or they could happen at the same time because the directives come from different sources. These changes can be overwhelming at the teacher level, let alone what students might actually pick up during this process.

Each time something changes, we lose valuable time we could be committing to mastery. Teachers leave the class for professional development to learn the new material, and it takes significant time before they are comfortable teaching a new system. Students suffer because they're learning from a teacher who may not yet be solid on new material. By the time the teacher gets comfortable, a new mandate may be just around the corner! Meanwhile, who's to say that the latest curriculum and technology are better than the previous one or that the teacher will even stick around? (Another major difference is the way Japan values teacher retention—more on this a bit later in this chapter.) Innovation can be great, but it can also have its costs.

Learning with the Heart, Body, and Mind

Social-emotional learning (SEL) is a buzzword in the US educational landscape. *Social and emotional skills* refers to the tools needed to navigate the social situations that children face at school and will face as adults. For example, stress management, decision-making, and conflict management all require social-emotional skills.

SEL language has worked its way into the curricula of many schools. Including these elements in an explicit way in a school's goals and mission statement demonstrates that they recognize the need to address social and emotional issues within the school setting rather than leaving them for parents to address entirely at home. However, each school can have a slightly different definition of SEL.

The federal government doesn't offer guidelines that every state must follow, but the federal Every Student Succeeds Act (ESSA) does offer funding to address SEL within each state's learning standards. Examples of ways to implement SEL include conducting research on student absenteeism, administering parent and teacher surveys, making the school inviting, and funding professional development on SEL for school staff.[3]

It's clear that there's no one right system of education. But one thing the top-rated countries in education have in common is the highest standards for teachers. Those who become teachers in Shanghai, Japan, and Finland are the best students in their class, clamoring to join the esteemed teaching profession. In contrast, in the United States, those top students often are lined up to become doctors or lawyers.

Japan, Shanghai, and Finland all get excellent results with very different systems. Japan emphasizes problem-solving and being a team player. Shanghai is test driven and heavily about competition. Finland has almost no standardized testing and aims for a holistic education.

In Japan, students who have completed all their course work in teacher education take rigorous teacher-credentialing exams. Before a prospective teacher is licensed and hired, she has to pass an exam given by the board of education in the prefecture (Japan has forty-seven prefectures, similar to our fifty states). This exam is comparable to the difficulty of passing the bar exam for prospective lawyers in the United States. It includes testing on subject matter and teaching methods, and teachers must pass an essay portion and an oral interview. Most of these aspiring teachers don't pass on their first try, and some give up because it's so difficult. In 2014, less than 14 percent of junior high teacher applicants and just over 24 percent of elementary school teacher applicants passed on the first try.[4] Some years, the passing rate has been as low as 6 percent. There's so much competition for teaching positions (200,000 applicants for 38,000 openings in public schools each year) that the profession consistently attracts passionate and dedicated individuals.[5] However, according to 2018 statistics from the Japanese government, there is gender disparity in the teaching profession in Japan: 62 percent of elementary school teachers are female, while only 32 percent of high school teachers are.[6]

For elementary school, Japanese teachers also have to prove their physical dexterity by spinning on a playground bar and swimming multiple strokes and laps. They also have to sight-read and play the piano and recorder because Japanese teachers teach music as well. Why? Because these teacher leaders are the role models for our next generation. They get in the pool and teach the kids to swim, they get on the bars and twirl with them, and they sing and play on the piano the songs their students learn to play and sing.

Every ten years Japan's teachers must take classes on contemporary issues in education and their content area to renew their license.[7] There are also regular evaluations and critiques; anyone who doesn't pass is retrained or directed to a new profession. Teachers who are underperforming are pulled out of the classroom for an entire year of more training.[8]

In China, the minimum requirement for becoming a teacher is an associate's degree. However, 95 percent of teachers in Shanghai have a bachelor's degree, mainly from East China Normal University or Shanghai Normal University (universities specifically for teacher education). Candidates who successfully pass teacher training must take a three-part certification exam, which covers written tests (in pedagogy, psychology, and teaching methods), a Mandarin test with spoken and listening components, and an interview with master teachers and local school district officials. In addition, they have to pass a district-level exam on their specific content area.[9] In China, teachers must be recertified every five years. If their performance isn't up to speed, they go back for full-time training.[10]

As different as they are, all three of these systems put a ton of trust in their teachers. Across Asia, teachers are revered by the children and the community, and it shows in many ways. The whole image of authority is very different between the East and West. In the United States, parents and kids call the shots. In Japan, students bow at the start and end of every class period. Teachers walk their students out to the school gate every afternoon for a formal good-bye, modeling mutual respect and caring. Teachers put students first and are fully responsible for student outcomes. They deserve every bit of the respect they're shown. In China, too, there is a healthy deference to the teacher. Each day starts with students saluting the teachers as the kids enter the school building. The end result is that there are very few problems with kids speaking out of turn or being disruptive, whereas in the United States, it's not so uncommon.

Both sides could use a little shifting toward the middle on this one. Our educational choices need to be considered and intentional with measured consequences well thought through.

Just about everyone can name a teacher who had a great impact on their lives because that person taught with heart. These teachers went above and beyond to show us they cared about us as individuals. Having that connection with a teacher and building trust is what allows a student to thrive.

The most capable individuals should be recruited into the profession. Respect for teachers can attract people into the profession. Keeping teacher salaries high in relation to other professions with similar training is also key to recruiting the best and the brightest.

When comparing the United States and Finland, Finland has the United States beat on both counts. Finnish teachers exercise great amounts of autonomy as professionals. This is possible due to their extensive preparation in research and pedagogy in order to assume a teaching position.

Teacher pay is relatively modest in Finland, with elementary teachers making 74 percent of the pay of people with similar levels of education; this rises to 81 percent at the junior high level and 91 percent for high school. However, according to 2015 data from the Brookings Institution, for teachers in the United States to even match these salaries, their average pay would have to be increased 10 percent, 18 percent, and 28 percent, respectively.[11]

According to 2017 data from the OECD, starting salaries for junior high teachers are higher in the United States than Japan ($43,000 versus $29,000), and by the time they reach fifteen years of service, the gap between teacher salaries in the two countries narrows slightly ($61,000 in the United States and $51,000 in Japan).[12]

In the United States, we need to prioritize our spending dollars to incentivize and recruit the best and the brightest into the profession so they can be our most capable and trusted partners. And this financial investment must go hand in hand with recruiting the brightest and paying them respect. Our future, quite literally our children as they become adults, depends on it.

I quickly found out the importance of collaboration among Japanese teachers. The culture is collaborative, and the teaching profession follows this lead. It's not about being Teacher of the Year; it's about their entire school performing well. This educational ethic hit home with me early on when I called the elementary school to leave a message for Charles's teacher. "Hello. This is Teru Clavel, grade 1, class 2, Charles's mother. Thank you for all your care [*itsumo osewa ni natte ori masu*]."

"*Hai!* [Yes!] Clavel-san, *itsumo osewa ni natte ori masu*," a teacher (not Charles's teacher) would reply.

"I am so sorry to burden you, but I forgot to write in the *renrakucho* [daily parent-teacher journal] that Charles had a bit of an upset stomach this morning, so he may not want to eat a full lunch."

"Oh, of course, Clavel-san. I will let Kaneko Sensei know."

"Thank you so very much. *Dozo, yoroshiku onegaishimasu* [With gratitude, thank you very much]."

After we hung up, I reflected on a couple of elements of our conversation. First, a teacher answered the phone: Japanese schools have very little in the way of administrative staff, which is one way they save on their budgets. There was no receptionist in charge of picking up the phone; it was often the principal or vice principal answering or whichever teacher was free at the moment. Second, every time I called, any teacher who answered knew who my children were, even when they'd never had them in a class. The first time I thought it was one teacher with a great memory. By the third time, I had learned about the collaborative culture in Japanese schools, which helped to put my own experience into context. I loved knowing that my kids were emotionally safe and cared for at school. My kids' teachers and I were partners in my children's successes. We relied on each other to do our part.

Teachers in Japan don't stay in their classrooms after school; they work together in a single teachers' room (*shokuin shitsu*), getting to know every child in the school—their strengths and challenges, reasons for absences, family situations. In this room, the desks are side by side in two separate rows facing one another, like long islands separated by walking aisles, the way they would be on a trading floor.

Although the curriculum and books are standardized, Japanese teachers have a good amount of autonomy to create their own lesson plans, and they often do so by teaming up with other teachers. They receive feedback from other teachers on new lessons before teaching the students, and they may form groups of teachers to deal with problems that come up.

It was completely normal for me to get a call from my children's teachers in Japan from the school phone number at 7:00 p.m., dinnertime. In fact, we rarely got phone calls on our house phone in Japan other than from the school. Whenever the phone rang, I grew to assume it was a teacher.

Do they ever get to go home? I wondered with a bit of guilt.

The OECD data show that while the total number of hours children are required to be in school per year is fairly consistent across countries, instruction time per teacher varies greatly. The United States is toward the top of the spectrum. To share one point of comparison, US teachers spend about 27 hours each week teaching students, while the international average in OECD countries overall is 19 hours. In Shanghai, classroom instruction averages 15 hours a week, with about 20 hours a week for nonteaching activities.[13] Elementary teachers in the United States spend 1,004 hours per year instructing students, while in Japan they spend 742 hours teaching.[14] That said, Japanese teachers spend just over 30 percent of their time teaching while US teachers spend over 50 percent of their time in the classroom. Japanese teachers spend the remainder of their time doing administrative, coaching, and preparation work.

When the new school year began in our second year in Japan (the Japanese academic year begins on April 1 and runs through mid-March), the kids found that some of their favorite teachers were gone. We were heartbroken, but it turns out that teachers in Tokyo can be moved around every three or four years to keep school quality equal; this way, no school always has all the "best" teachers and no school always has the "worst."

In Japan, the local school board hires teachers and can place them anywhere within the prefecture for the same salary. Teacher salary has nothing to do with local taxes; teachers are paid by the national and prefecture-level governments, so those in rural and urban areas are paid similar salaries. The school board assigns a larger number of the best teachers to struggling schools in the hopes of bringing them up. Teachers can also petition the school board to be assigned to a specific school in the prefecture. Japanese elementary school teachers can be moved around from any grade, first through sixth, to another.

This is all part of their professional development, and it allows teachers to be familiar with the full spectrum of educational requirements from grade to grade. This range contributes to the horizontal and vertical alignment. The teachers in a grade are on the same page about the learning (horizontal learning), and teachers at all levels above and below know what's coming and what has already been covered (vertical learning). Japan does this masterfully.

Japan invests in retention and opportunities for teachers to advance, and it offers tenure from a teacher's first job. The teachers' gathering room and principal provide considerable support for problems teachers may face. Teachers get sustained mentoring for the first several years of their careers. In both Shanghai and Tokyo, they spend time in each other's classrooms, learning from each other and providing feedback. Experienced teachers are assigned newer teachers to mentor.

In the countries with the highest PISA scores, teachers rarely leave the profession. In high-achieving school systems such as in Finland and Singapore, annual teacher attrition rates typically average as low as 3 to 4 percent.[15] Even with all the demands on their time, Japan's annual teacher attrition rate is a low 1.35 percent.[16]

In the United States, the national annual attrition rate is about 8 percent. We need about 90,000 new teachers to enter the profession every year to account for the ones who leave due to retirement or other factors. Contrary to popular belief, though, the ongoing teacher shortage in the United States does not stem from a low number of teachers joining the profession but those leaving.[17] Research from Richard Ingersoll at the University of Pennsylvania, Lisa Merrill of the Research Alliance for New York City Schools, and Daniel Stuckey at the Relay Graduate School of Education shows an increase in annual teacher turnover in US public schools from 12.4 percent in 1991–92 to 15.7 percent in 2012–13.[18]

The High Cost of Teacher Turnover in the United States

Teacher turnover has negative impacts on the academic outcomes of students, a school's fiscal performance, and job satisfaction of other staff.

Research shows that high teacher turnover contributes to problems for the nation's poorest students, who need excellent teachers the most. Students of color, special education students, and English Language Learners are especially affected.[19]

In their 2017 report for the Learning Policy Institute, Desiree Carver-Thomas and Linda Darling-Hammond bring together statistics on the schools most affected by high turnover. According to their research, turnover rates are:

- 50 percent higher for teachers in Title I schools, which serve more low-income students
- 70 percent higher for mathematics and science teachers in Title I schools than in non–Title I schools
- 70 percent higher for teachers in schools serving the largest concentrations of students of color
- 90 percent higher for mathematics and science teachers in the top quartile of schools serving students of color than in the bottom quartile
- 80 percent higher for special education teachers.[20]

The 8 percent annual attrition rate accounts for close to 90 percent of annual teacher demand.[21] In addition to the immediate turnover upon entering the profession, a large number of teachers exit the profession within five years, averaging up to 30 percent nationally.[22] Halving the teacher attrition rate would, in effect, end teacher shortages on a national level.

As for the fiscal costs of high teacher turnover, Carver-Thomas and Darling-Hammond estimate the costs at $20,000 or more for replacing each teacher who leaves an urban district.[23]

We need to change the conversation about teaching and teachers in order to inspire future generations. At Cleveland Humanities Magnet High School in the Los Angeles Unified School District, a public school in the nation's second-largest school district, I spoke with a dynamic young history teacher, who looked just a tad older than his students, about his own background. He had gone to the same high school where he was now teaching. I was inspired watching his lessons on civil rights.

"Why did you become a teacher?" I asked.

When he replied, "I always knew I was going to come back," I felt that I had asked a really dumb question. His frank answer moved me. He'd been so inspired by his own teachers that he wanted to become one of them. That is exactly the kind of teacher I want in my kids' classrooms.

As parents, we need to work *with* teachers to help them succeed. They hold our children's futures in their hands. In Japan, this was part of the unspoken rules of parenting. Mothers bore the greatest burden and responsibility when it came to supporting their children's education. At times, the demands on Japanese mothers felt surreal, like something out of reality TV.

CHAPTER 10

Wonder Woman

The Mom Behind the Scenes

When I arrived in Tokyo with my family, I knew that the demands on parents (read: mothers) were going to be extensive based on my experiences with Victoria's preschool interviews. Parental involvement was part of every child's school experience. But my first lengthy brush with the PTA opened my eyes to just how demanding it could be.

At the end of our first school year in Tokyo, I attended a parent meeting at Kogai Elementary where the executive committee discussed how next year's PTA committee and class parents would be chosen: by random lottery. The PTA system started in Japan after World War II, based on the US model, with the idea of promoting democracy in Japan.

A woman raised her hand and stood. "I very much appreciate this school and all it has done for my family. I will always be devoted to it. I have noticed my child flourishing from all the attention this community has given. I attribute this to the excellent support from this school, her teachers, and the families here and especially the PTA. I am also thankful that through this, I have been able to work and provide for my family. It makes me so thankful to be a part of this community."

I smelled it: a *boom* was coming.

Japanese people beat around the bush whenever there's something possibly piercing to say, surrounding it with gratitude and compliments and platitudes. The longer this woman spoke, the tenser the room got. She was going somewhere big with this.

"I've had the opportunity to support my family," she continued, "and because of this, it would be very challenging for me to donate my time to the PTA at this moment because I want to be sure the PTA gets 100 percent commitment from anyone involved, and I think there are many parents who are currently far more capable than I am."

My eyes widened. I empathized with her concerns, and I had often wondered what I would do if I had to work full time in Tokyo while attempting to fulfill my duties at my kids' schools. But this kind of protest was so rare in Japan that I worried for this woman. Would she now be branded with a scarlet letter? Would she be known as the selfish mom who didn't care enough about her daughter's education? I furtively looked at the other mothers around me, seated around this science-lab-turned-meeting-room. I waited for the reaction from the committee.

At first, there was just silence. No one on the committee wanted to speak, for it too would have to be couched in all sorts of verbal gymnastics to sound positive and supportive while also getting across the point they were bound to make.

Eventually the committee's response came out; it went something like this: "We are so happy that your employment is going well, and that you approve of the education and support your daughter receives here. Participating on the PTA and contributing to the well-being of our children is something we all appreciate dearly. We understand your concerns and we are certain you would rather not be in this position because you are dedicated to your child. However . . ."

The parents in the room looked as if they were watching a tennis match as the ball volleyed back and forth. I was gobsmacked.

". . . in order to be excused from PTA service, you must either provide a doctor's note to show that you have a significant health problem or that you are pregnant or trying to conceive."

A doctor's note saying you were trying to conceive? *Wowza!* I sucked in my breath and waited to see if the mom would have the nerve to rebut this unrebuttable instruction. *She did!*

"Thank you for the explanation and for all your commitment! I can understand this policy, and I do appreciate everything the PTA does. The festival last summer was so wonderful, especially that you got the fathers involved with the fried noodles stand. Every time I get a letter home from the PTA, I feel such gratitude for all the work you have done and the high level of energy devoted to its activities. However..."

I could hardly stand it. This was the bravest woman in the city.

"...I still have to work."

Silence. It never got any more direct than this. Each brief point and counterpoint took an effusive parade of kind words around it, but this was as contentious as it gets in Japan.

"Your daughter must be benefiting greatly from seeing her mother work so hard. It's an admirable role and a hard plight for you. We are so glad you're here and that you've been able to enjoy events such as the fair. We don't wish to add any extra challenges in your life. However..."

I think the only reason it ended was that they had verbally exhausted each other. Scarlet Letter Mom continued politely arguing her point but never did get the exception she was hoping for. Her name would be thrown in the paper bag with everyone else's.

At my children's schools, moms were expected to serve on the PTA for at least one full school year for each child they have in the school. Your enthusiastic participation is a sign you value the education the school provides. In some schools, having a full-time job could be a legitimate reason to postpone service, but not at Victoria's school. And only women are expected to serve, though every now and then men also volunteer (and usually end up in leadership roles).

Although participation in the PTA is technically voluntary at public schools, there's extreme pressure on mothers to join and participate or to stand up in front of a room full of people to explain why they can't.

In some instances, the pressures of the PTA are so great that some Japanese moms have begun hiring proxies to stand in for them. Service providers report receiving requests for proxies to take notes at meetings, as well as to fulfill duties such as setting up and cleaning up after events, acting as crossing guards for children walking to or from school, secretarial duties, and more. One company in Tokushima says it gets about fifty requests a year related to PTA duties, and they charge the equivalent of $42 per hour plus transportation costs.[1] While this company, called Classy Co., says it won't assume anyone's identity, other companies have no such restriction—even offering to study the family's history to pretend to be the mother or father in question. Essentially they are stunt doubles for the PTA.

At Victoria's traditional preschool, this would never have flown. Attendance was often taken at PTA meetings.

The most convenient time to serve in the PTA is a calculated decision. While first grade is easiest, it is also the first year of elementary school, and many parents are inexperienced with the ins and outs of their child's school. In contrast, by the time children get to fourth grade, most parents are well versed in the school culture, but many Tokyo students in that year are studying at cram schools (called *jukus*) for the middle school entrance exam, so many families' energies are tied up in supporting their kids that way. Students drop out of extracurricular activities (including sports) during the year before their big entrance exams. There can be no distractions; those years are all about studying.

Mothers can of course volunteer for the PTA without waiting for their lottery turn. As in the United States, some moms (and the occasional dad) relish the opportunity. Others accept it for its social aspects or the chance to have more of an up-close relationship with teachers. Still others keep their head down and even eyes closed hard, like me, and pray not to be chosen. The overall mood is that it's a big, big responsibility.

Scarlet Letter Mom got lucky that year; her name was not pulled out of the paper bag. I was relieved for her, though part of me was disappointed that I couldn't witness her ongoing fight. There was something exhilarating about watching her challenge the system. It felt like she was doing it on behalf of all the mothers there.

PTAs in Japan don't have the "bake sales and school dance decorating" responsibilities of their US counterparts. The role is fundamentally different. According to Andreas Schleicher, OECD director for education and skills, "In the US, parents are often engaged in the *social* mission of the school." This often limits the mandate of the PTA to fund-raising, which might mean supporting students' participation in enrichment activities such as class trips or buying sporting equipment.

PTAs in Japan don't fund-raise, though parents do pay 350 yen per month (the equivalent of roughly three US dollars) or so to be a member.[2] They support the school in its everyday functions, not just in special events. They write newsletters, collate papers for teachers, organize the safety patrol, and find presenters to teach workshops, in addition to organizing festivals and gratitude assemblies for teachers. They work alongside teachers and principals to keep the school running smoothly in all ways. It's a demanding, serious job, and they are expected to be on call all the time. The responsibilities of the PTA are clearly delineated and separate from those of the school's teachers and administrators. It's passed on from year to year, so there is little (or no) variation.

The Japanese PTA system is fundamentally different from its US counterpart because in Japan, every aspect of a child's experience at school is already well covered and funded by a tested curriculum, experienced teachers, adequate teacher salaries, and a shared vision of the importance of education in the country as a whole. There is so much adult support surrounding the success of the student in Japan.

In addition, children often receive supplemental educational support from tutors or outside classes. Whereas we think of tutoring for students who are struggling to pass, it's seen as enhancement in the top East Asian countries. Some Japanese cram schools, like the big chain Sapix, focus on entrance exams for specific prestigious schools, while others focus on overall academic maintenance.

As 2016 research from Yoko Yamamoto (assistant professor of education at Brown University), Susan D. Holloway (professor of education at the University of California at Berkeley), and Sawako Suzuki (professor of education at St. Mary's College of California) states, "Mothers may view the management and expenditure of resources on such educational opportunities as a more effective way of being engaged than interacting extensively with their children's regular school."[3] Therefore, Japanese mothers are very involved in activities to support their children, but in a different manner from the way US parents are. They are more like silent partners.

Japanese parents typically do not volunteer for activities in their children's classroom, for example.[4] When parents do help out at school, it's often in administrative tasks like helping teachers photocopy and collate papers. Japanese parents would never vote on a new curriculum, for example, as many US school districts may ask of their parents, nor would they come into the classroom to lead early elementary reading or math circles.

A few months before starting year one of three at Victoria's preschool, the headmaster distributed a spreadsheet of fifteen items to hand-sew for her in preparation at one of the many mandatory preparation parent meetings before preschool started! It was insanely detailed, with hand-drawn illustrations like blueprints with measurements down to the centimeter and directions to use Velcro, not buttons, for the first year when children may not yet be able to manipulate them. The experience was so unlike the "two glue sticks and a pair of safety scissors" lists in the United States.

Over time, I came to appreciate the supporting role of the PTA at Japanese schools. But when I first found out that *every* mother had to volunteer for something at Victoria's preschool for six months to a year, all I felt was pure anxiety. My Japanese reading and writing were somewhere at the upper-elementary level, and I lacked confidence in my spoken honorific Japanese, in addition to the burden of the major time commitment. I felt unprepared to jump right in.

At Victoria's preschool, I was on the committee that helped prepare for the annual anniversary celebration, which was like a carnival day run entirely by the moms, with approval and oversight by the school administration. About thirty women were involved through specific roles, including the executive committee (president, vice president, logistics leader, accountant) and about five smaller subcommittees (merchandise, face painting, games, food, bazaar shopping), as decided by *janken* (rock, paper, scissors). No one got preference for the popular committees or the ones with the lowest time commitment.

My good fortune landed me on the games subcommittee. I always loved the wishful penny toss and water-gun-spraying-into-the-clown's-mouth type of games at amusement parks. The games group consisted of four women, one of whom coincidentally was the only other non-Japanese-born mom in the entire school, Eve Kagimoto, a Cambridge-educated British woman who'd married a Japanese man. Another mom spoke with a thick Osaka accent, and the last mom had literally been a teen rock star like Selena Gomez. She hadn't gone to college because she was a star at age fifteen.

We were all misfits in this prestigious Tokyo preschool. One mom even approached me and said with a snicker, "Your group is going to be a disaster. Two foreigners, a country bumpkin, and a pop star? Good luck." It seemed the other parents made the incorrect assumption that we were not as smart or capable as they were.

Our subcommittee was a blast, and, boy, did we prove everyone wrong. We met twice a week at my house for about three hours each time, and we really enjoyed it—I actually looked forward to our meetings! I was in charge of making rods for the fishing game and colorful puppets on sticks for a manual five-station version of whack-a-mole. It was a role that I took seriously.

I was also the "sourcer," who, on a minuscule budget, procured quick-gratification prizes: candy, stickers, and a palm-sized pinball machine with a life span of maybe one hour. I used previous years' spreadsheets to determine which toys were "most effective," what materials could be used, what prizes were more likely to get broken, and so on. Because we needed to conduct quality control on every single one of the thousands of trinkets, we created our own assembly line. Our committee also organized volunteers to run the games stations on the day of the fair.

With my design background (I had been an interior designer in my later twenties and most recently hosted a TV show for HGTV BC [Before Children]), I was also in charge of creating the games ticket that hung around the preschoolers' necks; it doubled as a four-page coloring book the size of a medium-sized index card. We were good about leveraging our strengths and working together. I had to prove that we misfits could make exemplary puppets and coloring books.

We presented our games group's ideas at a whole school meeting to about 150 mommies, wearing navy suits to the meeting as instructed, no exceptions, by the annual anniversary committee president. (By that point, 80 percent of my dresses were navy.) At our smaller thirty-person monthly meetings, very serious women with clipboards delivered practiced presentations about lunch preparations, decorations, face painting, and school-themed shirts.

We quickly ran out of room to store everything. The average Tokyo rental is no more than 425 square feet.[5] (The "tiny house" phenomenon is more than just a cute idea there.) We were to schlep things back and forth between our homes and the school to work on them. Because I was on an expat housing allowance, my home was a bit bigger, so we ended up storing things for the carnival there. Plus, I lived just down the street from the preschool, so it was convenient. The items took over my entire living room.

Everything was supposed to be approved first by the committee and then the school administration. If we wanted to add anything (streamers, costumes, whatever), we had to first present it to the committee, and then they'd take it to the school, which meant a two-week turn-around on any little request or change we wanted to make. There were arguments and tears and drama. I was living my own episode of *The Real Housewives of Tokyo*.

By the end, we quit asking for permission and went ahead with add-ing little things we didn't think anyone would care about or notice. Ap-parently they did notice. "I think we ruined it for everybody," Eve told me two years later. She still had a younger child in the school, but we had moved on by then. "Now the process is even more meticulous and strict about getting approvals." Our small acts of rebellion hadn't been received with much humor.

That said, our final product was gorgeous. The classroom was decorated with a circus theme, with red-and-white-swirled streamers hanging from the ceiling in the shape of a circus tent. It all went off beautifully, and the kids loved it.

On a personal level, my online Japanese trinket shopping skills had improved considerably, I learned so much about my mother's culture and therefore myself, *and* I formed lasting friendships with the women in my games group.

While the carnival didn't serve any strict academic function, it served a more important purpose in the eyes of the preschool, one that had been carefully considered based on the school's focus on family and play as the most significant form of learning during the formative years of early childhood education. The yearly carnival was a grandiose ges-ture of mothers' dedication to our children. Every meticulous minute of investment was a physical show of love. I grew to take pride in the role the PTA played in supporting our kids. In the United States, how often do we feel that our kids appreciate us? Here, at this preschool, the children were taught to do so.

At the formal graduation ceremony, again donning the requisite navy formal wear, we moms performed a song on stage like a choir for the students and their fathers that we had been rehearsing for several months. Yes, all the moms gathered before preschool pickup a handful of times for mandatory rehearsal. There wasn't a dry eye on that stage, and we were forewarned that we should carefully tuck away tissues to dab our tears. This was our farewell and gratitude for the past three years of devotion to our children. The lyrics are from a song titled "Arigato" ("Thank you"), which is the theme of a popular morning TV drama. The show, named *Gegege no Nyobo*, aired on the government-sponsored station NHK in 2010. We chose this song because it opens with a simple yet beautiful image of holding hands, which evoked our daily walk to school these past three years, holding our child's precious hand as we navigated the streets of Japan together:

> *I want to say "thank you" and look in your eyes*
> *Your hand holds my right hand more gently than anyone else's . . .*
> *We have spent time together, taking a path with ups and downs . . .*

Now that our little ones were growing up, they'd be traveling to school all on their own. We'd never get those sweet preschool years back. As the song continues, it speaks to how our relationships with our children have evolved during these short years, and to our own nostalgia as we watched our little ones grow up:

> *"Your dream" changed into "Our dream"*
> *Today will be a piece of precious memory . . .*

Even now, I cry every time I sing the lyrics. And to this day, Victoria and I sing the song while holding hands, walking down the street wherever we may be. It reminds me of the three-year daily ritual of walking Victoria to and from preschool with her little hand in mine. I will forever cherish this memory. And I appreciate the way the preschool created this special moment for us.

*　　*　　*

The larger issue the PTA unearths in Japan is this: women are under significant pressure to "do it all," while having fewer career options and receiving lower wages than men. Stay-at-home moms are still idealized, but more and more women are working while simultaneously performing all the tasks their grandmothers did when *they* were stay-at-home moms.

When I was eight years old, my mother's younger sister got married and moved to Tokyo with her husband. From then on, rather than spending summers in Osaka with my grandmother, I went to Tokyo to stay with her almost every summer until I graduated from high school. I loved staying with her, her husband, and, eventually, their two babies and then elementary school–aged children in a compact two-bedroom apartment with one bathroom.

I relished every moment. I looked up to my aunt as the stay-at-home mom who was completely devoted to her children. She was the fun-loving proxy to my intense and serious working mother. It felt nice to have a sit-down breakfast and dinner with the whole family, in contrast to meals in New York City, where I often ate spaghetti with Ragu sauce alone in the evening while my mother was still at work. Her hours were long and unpredictable. Sometimes I had a babysitter, and sometimes I just watched TV until she came home, at which point we'd study Japanese and I'd practice the piano.

My aunt's family also represented the one I never had as an only child. After she had children, I played older sister to her children, who were thirteen and fifteen years my junior. I enjoyed pushing their strollers, attending their swim lessons, giving them baths, feeding them, teaching them how to ride bicycles around a Tokyo city block, and taking them to Tokyo Disneyland. Being in Japan represented many things to me every summer, but this surrogate family informed a lot of my ideals on family.

Back in New York City, when I went to friends' homes and their parents were around, I couldn't help but feel both jealous and curious. What did these moms do all day? Did they help their children with their homework? Did they spend all night baking a cake for their child's school birthday celebration? I fantasized about what it must be like to have a mom who didn't work. Before I knew a Chipwich was prepackaged, I wondered if the moms had painstakingly baked chocolate chip cookies and scooped up vanilla ice cream to somehow create a perfectly filled cylindrical ice cream sandwich.

In contrast, when it came to my birthday, the party planning was my responsibility. In the sixth grade, I planned a party at Rye Playland. I ordered two full-sized school buses from a transport company that I found in the Yellow Pages, and I instructed my mother to have cash on hand to pay for them and the Playland entrance tickets. I sent out the invitations to everyone in my grade myself. Among the most memorable gifts were Kareem's *two* tins of David's cookies and Ian's citrine-colored stone bracelet (I still have it), which came with a letter professing his love for me. The day was wonderful, but I wondered what it would have been like to have my mom take care of all the details.

Certainly there is a middle ground between my experiences as an only child with my mom and my precious time in Tokyo with my aunt's family. I think I have often lived my life now as a mother trying to find my way between these two extremes.

Although Japanese businesses have to offer maternity and child-care leave, women also describe "pregnancy rotas"—unwritten rules about when women should get pregnant so that several employees aren't out on leave at once. Women have described being told that it wasn't their "turn" yet or that they'd missed their turn due to infertility or personal decisions to wait.[6]

The social and economic regulation of childbirth may be a contributing factor to Japan's low birthrate, which is currently at 1.4 births per woman. The population of fifteen- to sixty-four-year-olds is expected to fall from 77 million in 2015 to 45 million in 2065.[7]

Meanwhile, women are blamed for the low birthrates, with the argument that many younger Japanese women are now focused on their careers rather than starting a family.[8] My experiences in the Japanese school system pointed to the heavy demands on women once they have children; they are expected to put their kids' education first. These discussions strike at the heart of the ways that Japanese culture struggles to adapt to changes to the traditional social order.

Seventy percent of women in Japan quit full-time jobs after the birth of their first child, at least for a while, even though there is guaranteed maternity leave and child-care leave that lasts until the child is one year old. Fathers are also entitled to take a full twelve months off at a reduced salary, though only 2 percent of fathers took this leave in 2015.[9]

The High Cost of Being a Woman in Japan

While women in the United States experience a gender pay gap (we earn eighty cents to every dollar a man earns on average),[10] the gender pay gap for Japanese women is even worse. More than 68 percent of working-age women are employed in Japan, though mostly part time and for low pay: women made up 77 percent of the part-time workforce in Japan in 2012, and they earn 26 percent less money than their male counterparts. Japan has the third-worst gender pay gap among OECD nations, beat only by South Korea and Estonia.[11]

Prime Minister Shinzo Abe has made it a mission to increase Japan's workforce overall by encouraging more women to work. He has also supported efforts to get more women into positions of power, a directive that's been nicknamed "Womenomics."[12] In 2017, the OECD reported that women still occupied only 12.4 percent of managerial positions in Japan, compared to the OECD average of 31.2 percent.[13] Even within Abe's own cabinet, only two people in his twenty-member cabinet were women as of 2018.

Japan ranks dead last among major economies, with a low 9.5 percent representation of women in the national legislature in 2017, while the OECD average is 28.7 percent.[14] However, Japan's figure represents a notable increase compared to its 1 percent rate in 1990.[15]

When Channel News Asia interviewed me about this issue, I explained the impossible situation for women: they're needed in the workforce, yet society expects them to be homemakers.

Although the gender pay gap in the United States is not quite as large as Japan's, it's still significant, and fueled mostly by the same factor: motherhood. A recent study showed that there's a specific time in life that corresponds with lifelong pay gaps in the United States.[16] Women are often occupied with child-rearing during the key years of their career trajectory. "Women who have their first baby either before 25 or after 35—before their careers get started or once they're established—eventually close the pay gap with their husbands," writes Claire Cain Miller in the *New York Times*.[17] Men's salaries keep going up in those years, while women's decline.

During a meeting at Victoria's school, when the mothers were asked to share what they wanted to be when they were their child's age, most said things like baker, florist, ballerina, and singer. I said "president," maybe just for effect, or as a psychology experiment. I heard audible gasps. *The audacity!*

Things haven't changed much in that regard since my mother was a girl. When she left Osaka to attend a competitive university in Tokyo in the 1960s, her mother told her, "You will never find a husband if you are overeducated."

Discussions about how to educate a girl versus a boy felt foreign to me. I noticed that preschool moms often prefaced their comments with "Because she's a girl . . ." before talking about schooling. Whereas women make up about half of the undergraduate classes in our Ivy League schools, they make up less than a third of the student body at the top three universities in Japan (Universities of Tokyo, Keio, and Waseda), which perpetuates gender expectations. Here's an interesting tidbit, though: Japanese girls far outscore American boys in math, reading, and science according to the 2012 PISA scores.[18]

I noticed that gender roles carry through to all kinds of activities. At James's baseball practices, I quickly learned that in sports, moms are the nurses, snack preparers, and tea servers, and the ones who clean the bathrooms and toilets, while dads are coaches or umpires.

One area where I felt inadequate compared to other preschool moms was in the lunches I prepared. (The elementary school provided hot lunch daily, but not the preschool.) Japanese moms prepare food for their kids like it's an art form. Their kids' lunches were *onigiri* (rice balls) in the shape of panda bears, or eggs cut into cow faces with a coordinated family of colorful and edible farm animals. I must admit to having purchased several "how-to" books on this very art form and the associated panda-cutting templates and the like. Ultimately, I had my limits. Victoria brought in peanut butter and jelly with the crusts cut off. On my "fancy" days, I prepared a ball of rice with some fish flakes at the center, wrapped up tightly in plastic wrap. This was always accompanied by a small box of cut fruit.

Somehow Victoria's simple "American" PB&J lunches were such a novelty that parents started asking me how to make them. Rather embarrassingly, it became a popular item in her class!

Our time in Japan offered me many opportunities to grow as a mother and as a professional. In Tokyo, my passion for education and globalization translated into a new career for me as a freelance education journalist and public speaker. I wrote articles, appeared on TV, and gave talks at high schools, universities, and corporations about the importance of having a global perspective and educating our children with this philosophy in mind.

I thought often about the differences between what "parent involvement" means in Japan versus the United States. In Japan, the parent role is very clearly defined. In the United States, it depends on the family, teacher, school, district, and state. But it would do us a world of good to get all parents to participate in the most useful ways possible to support classroom learning. With parents and educators working as a team, children can flourish.

PALO ALTO

2016–2018

James: 12 to 14 years old

Charles: 10 to 12 years old

Victoria: 7 to 9 years old

CHAPTER 11

The Twilight Zone

Our Worst Year Yet, in the
Best-Ranked School District

It's time, I thought during our third year in Japan. *We need to get back to the United States.*

The kids had spent the better portion of the past nine years overseas—which was Victoria's entire life and the majority of both James's and Charles's lives. Sure, we had come back home over holidays and summer breaks, but it was time my kids went to school full time in English in the United States. My goal had always been to have them attend college in the United States, so middle school seemed the perfect time to move back. They could find their way and get adjusted to the US education system during middle school to be fully up to speed for high school, when rigorous academic learning and grades mattered for college applications.

Overall, it seemed they had thrived during every leg of our journey. Maybe they just didn't know any better. There had been ups and downs for each of us, but the experiences made us more resilient, academically confident (the kids as well as me!), curious, and independent. And our off-the-beaten-path experiences will always bind us. Each of the children hit cultural and language exposures at different times in their development, so they each have different strengths, weaknesses, and attachments to each of our host countries. I will continue to be fascinated to see how this plays out throughout the rest of their lives.

It was especially important to me for my kids to know what it means to be a US citizen actually *living* in the United States. Throughout our sojourn, I had tried to impose on the kids that it was because of our very US citizenship that we were welcomed by our host nations.

When I mentioned the thought of moving to my kids, they seemed to expect it. *No big deal.* It had become a way of life for us all. They were game for another grand adventure. *Can we live in London now?* But while they were fine moving on, *I* was tired. I didn't want to face another new language and culture, or learn to navigate a new school system. All I wanted was a hot bath in a home that was familiar. Yes, that would do just fine.

Luckily, Alex was offered a position in Silicon Valley. So after ten years abroad, we could finally come back to the United States.

I scoured the San Francisco Bay Area to figure out where we should live. I needed to find a place (a) where the public schools were great, and (b) the community was safe. I didn't want to take back all the independence I'd been able to give my children in Japan; I wanted to give them some degree of free rein.

I decided on Palo Alto. There, it was sunny all day, and my kids could bike to and from school with their friends on spotless tree-lined streets—a sharp contrast from the subways and concrete of urban Tokyo. It was also a college town in the backyard of Stanford University, in the heart of Silicon Valley. I figured we were in for a different and intellectually stimulating adventure. More than 40 percent of Palo Alto residents have a graduate degree.[1]

The only thing that concerned me was that the population of Palo Alto itself is quite homogeneous in terms of socioeconomic status, considering the high cost of living in the area. It's an ideal place for professors, software engineers, and investors to raise their kids, but it's not accessible to most working-class families. Housing prices are astronomical. According to Zillow, the median listing price for homes in

Palo Alto as of 2018 was $3.2 million,[2] and the high property taxes go a long way toward funding the local schools.

I looked at a handful of private schools and even submitted some applications where they could attend school with the children of Silicon Valley's top executives; 74 billionaires live in Silicon Valley (only New York City and Hong Kong are home to more billionaires, with 103 and 93, respectively).[3] All three kids sailed through the entrance exams and school interviews. But as we toured, I had the same concerns about private schools here as I did in New York City: Silicon Valley was already a world of privilege without adding the private school wealth into the mix.

I considered the public schools as well. I met with parents and teachers, and I went on school visits to get a sense of whether my kids and I would fit in. In the end, I opted for public schools. It was important to me that my children attend schools with a more diverse student body that represented the surrounding community and country. I didn't want to embed them among the Silicon Valley elite.

When we arrived, I could hardly believe how exciting it felt. California! The dreamy land of high school movies like *Fast Times at Ridgemont High*, *Stand by Me*, and *The Karate Kid*. Except the movie we landed in wasn't quite the genre I expected when we'd paid for our tickets. It felt more like *The Twilight Zone*.

I was in for a rude awakening. On the first day in the Palo Alto Unified School District (PAUSD), it was 40 degrees, not warm and toasty. School drop-off was filled with dads wearing flip-flops and Google T-shirts, a far cry from the Birkin-toting moms in Shanghai and the PTA moms of Tokyo. I was excited to meet Charles's teacher, but then tried not to panic when it became clear that she was very pregnant—last-trimester pregnant—and there wasn't yet a plan in place for her replacement.

Later that week, I attended my first PTA meeting where it was "suggested" that I donate $3,000 to various school funds. Three thousand dollars?! I was even more concerned when I realized that one of the previous year's line items included a $30,000 expenditure for ergodynamic chairs for the fifth grade.

I planned to overlook the exorbitant fund-raising for quirky chairs, since the quality of the education should be truly excellent. Right? The school district was the best ranked in California, the nation's largest state by population, according to Niche.com. The district's recognition gave me the confidence that my children would continue the excellent educational path they were on.

The school district has around twelve thousand students in twelve elementary schools, three middle schools, and two high schools. Judging by test scores and teacher résumés, the district looks top-notch. I'd seen the numbers bear out before, as in Shanghai's amazing performance on the PISAs. But I quickly came to learn that I could not put that same trust in Niche.com, or GreatSchools.org, or any of the other school-ranking databases in the United States. This "#1 school district in California" was nothing like I expected.

California: Land of School Funding Inequality

In the United States, the large majority (90 percent) of funding for schools comes from the local and state levels, mainly in the form of state and property taxes. Only 10 percent is provided on average by the federal government. This means that some districts and states are at a distinct disadvantage, depending on the tax base. These funding disparities particularly have an impact on students of color. School districts serving the largest populations of black, Latino, or Native American students receive roughly $1,800 (about 13 percent) less per student in state and local funding compared with those with the fewest students of color.[4]

California is considered to have a regressive school funding system on the local level because of the large disparities in income on that level. However, in 2013, California enacted state measures to spread funds more equitably across districts with higher needs.

The Education Trust analyzed data for the state's more than six million public K–12 students in 2015. Fifty-nine percent of the state's students qualify for free or reduced-price lunch, and 20 percent are living below the poverty line. After adjusting for the additional needs of low-income students, the Education Trust finds that the districts in California with the highest levels of poverty receive 2 percent less than districts with the lowest levels of poverty.[5]

What I learned from my time in Palo Alto is that *all* data that contribute to *any* school rankings need to be pulled apart to consider all the variables. One way to understand this is to say that children's academic performance needs to be looked at holistically and not as a single data point—for example, how much of their score is based on in-school learning versus what the students are absorbing from their educated parents, tutors, summer programs, and peers; extracurriculars; library books; and the like. Sadly, these assessments do not give teachers timely qualitative feedback to understand what makes each child tick, to be able to motivate that child, and to develop a safe, strong, and trusting relationship with her. For actual actionable growth, it's not the numeric score that matters so much as the explanation.

At the first middle school parent education meeting, I found out that seventh-grade students would read just three books in English class all year and that they were allowed to select any books they wanted for free reading. They could even pick the same book again and again all year long "because they'll learn something different from it every time"!

In addition, the teacher would critique only three essays in the course of the year because, she explained, "each teacher has 125 students and there's not enough time." And this is at one of the best-funded public schools in the country. When I looked for the statistics later, I found that per-pupil spending for 2016–17 in our district was $19,386, several thousand more per pupil than the statewide average of $11,619 for other California unified school districts.[6]

I was dumbfounded by the way teachers openly spoke about how little they expected of students—not because the students were incapable of more, but because it was too time-consuming for the teachers. At a twelve-person parent-teacher council meeting at the middle school, one tenured teacher nonchalantly explained his philosophy on grading: "Well, these kids come in so smart. If they already know everything I'm supposed to teach them when they walk in, then they get an A off the bat." When I jumped in with disbelief, "Then increase your learning expectations," the principal quickly moved us on to the next topic on the agenda to avoid the gloves coming off. But these kids would be bored, bored, bored. And why would they ever want to sit in class?

In fact, teachers seemed to realize they were on their own to figure out what was acceptable and what wasn't; there was almost no oversight because the school was on its fourth principal in four years. At another council meeting, a middle school teacher complained, "None of us knows what's going on in other classrooms, including grading policies. One teacher could be using mastery based, another could be using letter grades, and we all have different requirements for how students achieve their grades."

"Teachers aren't required to use the same grading system," the principal said. "It's not recognized by California's Education Code." It wasn't enough to do the right thing; it required a law.

"Oh, I don't care about grades!" one parent chimed in. "They're not important."

It felt like no one was paying attention and somehow students were expected to churn out impressive scores despite the lack of instruction or oversight. Yes, to reiterate, this is *the* top-rated school district in California, the largest state in the United States, in the cradle of the greatest STEM (science, technology, engineering, and math) minds in the world.

Maybe it's just crazy because it's the beginning of the school year, I thought.

Things got worse, though. Charles had five teacher changes in his fifth-grade classroom. All five Palo Alto secondary school principals resigned within the first year we were there. The superintendent resigned (or was pushed out) after a mistake causing a multimillion-dollar budget shortfall for the school district. But the silver lining? Charles was thrilled to have watched no fewer than ten movies in full at school, including *Rango, The Lego Batman Movie, The Incredibles, Despicable Me, Megamind,* and *Cloudy with a Chance of Meatballs.*

It felt like chaos.

In 2016 my kids were in the second, fifth, and seventh grades. I found it hard to find my place among the families whose kids had been playing together for years. Communities were quite entrenched by elementary school. This was different from our previous experiences, where I had always had a child starting preschool, and many of us were looking to make friends with the other parents. And within expat communities, antennas are always out for making new friends as old ones leave.

But one of the things I did appreciate was the opportunity to meet so many families from international backgrounds. When I attended the meet-and-greet during Victoria's first day of school, I was immediately struck by the variety of languages being spoken around me: Portuguese, Hindi, Hebrew, French, Mandarin, Polish, Japanese, Spanish.

The diversity in Palo Alto contrasted sharply with my previous surroundings in Japan, a 99 percent ethnically homogeneous country with small numbers of immigrants and foreigners. With so many interesting people around, I believed that I would settle in and make mom friends, just as I believed my children would figure it out too. But as the first few weeks got underway, I felt more uneasy. Neither James nor Charles adjusted particularly well to their schools.

My kids' new experiences at school also had a significant effect on our home life. Both Charles and James were seemingly desperate to fit in to their new social environments, which included an emphasis on sports that was new to us. They were the cool kids in China and Japan because they were good at school. Here, to be accepted, you had to be a jock. Following, playing, and watching sports suddenly took prominence. So I went along.

Unlike our leisure time in Japan, suddenly the boys were insistent on watching NFL games, which were interspersed with erectile dysfunction commercials and scantily clad women advertising resorts. I never expected having to explain to my grade-school kids why the man on TV needed to take a pill before he started "kissing" the woman. These kinds of commercials didn't exist in China or Japan. Even the wildly popular and addictive online video game *Fortnite* may get banned—yes, *banned*—in China to protect its youth.

Here, kids weren't protected from anything. There were similar messages all across the radio, awards shows, bumper stickers—you name it. I was going to have to initiate talks about sex, drugs, and drinking before I knew my kids were really ready for it and before the rest of society took care of it for me. *US parents have been dealing with this all along*, I realized.

Even at Stanford, currently the most selective college in the United States with a 4 percent acceptance rate, we saw the priority on sports. In June 2016, we had proudly watched President Obama's motorcade leaving Stanford after the Global Entrepreneurship Summit. Now, in that same spot on El Camino Real right across from Palo Alto High School stood a giant billboard of NFL football player Christian McCaffrey, who graduated from Stanford early to turn professional after his junior year. It's there to advertise Stanford's athletics program. Every time I drove by it, my heart dropped. *Where was the billboard advertising its thirty-one Nobel laureates? Do we really value sports more than we value brains in the United States?*

And I mean that question quite literally—kids play contact sports even after the damning evidence from autopsies of deceased athletes that *nearly all* professional football players (and many other types of professional athletes) wind up with brain damage from multiple head injuries.[7]

At a Stanford open house, an admissions officer bragged that Stanford had the most Olympic athletes of any other US college instead of showcasing their graduates' intellectual accomplishments.[8] It was not mentioned that Stanford graduated one hundred and two Rhodes Scholars between 1904 and 2018. Stanford came in fourth after Harvard, Yale, and Princeton for the most recent ten-year period.[9]

This is an issue in high school sports as well. For example, in 2017, the Katy Independent School District in Texas built an additional $72 million football stadium to go next to its existing stadium,[10] despite the fact that the district is in significant debt and the schools are overcrowded.[11]

This spending reinforces the message for parents that their kids need to invest their time and prioritize becoming elite athletes. College recruiters start early, with many trying to lock students in *even before high school starts* in spite of recent NCAA regulations to the contrary. What does that say about how much they care about grades or a student's own development and free will? When we arrived from Asia, we had a shelf full of medals for academic accomplishments. And if we don't encourage our kids to paint and write poems and go to museums and concerts as often as they watch sports on TV or kick a ball, then our world-renowned concert halls and museums and university humanities departments will lose their funding.

Despite how important I find it not to shelter children from life, I found it dizzying to try to talk about current events in the United States. In Japan, I was happy when my kids read newspapers. Here, I had to consider what they were reading within the context of what they were observing. A presidential nominee was bragging about "grabbing" women. Vile sound bites filled the news, and I worried about what they were hearing from their classmates.

School shootings have become a common occurrence. I even got a taste of mayhem when Charles called me from his classroom phone panicking, screaming incoherently about what he should do as there was an active shooter in the school building. "Mama, should I just run home now, Mama? Please, Mama, help me. Help me, Mama!" I heard kids in the background crying out, terrorized. I ran to my car and drove shaking in terror because my child's life was in the balance, only to learn that it was a false alarm: the substitute teacher hadn't been prepped on how to handle emergencies.

Teachers also spoke entirely differently from what my children were accustomed to. James came home to tell me with dismay that one of his teachers kept using the word *crap*—the textbook was *crap*, the homework was *crap*. And other teachers spoke so disrespectfully ("I'll stick that pencil where . . .") to the students. James was confounded.

This was culture shock. The United States, and especially *this* United States, was nothing like what I had been nostalgic for over the past ten years. What I thought would be the most familiar was suddenly more foreign to me than Shanghai and Tokyo. I had few expectations for Shanghai and Tokyo, yet I returned to the United States with many because I thought I knew what I was returning to. I didn't realize how much the past ten years had changed me—and how the United States had changed.

I was dumped in the land of capitalism, individuality, and freedoms— the opposite of the collective ideology of Japan, the opposite of nurturing, protecting, and investing in the next generation—the future. Everything there was smooth and predictable in comparison.

Suddenly it was the squeakiest wheel that got the oil, and I needed to learn how to advocate for my children.

Getting the Facts on Your Local School

- What do the school's five most recent annual state reviews reveal about its academics, socioeconomic and racial makeup, teaching practices, and the like? For example, what is the percentage of students up to grade level in reading? How has it changed historically?

- How often (if at all) do teachers meet with each other at the same grade level (horizontal alignment) and at grade levels above and below (vertical alignment) to ensure students are prepared for what's next?

- How, and how often, do parents and teachers communicate with one another?

- What are the time and financial commitments expected or requested of parents?

- What is the curriculum by subject area, and how often is it changed or reevaluated, and why?

- How are the students assessed, and how often and how is this communicated with students and families?

- What are the daily and weekly student schedules? Does the school operate on a block schedule, the same schedule daily, or a rotating daily schedule?

- What does the PTA do? Who runs the PTA, and how is leadership decided? How did the PTA spend its funding the previous year? How involved is the parent body in the PTA?

- Are there specialized or subject-specific teachers? If so, how often do they meet with which students and for what?

- How does the school offer science, visual art, music, and physical education?

- How are the needs of students with special needs met? How, and how often, are these students evaluated?

- How is technology used? And how much class time is spent using technology versus not? What policies about technology does the school

have? Are kids allowed to bring cell phones to class? What kinds of devices and apps are used during class time?

- Do students learn to write cursive?
- How much time is spent on mandatory state-testing prep? How are the
  results used, if at all, by the school and teachers? Can individual students opt out of the tests? If so, what are the consequences of doing so?
- What resources are available at your child's school: library, tutors, academic counselors, psychologists, clubs, parent groups, before- and
  after-school activities, college prep courses?
- What opportunities do parents have to observe classes?
- How does the school define civic responsibility? Do students learn the
  rights and responsibilities of citizenship through the curriculum or
  other school activities? (See Appendix B for more on civics.)

Somewhere along the line in Palo Alto, the balance of power shifted
from teachers and administrators to active families and PTAs. This
manifested itself in all kinds of issues, which I experienced in our first
year there. I thought that administration often acquiesced to the demands of the most vocal parents rather than prioritizing the requests
that could contribute to the learning of all students.

I had never understood the concept of "child advocacy" before—
adults advocating on behalf of students. In every other country, I had
trusted that the teachers and principal wanted the best for my children
and understood their needs. I never had to lobby against a decision a
teacher made or ask for my children to be educated at an appropriate
level. Here, I began understanding the pushy parents—the ones who
were always in the principal's office wanting something.

In the case of James, my "Welcome to Palo Alto" moment was having
to plead with no fewer than five groups of teachers and administrators
to place him in the proper math class. He had no track record, so the
district was loath to place him in a class two years above grade level.

My persistence prevailed, but I think most others would have given up. It was evident that the district was tired of pushy parents like me. Charles too was far ahead of his fifth-grade math class (there were no upper-level math classes available at his elementary school), so he was told to just read books quietly during class time.

I spoke to another mom about it, and she just chuckled at *my* learning curve: "Oh, you trusted the *school* to teach math?"

The schools weren't doing an exemplary job educating the kids, but the parents of Silicon Valley *were*. One member of the school board called it the "broken feedback loop," meaning teachers believe they are doing a great job because their students were performing so well. But Palo Alto parents refused to allow their kids to fall behind. Many of them were highly educated, ambitious, and wealthy. I attribute much of the 100 percent graduation rate to *their* efforts. *They* kept up the high enrollment in AP classes. This district's success came down to one thing: the parents.

Which was both good and bad.

I had mixed feelings about the strategy that parents were employing in Palo Alto. On the one hand, they were supplementing the school's patchy academic offerings with private tutors and other enrichment activities. They were educated people who were reading and discussing books and current events with their kids and reviewing homework. On the other hand, they were mostly going over teachers' heads and straight to the principal or superintendent's office with any complaints or requests.

What happened to following the chain of command? I imagine much of this is due to accessibility—a few clicks, and you can email anybody and multiple somebodies in one fell swoop. I certainly experienced a great deal of frustration trying to work with my kids' teachers to resolve issues, such as the complete lack of support for new students entering the middle school in the seventh grade and the high teacher turnover that Charles experienced in fifth grade. Communication was limited; parents were supposed to use an email template supplied by the PTA and then wait forty-eight hours for a response. Two days can be a long time in the life of an adolescent. Often I didn't even receive a reply. It was evident that teachers were stuck in a game of tug-of-war among pushy parents, district mandates, limited funds, and other demands on their time.

I played along and successfully campaigned to get Charles moved to a higher-level math class when he started middle school, but he could have literally learned no math at all that year without this intervention. Teenagers often already think they know everything. At the same time, I thought about the fact that Palo Alto's parents had social capital and networking skills that parents elsewhere normally didn't. How many children in other school districts were languishing because their parents didn't have the time or know-how to navigate the system or because administrators didn't feel the same pressure to listen to them?

At the student level, the teachers' catchphrase at the middle school was *advocacy* (different from child advocacy), which referred to children advocating for themselves. I often wondered if this was more about trying to keep parents out of the classrooms than about helping students develop this lifetime skill of self-advocacy. I couldn't understand why there weren't greater efforts for equal and open communication among teachers, students, and parents. Without it, the odds for success are stacked against the child.

One of the hard truths I came around to in California was that I'd been a little naive about the US education system in general. I knew it had problems and there was plenty to work on, but until I was walking through it with three children, I had downplayed in my own mind how deeply rooted and systemic the problems are. Maybe the biggest concern isn't a lack of dedicated teachers, or parents who don't value education enough; maybe the most significant problem is that we've let the public schools sell out our kids to the highest bidders.

CHAPTER 12

Who's the Boss?

*Education in a Nation Where Capitalism,
Individuality, and Freedom Prevail*

One night as I passed by Charles's room, I saw glowing light ema-
nating from under the covers of his bed. "What do you have under
there?" I asked.

"Nothing."

"Show me."

He reluctantly handed over an iPad—a PTA-funded iPad that I
didn't even know he had. The fifth-grade teacher had given them out
to all the kids, with no limits on the games or apps they could use.

"She told us we could read all our books on here," he explained. "And
we can download whatever apps we want."

I was stunned. Charles had the iPad for at least a few days before I
happened to walk in on him using it. He didn't tell me because he knew
there would be rules once I found out about it.

When I met with the principal later that week, he had no idea
that Charles's teacher had distributed iPads to all the students. This
sounded the alarm for me. *Who was steering the ship at Charles's school?*

Later, when visiting a Blue Ribbon School in Utah (a highly rated
public school; see the glossary for more information), I had a similar
moment. After spending time in classes, I mentioned to the principal
that I had watched the students using virtual reality (VR) goggles in
class. He had been totally unaware that the teacher was using this

technology as part of the curriculum. It wasn't necessarily the use of the technology that caused me concern, but more so the fact that there were obvious gaps in oversight and communication between teachers and the school leadership.

The haphazard way technology was introduced in the classroom represented a lack of cohesive oversight in the Palo Alto schools. I noticed a lack of alignment in many other ways too: how teachers assess and grade, their standards of mastery, their expectations for behavior, and the technology and apps they use in class and for communication with parents. I couldn't understand how students were expected to spend their time navigating a mess that was created by a system meant to be teaching them.

I was used to the governments in Japan and China having a somewhat heavy hand, especially when it came to children's education. But I had come to appreciate the benefits of that intervention. In particular, I appreciated how the collective ideology of Japan led to everything being smooth and predictable. There were rules, and people followed them. Japan employed a long-term approach that didn't rely on ever-changing initiatives. This meant that the children's learning was both protected and prioritized above all else.

One of the qualities I had liked right away in Japan's public schools was the standardization of the curricula and materials. The nation's Ministry of Education has implemented a centralized curriculum that gets reevaluated every ten years, not on the whims of the school, school board, district, state, federal government, or newly elected official.[1] Teachers in Japan know exactly what kids covered the previous year. Textbooks are time-tested and not constantly changing. In Japan, elementary textbooks are more like magazines: thin paperback books packed from cover to cover on every subject, unlike the massive textbooks and supplemental materials students often receive in the United States that are impossible to cover in full in a year. Here, teachers skip around and are never trained on how to decipher which material to teach. There, it's all covered on a predictable schedule.

In China and Japan, school funding, sourcing, and allocation are clear because a top-down system actively supports families, no matter their income. The government gives every possible chance to the children in poorer districts and areas of the country rather than punishing them with less funding, fewer services, and less qualified teachers.

A 2017 article in the business section of the *Atlantic* declared that "Japan might be what equality in education looks like" because schools are funded equitably, according to an assessment of the needs of its students.[2] Schools in Japan are not dependent on local taxes or state grants the way US schools are funded; in Japan, there is no purely academic advantage to living in a school district with wealthier parents.

Palo Alto has world-class schools, after all, right? When I didn't find this to be the case, I was at a loss. How did the local schools achieve such high ratings if the problems I experienced were any indication of what was going on?

I was in for some big surprises.

This lack of equitable funding among school districts, even for those located only a few miles apart, raised alarms for me when I arrived back in the United States. Families able to afford to live in affluent areas with high local taxes—like Palo Alto—have an advantage over the rest. And since many of these families are highly educated, they pass this advantage on to their children as well. Children from these families come out on top; they possess all kinds of capital, from financial (money to live in the right district, pay tuitions, hire tutors, play for travel sport teams) to social (friends and connections) to cultural (previous experience and understanding of how to work the system). Palo Alto parents had all these kinds of capital in spades.

But just a short drive away from my kids' well-funded schools in Palo Alto was the Ravenswood City School District in East Palo Alto. In 2018, the district had a $5 million budget shortfall that is expected to lead to cutting the equivalent of eighty-three full-time staff positions.[3]

According to the California Department of Education, 88 percent of its students qualify for free or reduced-price lunch and 55.6 percent of the students are English Language Learners.[4]

By comparison, in our district, 12 percent of students qualified for free or reduced-price lunch in 2017–18. And less than 11 percent of students in the district were learning English as a second language that same year.[5] (One reason Palo Alto numbers are that high is because of a 1986 court-ordered program, the Voluntary Transfer Program, that brings students from neighboring underserved Ravenswood School District to Palo Alto.[6])

In spring 2017, I observed an eighth-grade social studies classroom for several hours every week at a local middle school in this neighboring district. Bars covered the classroom windows, and I was informed that several of the students had part-time jobs, took care of their younger siblings, were living in foster care, or had parents in prison.

I was confused when, at the end of class, the teacher said, "If anyone needs to borrow a textbook, come see me."

"Why do some of them need to borrow textbooks?" I asked the teacher once the students were gone. "Did they lose theirs?"

"No, it's for the kids who don't have smartphones. Our school doesn't have enough textbooks for everyone. All the text is online, so most kids just read the book on their phones. The ones who don't have phones can borrow a textbook to take home."

I'm not sure if I managed to hide my horror. Probably not.

First, I was dismayed by the idea of students reading books on their phones. How much learning is really happening when you're scrolling along on a six-inch screen while chatting with friends on the latest social messaging app? What happened to annotating and highlighting?

At the same time, many of these students were using small Bluetooth-connected earphones to listen to expletive-laden rap music *during* class anyway. I could hear it from ten feet away. Then I was dumbfounded that the teacher ostracized the kids who either couldn't afford smartphones or whose parents hadn't allowed it. The other kids didn't have to lug around heavy books, but this small group of students did—and they had to go to the front of the class and make their situation public.

When I visited California Senator Kamala Harris's office in 2018 to discuss education funding at the federal level, her aide leveled with me: "In this country, the school districts that need the most money have the least money. The school districts that need the best teachers have the worst teachers. The places where we need the highest standards have the lowest standards. Everything is inverted in our system."

Separately, a Democratic staff member of Congress specializing in education policy revealed to me there wasn't much the federal government could do to affect state policies: "The reality is that states don't have to listen to us." Funding mostly comes from state and local budgets, and districts decide how to use that funding. It's up to parents to hold school administrators and school board members accountable for spending the money well. Yes, it's up to the constituents. And this comes full circle to the poorer districts not having access to the resources necessary to pull themselves out of their condition without intervention at the state level.

The pervasive use of technology in classrooms represents how the corporate interests of technology companies and the need for individual "personalized learning" are presented as paramount to the fundamental educational needs of children; I disagree.

I had managed to escape school-induced battles over technology in our house thus far, but all that suddenly changed in California. "Put your Chromebook away! It's time for dinner," I would tell James, and he would say, "My teacher hasn't posted my grade yet" or "I need it for my homework."

Teachers really did post homework assignments and grades at all hours, so James kept going online with his school-issued Chromebook to check if things were up yet. When I broached the subject with the school, I was told that I should just impose limits on their online time and to make them wait until the following day to check for grades. But I couldn't help but wonder, *Why has the school set me up for conflict?* They put devices in my kids' hands with an easy work-around firewall, allowed teachers to post at all hours, and then expected me to deal with the strife that caused at home.

Talk about a science experiment gone awry. Just as students have deadlines for submitting their homework, so too should teachers have limits for posting assignments and grades. I have yet to find a school with a comprehensive home *and* school tech policy, when this *must* be a joint effort if the school is going to require tech usage for homework.

This scenario would have been unimaginable in my kids' schools in China and Japan. In the boys' Tokyo elementary school, there was one computer lab, with monitors covered with dust. Students learned about computers, but technology was not integrated into their academic lives; there were no computers in their classrooms or tablets assigned for home use. Now, teachers may use them, but the ratio of one computer to one child is nowhere on the horizon.

When I visited the Scarsdale School District in New York State, I noticed that the district placed great importance on having the most up-to-date technology. Its high school computer lab would fit in perfectly on the Google campus in Silicon Valley. The district's technology officers explained to me how thoughtfully they integrated tech into the school's curriculum. The newness of the technology wasn't the most relevant thing; it was the careful attention the district paid to how technology fit into their overall educational mission.

In China and Japan, technology use in classrooms is among the lowest in OECD nations. "If you look at the best-performing education systems, such as those in East Asia, they've been very cautious about using technology in their classrooms," said Andreas Schleicher of the OECD. "Those students who use tablets and computers very often tend to do worse than those who use them moderately."[7]

In their 2014 article in *Psychological Science*, Pam A. Mueller of

Princeton University and Daniel M. Oppenheimer of the University of California, Los Angeles, push back against the common practice of students in universities taking notes on laptops or other electronic devices. While students are able to record a larger quantity of words when using a laptop, their ability to retain content is reduced. As Mueller told NPR, "When people type their notes, they have this tendency to try to take verbatim notes and write down as much of the lecture as they can. The students who were taking longhand notes in our studies were forced to be more selective—because you can't write as fast as you can type. And that extra processing of the material that they were doing benefited them."[8]

In our August 2017 interview, Schleicher pointed to Japan as an example of a balanced approach to technology: it is mostly found in schools as a means for collaboration among teachers. He contrasts this with many Western countries, where, he says, "we use it as a substitute for existing practices" rather than as a complement to pedagogies that are already in place.

In Japan, parents communicated with teachers primarily through phone calls, the daily teacher-parent journal, and in-person meetings—not emails, texts, or apps. *Are they behind in Japan?* I wondered. Both China and Japan will certainly move in this direction, but with planning and intentionality, no doubt, and not to the detriment of face-to-face communication or in the haphazard way I was experiencing it in Palo Alto. Tech was even less a part of my kids' lives in Shanghai, where the Internet at that time was unreliable, slow, and heavily monitored by the government's Great China Firewall.

For me, technology run amok came to symbolize the conflicts I felt on returning to the United States. Palo Alto was smack dab in the land of capitalism, individuality, and innovation. Often corporate profits seem to be more important than our social responsibility to protect and nurture our most vulnerable yet invaluable asset: our children. I wanted to see tested-and-true methods where technology was thoughtfully integrated, not used as a sloppy substitute for meaningful learning.

But in the middle of the world's tech capital, reversing the use of tech seemed like a lost cause, especially in the realm of education. In Silicon Valley, the very tech executives who push these $200 Chromebooks to school districts send their kids to these schools.

Tech billionaires push their wares into classrooms while also building their own schools; Google and Oracle have charter schools on their campuses, Mark Zuckerberg is building one near Facebook, and Elon Musk has one in LA. These schools offer to "fix" our education system through personalized, customized education for every child in the world. When I hear these terms in the same sentence as *students*, I wonder how children will ever function in a world that does not always cater to them.

One afternoon when Charles was in fifth grade, he handed me a printed-out essay he had written. "But, Mama, promise not to get mad at me. Don't look at the capitalization or punctuation. The shift key is a total pain on an iPad. But the spelling is okay."

He was learning how to craft essays finger-tapping on an iPad with auto spell-check, unfiltered and immediate access to fake news, and cut-and-paste functionality?

At a parent education session in Palo Alto run by the middle school's chief technology officer, parents were told to sit by their child every afternoon or evening with a timer and monitor everything they did. Daily! I couldn't believe my ears. I was being asked to police my child because the school was giving him an addictive entertainment machine (read: *Fortnite*) on which he could also do minimal amounts of homework. This was totally contrary to my belief in offering my kids opportunities for autonomy and self-regulation. It was also dissonant with what we know about the adolescent brain: that its critical thinking skills and judgment are not developed enough for unfettered access to technology.

Opening Pandora's box to social media was not on my wish list either. Even adults have a hard time navigating a social world that's ruled by "likes" and "retweets"; online personas are often filled with bravado, and lives are curated to seem much cooler than they really are. At ages when children need to develop their social communication, the focus has to be on in-person interactions, not on trying to "go viral."

Even the lack of handwriting was a stolen piece of childhood. Once upon a time, we would recognize a note from a friend by the handwriting, which revealed bits of personality through each curvy *s*, each carefully drawn bubble letter, and each intentionally scrawled signature. Handwriting is a piece of identity that keystrokes can't match.

Family time in our household was now tainted by arguments over the ever-present screens that had been such a minor part of our lives before. Communication with the school that used to end when the student left the building was now 24/7. I refused to give my kids smartphones, much to their massive dismay. But when the school issues technology, what could I do?

Oh, how I missed the days of graphite-blackened sleeves and filled notebooks.

Because the US federal government has a largely hands-off policy when it comes to schools, it does not regulate other forces that influence schools, including technology companies and other corporate interests with powerful lobbies.

Behind closed doors, our educational and government leaders allow tech companies, testing companies, and book publishers to take over our classrooms, replacing the textbooks and curricula every couple of years, generally without even consulting significant numbers of educators and the actual teachers in classrooms. Whose interests are being met? Often it's not the students' or the teachers'. These are financial deals that boost profit margins and benefit shareholders who want to get into our schools.

When corporations offer free playground equipment, free access to lessons, grant money, and sponsorship money for after-school programs, administrators convince themselves it's a win-win relationship. Often these are short-lived programs because the district cannot fund them on its own later. For example, Google for Education has granted over $160 million to educational causes "to help more people—especially those in underserved communities—benefit from the promise of technology, in the classroom and beyond."[9] Apple has various programs in US public schools to promote its products, including its Apple Distinguished Schools program (which has recognized 470 schools in thirty-four countries) and ConnectED, as well as curriculum like Everyone Can Code. Korkat.com even offers an entire free *book* of places schools can apply for grants for playground equipment (including corporations such as Nike, Mattel, Lowe's, and General Mills). Powerful companies are masters of product placement in our schools.

And our teachers and principals fall prey to corporate entities because *our schools do not receive enough funding and do not allocate it properly*. At times the drive toward more tech is coming from well-meaning school administrators and teachers who want to help students compete in the job market later or on their college applications.

However, not all students need to learn how to code. Fluency in Google Slides and Photoshop—at the expense of foundational lessons, textbooks, and teachers—might sidetrack valuable resources that could be better spent on teacher salaries, the arts, and everything else it takes to make a school work.

The explosion of education technology in our classrooms is being driven by an implosion of traditional education companies like textbook publishing. Driven by profit, the nation's largest publisher of textbooks, Pearson, is selling off its textbook division because it is not as profitable as its online and assessment offerings.[10]

Parents are also often unclear about the effective uses of ed-tech. They get excited along with their kids when they hear about Chromebooks for all the kids, subscription-based programs and apps kids can use at home, and so on. They think they're giving their kids an advantage over schools with lower budgets and less tech.

To gain some perspective on the potential of technology to revolutionize education, I attended the ninth annual summit on ed-tech, ASU+GSV, in 2018, coorganized by Arizona State University and Global Silicon Valley. The registration for the conference was over $3,000 (the "discounted" rate was $900 for educators), high enough to exclude teachers and most administrators from the conversation altogether. This event was clearly meant for businesses, tech investors, university administrators, and politicians. And me, apparently.

With nine hundred speakers and presenters (including John Legend and George W. Bush, along with education experts like former Secretary of Education Arne Duncan and "grit" expert Angela Duckworth), there was a great deal of energy in the room. It was all about innovation! Personalized learning! Scalability! Equal opportunity! I almost drank the Kool-Aid myself except it too was out of my price range.

Among the business leaders presenting were Jack Lynch, the CEO of Houghton Mifflin Harcourt; Mark King, the president of Adidas North America; Nick Gaehde, the president of Lexia Learning; and Andrew Rosen, chairman and CEO of Kaplan.

The technology being promoted was unproven by anyone other than the companies' own marketing teams that produce convincing white papers. There were no longitudinal academic studies showing any measurable positive effects. The largest corporate sponsors of the nonprofit Common Sense Media—which produces much of the research, ratings, and reviews we depend on to evaluate tech for kids— are the major tech companies! There's a major conflict of interest here despite their insistence that there isn't. Know your resources, and who is behind them.

I have never been against tech. I rely heavily on it for my own professional and personal organization. I *do* think there could be invaluable uses for tech in the classroom. We just don't know what they are yet. US schools and our children are running headfirst into the unknown. Tech should be an add-on tool, not a substitute for established elements of the curriculum. Watching a student-created slide show or film can be ooh- and aah-inducing, but was it challenging to their brains? *Can we please get the basics down first?*

Tech Transparency

To better understand tech in our classrooms, demand transparency. It should be clear who is getting funding for what initiatives at all levels, from the classroom teacher who could be subsidized by Apple all the way up to legislators whose campaigns are funded by major education lobby groups. Ask why this initiative is necessary.

When there are new mandates and school board elections that directly affect our school districts, we need to be vocal about asking where they're coming from and who has a financial stake in them.

- What's the catalyst?
- What is the life cycle of these reforms?
- How will it be funded, and for how long?
- Is there any longitudinal research showing them to be effective?
- What's the assessment of the plan?
- What professional development is planned to support those efforts?
- Will teachers require time away from the classroom to train?

Based on my experience and extensive research, my advice is to petition for tech to be removed entirely from elementary and middle school classrooms (aside from computer labs) until schools have long-term tech plans that include fierce oversight, continued funding, professional development, clear intentionality, and 100 percent transparency with every stakeholder in each student's life. Otherwise schools need to wait for longitudinal research that demonstrates that it's good for kids' brains and long-term knowledge retention. Tech should never replace human interaction in our classrooms. It's extreme, for sure, but I saw how this opposite extreme worked halfway around the world to great effect.

Another "Who's steering the ship?" moment occurred when I started receiving daily notifications from Charles's fifth-grade teacher via the ClassDojo app. According to the app's website, it is used in 90 percent of K–8 schools in the United States.[11] Although I hadn't given permission for my children's private information to be shared in any app, suddenly I was getting daily reports about how Charles scored on ten different behaviors (such as staying on task, helping others, and participating in discussions). The goal was to get at least 90 points out of 100 every day, and Charles was failing every day.

I could not wrap my head around a teacher spending time typing in a play-by-play on her smartphone rather than speaking with my child face-to-face about social skills. *The irony!* Would you ever take a job if you were being judged on behavior every moment of your day? Talk about anxiety-inducing practices—at the age of ten! For us, the problem was that Charles was starting to think school was stupid. He actually used the word *stupid* to describe the app, the learning that it was supposed to inform, and the overall classroom management.

How was I supposed to convince him otherwise when I had the same feeling? I needed to keep him engaged and make sure he respected his teachers, but I was losing respect for them myself.

Despite their aspirational expectations for behavior, teachers for both boys did not challenge them scholastically. Once I realized how low the expectations were and I was unable to make much progress on that front, I took matters into my own hands. I signed the kids up for supplemental learning activities that included attending an after-school math program. Charles, ever the science enthusiast, studied with a Stanford astrotheorist. James, the family diplomat, attended an intense competitive Model UN/government program at Stanford. We also hired Mandarin and Japanese tutors so all three kids would maintain their language abilities.

We took advantage of the public libraries in Palo Alto to keep a steady supply of books flowing in and out of the house. Charles was a voracious reader, devouring anything he could get his hands on, and this was a crucial supplement to his lackluster reading list at school.

Keeping Kids Challenged in Middle School

There are many ways parents can help their children learn. Here are some of my favorite ways:

- Encourage your children to read the classics. I have used the book list at St. Bernard's, an all-boys school in New York City, for years. Regularly visit the library, and keep all genres of books around your home. Resist the temptation to get your kids an e-reader too early.
- Know your kids' subject-specific curriculum, but do not do their homework for them. Encourage their independence.
- Have a home base for all calendars and schedules of each member of the family. Discuss the day's events every evening at dinner, as well as what is to come the following day.
- Differentiate between your needs and your children's when you make decisions about things like getting a smartphone for your middle schooler. What are the pros and cons for everyone involved?
- If possible, separate your kids' study space from their sleep space. Put the desk in another room or the family office.
- Remove technology from the bedroom as much as possible. Be in charge of the home Wi-Fi. Do not buy a smartphone until your child

already has the self-control, organization, discipline, and study routines in place. Do not allow tech at the dinner table.

- When debating any topic with your children, ask them to argue with three valid points as they would in an essay. Then have them argue the flip side.
- Improve vocabulary by subscribing online to Merriam-Webster's word of the day, and discuss the word. Intentionally use large words.
- Stay up on the school gossip by befriending other parents.
- Subscribe to hard-copy news sources like the *New York Times*, the *Wall Street Journal*, the *Economist*, the *New Yorker*, and *Scientific American*, and keep them in the most heavily used family area.
- Model behavior that shows you value education and are a lifelong learner.
- Discuss what is meant by civic engagement and be prepared to raise a soon-to-be voter.
- Be as informed as possible about your child's friends, and invite them to your home while you are there. Get to know their families.
- Have regular communication with your child's teachers to keep abreast of all developments. You do not want to be the last one to know about something that could have been avoided. You also want to be aware of any accomplishments that should be celebrated at home.
- Be up-to-date on international, national, and local news, and discuss it with your children regularly.
- Make sure your kids are contributing to household chores.
- Find a tutor or study group whenever your child may need one for keeping up or getting ahead if your child is passionate about a subject.
- Watch educational TV shows and films and documentaries.
- Prioritize family time—without technology.
- Go to book readings at your local library and bookstore. Meet the authors.
- Have your kids participate in summer programs to avoid summer slide. Establish clear academic goals and routines.

- Grow acquainted with the opportunities in your community: library, community center, museums, and others.
- Encourage social responsibility and giving back to the community to develop empathy and humility.
- Practice global competence. Show an appreciation for and interest in varied cultures. Show your kids ways to protect the environment. Understand international trade, and expose your kids to these ideas. Study another language, and immerse your family in other languages as much as possible.
- Review all the practical skills in life that your child may not learn in school: how to do household repairs, how to do the laundry, how to sew, how to cook, how to balance a checkbook, and the like. Refer to the chart of chores in the box titled Contributing at Home at Any Age on page 156 for ideas.
- Make visiting museums and watching live performances a regular practice in your family. If theater is cost prohibitive, explore children's theater in your town for less expensive performances that your kids will enjoy. Perhaps your local library has passes for museums.
- Travel as much as you can, internationally if possible, and read up on the culture of the countries you are visiting before, during, and after the trip.

I was managing my children's academic life instead of leaving it to the school, as I had done in Shanghai and Tokyo. It felt like I was sending them to school to be social and learn the culture—though I wasn't 100 percent certain of this either—while I was home-schooling them for academics. What I really craved but found lacking in Palo Alto was a strong commitment to the fundamentals, with or without tech. I was looking for a stable curriculum, with continuity in the teaching and administrative staff of my kids' schools.

During this time, it hit home how decentralized the US education system is. States and districts have great leeway to set budgets, curriculum, assessments, and teacher credentialing requirements. We have few national policies or requirements that are applicable to all schools across the country; instead, we have what I would refer to as guidelines. In a large and diverse nation, it's not such a bad thing to have flexibility to adapt curriculum to the local context and history. But the lack of standardization leaves wide gaps in learning expectations as well as specific content to be learned. Student experiences can differ greatly not only by region and state, but even by district, school, and classroom. This lack of common standards makes it difficult to ensure that all students receive a great public education.

I call the US education system "the great Swiss cheese" because it has lots of holes that need to be plugged up. If you have the means, contacts, and knowledge as a parent to fill these in, you are among the privileged and your children can reap the rewards. Otherwise, you may fall through the cracks with attempts to fight a behemoth of a system that is working against you. It's not fair, and all of us must fight to correct these inequities. The future of our country depends on putting the right people in charge of education so they can ensure that *all* of our children's interests come first and corporate interests (profits) aren't even on the list.

This country *is* worth the fight. As critical as I may be of the US education system, I'm also devoted to its improvement because this is the country I love. I know we can right the ship.

CHAPTER 13

Cheers

To the Great Potential of the USA

M r. Routledge? I, uh, can't be in last period AP US History today because I, uh, am leaving school early. My mom is being sworn in as a US citizen." Anything to get out of class, especially on a Friday afternoon.

"Now *that's* an experience you can't replicate in a classroom!" he said, far more excited than I was. Yet he was right.

By the time I was in the eleventh grade, my mother had been living in the United States for over twenty-five years on a green card. Watching her raise her right hand and swear to uphold the laws of the nation—alongside hundreds of other immigrants with their families proudly waving the US flag and crying—was my first true exposure to the significance of US citizenship. I had been taking it for granted. Until that point, democracy was somehow my God-given right. But, no—the truth is that I was just straight-up lucky. Inexplicably, ridiculously lucky to have been born in a nation of promise and opportunity.

Who knew that my seemingly fresh-off-the-boat, thick-accented mom knew that there were twenty-seven amendments to the US Constitution or nine Supreme Court justices? I entered the room a bored teenager and left with a new appreciation of US citizenship.

Throughout my years living in Asia, I constantly reflected on my US citizenship. And it took on more importance when we returned to the United States because I needed my children to appreciate the gift they'd been given as a birthright. It was *their* turn.

I would venture to say that what makes America great is the promise of *possibility*—hope that you can be anybody or anything if you work hard at it. Heck, sometimes you don't even have to work hard; you can just play and win the lottery, literally—which is exactly what my practical, no-holds-barred mother told me to do any time I shared my ideas about working in fields she considered unlucrative: advertising, the restaurant business, interior design. "Teru! Go win lotto. You have better chance to make money," she would say with her simplified, thickly accented English.

Here in the United States, we don't have to determine our path when we're children, unlike in so many other countries where kids have to decide on a math/science or humanities track before high school. We can take our time and figure out who we are. We might decide to become a chef or a contestant on *The Bachelor,* or pursue a patent for a lifesaving medical invention, or become a conceptual artist using empty tomato cans, or even run for president. We can be innovative and creative. And the icing on the cake? Without investing in thousands of hours of schooling, we speak English, the most commonly spoken language in the world.

My own upbringing was strongly influenced by my mom's hardscrabble rise out of the literal ashes of post–World War II Japan and her ensuing tenacity to build a life as a self-sufficient woman in a foreign country. And like her, so many other immigrants continue to flock to the United States, creating the most richly diverse nation in the world. My mother's journey was living proof to me that the United States could open up the doors to the world.

I viscerally felt the limitations of the schools in Palo Alto, but I knew that there were schools in the United States that were thriving and producing engaged and motivated learners. I set out on a mission to see them firsthand. In the best of cases, these schools took me back to my days in Shanghai and Tokyo, where the learning expectations were high and the teachers, parents, and students worked together to practice the highest of learning expectations to reach each child's full potential. At several of the schools I visited, the leadership championed this.

I visited the Christa McAuliffe School, a gifted and talented middle school in Brooklyn that sends more students to New York City's nine highly regarded and competitive specialized high schools than any other middle school in the city.[1]

There has been city-wide protest about the school's heavy Asian student population (nearly 70 percent) and a push to open the doors to more disadvantaged students regardless of their test scores. Acceptance there is purely meritocratic and determined by simple scoring on three tests: English language arts, state math, and the Otis-Lennon School Ability Test. At my core, I do believe in a meritocracy, but I also believe that the pipeline to give every US citizen an equal opportunity starting from conception is completely broken.

Those who come from families of means should not be the only ones to make it to the top in this country. We are doing our nation a huge disservice not only by leaving so much untapped talent on the table but also by leaving those who were not given a fair shake with a deep sense of disenfranchisement. Our seemingly limitless opportunities in the United States can endure only if we all have access to consistent and reliable high-quality education, no matter our socioeconomic status, home life, or address.

Mastery was one topic that continued to fascinate me from my initial experiences in Shanghai. I looked for signs of how mastery is being achieved at US schools. In March 2018, I visited the Science Academy STEM Magnet, which is open for admission to all students in grades 6 to 8 who live within the boundaries of the Los Angeles Unified School District. It is a public magnet middle school for gifted students, specializing in STEM (science, technology, engineering, and math). Thirty percent of its students are socioeconomically disadvantaged.

When I entered the front office, I was gobsmacked by the number of trophies that decorated the entryway. These were not for soccer or basketball but for science bowls, robotics, academic decathlons, Science Olympiads, and the like. It's a *middle* school!

In 2018, 99 percent of the Science Academy STEM Magnet students met or exceeded standards on the math exam. Together with its 97 percent score on the English assessment, the Science Academy had one of the highest overall scores in California.

Principal Carlos Lauchu has fought tirelessly at the district level to get the funding and support his school has needed. His school showed me that when there is a firm, positive mindset of high expectations by the leadership, kids stay motivated.

When I walked around the classrooms, I observed sixth-grade students taking meticulous notes by hand that were reminiscent of those that I tried to produce during my caffeine-maddened days before finals. STEM Magnet coordinator and cofounder Jodi Huff explained that all students are required to take notes by hand.

Seventh-grade students take AP Biology, with the opportunity to take both the College Board AP Biology exam and the SAT Subject Matter test in Biology. Eighth graders enroll in both AP Chemistry and AP Physics courses that are divided into eighteen-week semesters. And though in the State of California Algebra 1 is typically a ninth-grade course according to the California Common Core State Standards, students at the Science Academy are well ahead. By the eighth grade, students are enrolled in Algebra 2, trigonometry, or precalculus.

I was struck by the thoughtful ways the school integrates technology. For example, I visited a physical education class where students were passing balls of different sizes with speed sensors in them, with instructions to throw the balls to each other in a different order every time. The teacher and students would analyze the data later in the classroom. I felt like I was witnessing Lamar's aerodynamic and infamous javelin throw from the lewd 1984 flick *Revenge of the Nerds*.

Similarly, at Polk Elementary in Ogden, Utah, principal Maridee

Harrison is committed to doing whatever it takes to give all her students the best possible education. She has turned her school around from receiving a C in 2013–14 to an A from the Utah State Board of Education for the second year in a row for 2016–17. Polk's scores place it in the top 3 percent of schools in Utah, one that spends just over $6,500 per pupil—the lowest in the nation. I met with her and toured her school in April 2018.

Although 52 percent of her students are socioeconomically disadvantaged, she refuses to let this impede their success.[2] She pulls out John Hattie's book *Visible Learning for Teachers*, her go-to manual, and turns to earmarked page 266, "A list of influences on achievement."[3] The top variables are student expectations, response to intervention, teacher credibility, and providing formative evaluations. Socioeconomic status ranks much lower, at number 45. She says that it's common for Polk students whose families can afford ski vacations in Europe to sit next to those who may be struggling at home, but that they all share the same high-level academic outcomes. She has a mission to never leave a single child behind.

All students carry a self-analytical data binder on how they are meeting their goals, updating their own personal growth trajectories and achievements weekly. The school hosts regular personalized teacher interventions for every child to ensure growth and challenge.

Harrison praises her staff for their continued and unwavering commitment to the potential of each student in the school. For its three hundred students, Polk has a full-time instructional coach, ninety-minute professional learning communities, complete alignment vertically between grades and horizontally between same-grade classrooms, individual goal setting, weekly formative assessments, teacher observations, discussions on social and academic issues, stronger teachers coaching less experienced ones, and regular discussions on clearly delineated and prioritized goals.

Ultimately, she says, "Success is different for everyone." But she makes sure they are all engaged and empowered learners for life.

* * *

Similarly, when I visited Carpenter Community Charter, a Los Angeles Unified School District (LAUSD) elementary school in Studio City, California, with standardized test scores far above the state average, I was handed a schedule for classroom observations and sent on my way.

As I was crossing through the school's large inner courtyard, I saw a man pushing around Chewbacca-sized garbage bins, whose zeal was reminiscent of one of Snow White's whistling dwarfs. I was intrigued, so I went over to him and said, "Hello. May I ask what you do here?"

"I'm the principal," he said as he immediately reached out a welcoming hand.

"I'm Teru ..."

"Yes, we've been expecting you! We have a big Halloween event tonight, so my maintenance staff is off this morning. I'm covering. Excuse me. I've had my hands full this morning," he said, rather tongue-in-cheek. I looked around, and it seemed that every single student and teacher was decked out to the nines in a Tim Burton *Nightmare Before Christmas*–themed get-up. Talk about community buy-in and early prep for the holiday spirit!

His enthusiasm for his school was infectious. It reminded me of the dedication I had seen among Japanese teachers and administrators, especially when they were singing and dancing in their poop costumes.

At Carpenter, I observed an overflowing fifth-grade classroom in which every student was pin-drop silent listening to their sparkplug of a teacher. I observed a science teacher who teaches every student in the school (just under one thousand). She not only knew every student's name in two of her classes that I observed, she engaged each of her students as if she was conducting an orchestra.

I observed a veteran music teacher conducting her class of third graders while they were sight-reading from sheet music. It reminded me of the fact that every child in Japan knows how to sight-read music, as does every teacher.

During another visit, this time across the country at the School Without Walls, a public magnet high school in Washington, DC, two seniors gave me a tour and introduced me to every teacher or administrator in every classroom and corridor and shared glowing personal anecdotes about each of them. School Principal Richard Trogisch explained how they are able to keep per-pupil spending down while providing students with a top-notch high school education: he pointed at his front office staff of two for a school of six hundred students. According to the website of the DC Public Schools, School Without Walls was expecting to spend $9,202 per student in 2018–19, well below the highest per pupil spending at a district high school ($15,253 at Coolidge High School).[4] School Without Walls won the Blue Ribbon Award for excellence in 2018.

In addition to keeping administrative fees low, Walls, as it is commonly known, relies heavily on the resources of neighboring George Washington University to supplement school programming and resources. Students can earn an associate's degree at George Washington University in their junior and senior years. They also mobilize any available parent capacity and GWU staff to volunteer or teach. Educators at Walls are committed to doing whatever it takes to keep their students and their school thriving. And the school has a low twelve-to-one student-teacher ratio, so each student gets ample attention. Teachers and staff lead by example and bring the best out of their students.

The leadership at Polk Elementary and School Without Walls maintain high standards for every student and offer them the supports necessary to succeed.

A commitment to high expectations and mastery for every student marked all the US public schools that captured my attention. At many of these school visits, I reflected fondly on my experiences in schools in China and Japan and how much I took them for granted at the time.

I have come to appreciate how big an impact the attitude of parents, administrators, teachers, and students can have on students' academic outcomes. Andreas Schleicher of the OECD chatted with me about differences in schools in the United States, Japan, and China. "Every child can learn," he told me. "Every child can reach those goals." He attributes the great success of schools in China and Japan to the fact that "in neither of the systems do you find options for failure. It's not just a mantra but a systemic attribute."

When I sat down with Stanford professor Jo Boaler, she expressed a similar sentiment: that schools in the United States are not designed to maximize each student's growth through trial and error. She compared the United States and Japan: "Teachers here feel like they should save kids if they struggle. That's the American way. In Japan they're encouraged to struggle." Her research on mindset points to the importance of having a growth mindset in reaching a high level of academic mastery.

As she had explained in an earlier TEDx talk, "What you have believed about your own potential has changed what you have learned, and continues to."[5] Boaler's comments appear among a spate of research on mindset in the United States in the past ten years. Mindset is an approach developed in the field of psychology, initially by Carol Dweck. A growth mindset indicates an open-ended understanding of our abilities, while a fixed mindset suggests that we believe that our intelligence and other factors are limited and basically unchangeable. Mindset research points to something already incorporated by our counterparts in China and Japan for at least several decades: students learn more if they are expected to learn more.

According to Boaler, the myth of the "math person" is leading to widespread underachievement in math in the United States. Drawing on the latest intersection of neuroscience and education research, she argues for a direct link between our belief in our potential to learn and our ability to learn. Boaler's research shows if children have a growth mindset, more synapses fire when they make mistakes, and their brains become hardwired to be more open to fixing those mistakes on the next try.

Part of a growth mindset is seeing value in failing; in other words, it's a learning opportunity. We can help our children embrace this mindset by praising their efforts over their intelligence and emphasizing the way many of the people we most admire (inventors, scientists, Olympians, and so on) didn't get things right on the first try but stayed committed to improvement.

China's teachers don't subscribe to the idea that only certain kids can learn math. Every child is expected to reach the same high standard. This ties directly to China's focus on cultivating and investing in the new generation, person by person.

How High Are Your Expectations at Home?

It's certainly easier to follow the status quo, but we need to expect and demand more when it comes to our kids' education. Here are ways to advocate for your child:

- Set up a conference with your child's teacher at the start of the school year. Get to know the teacher and allow the teacher to get to know your family and your child as early as possible, establish expectations, and learn how to work collaboratively with the school.
- If your child is coasting with an 80 average, understand and explain to your child that 20 percent of the content is not being learned and the cumulative effect of this loss.
- Have bookshelves in your house that hold important literature and knowledge (for example, works by Shakespeare, Dickens, Fitzgerald, and Plato; books on art history, Confucianism, physics).
- Do not make tech the default when your child is bored. Creativity and genius come from boredom.
- Make your household's learning expectations clear as part of your family's values. How much time do you expect your kids to spend reading and doing homework? What types of books do you keep at home? How much time is spent on technology? Discuss these family values regularly.

- Teach, practice, and model a growth mindset and be mindful not to impose your own hang-ups on your child. For example, if you say out loud, "I'm just not a math person," you are giving your child permission to feel defeatist in any endeavor before even trying.
- Read your school's curriculum, compare it to your state's Common Core, and identify the gaps that you can address at home.
- To elicit change at the school level, meet with other parents and raise concerns at the teacher, principal, superintendent, then board levels. See Appendix A for more on this.

During my time in Palo Alto, in addition to the academic concerns, I was missing a sense of *home*. Palo Alto did *not* feel like home. So after ten years abroad and two difficult years in California, I knew that it was finally time to go home: to New York City.

I wasn't sure what my kids' education would look like once we returned to New York, but I knew that I needed them to see more of what the United States really represents to *me*. I longed to return to a congested city on a grid with immigrants from all over the world—where over seven hundred languages are spoken in homes, schools, and on the subway.

With my mom now in her seventies, I also wanted to be nearby to care for her if she needed it. After all, I am an only child with a deeply rooted sense of Asian filial piety, and while my mom has always been healthy, I didn't want to have to travel back to Connecticut from across the country to see her during a health crisis. I was going to will myself home, one way or another.

It was the first in our five global city moves that *I* initiated, and I was so excited to come back after all this time. I was a different person from the one who had left this place twelve years earlier; I had learned to become a fighter, an advocate for my children. I had gained an understanding of privilege and how differently the world works for those who are not privileged. I'd researched and experienced so much about international education that I now felt a much deeper understanding of how it *can* work and a calling to share my knowledge with others. I developed friendships I will forever cherish and a sense of peace that I'd never had before.

New York is where I belong, after all.

While I was in New York shortly before moving back, I was walking west on Seventy-Ninth Street toward Central Park on a chilly afternoon. It was the perfect time of day, dusk, when the sun was setting. There were purple hues in the distance.

When I reached the corner of Seventy-Ninth and Fifth Avenue, I glanced to my right and stopped dead in my tracks, struck by the majestic and imposing Metropolitan Museum of Art just ahead of me.

Staring up at it, awestruck, I was reminded of all the larger-than-life lessons I had learned there in my youth. Reading *The Mixed-Up Files of Mrs. Basil E. Frankweiler* in the third grade, and then going to the museum to play out the scenes from the book. The art history classes I had taken in that museum—from learning about the frescoes painted in ancient Greece in fifth grade to van Gogh in sixth grade and Dégas in the tenth. This museum represented what was bringing me back to New York after twelve years away. I had not appreciated this place enough when I was young and had taken all its splendor for granted. I realized that no matter where I lived, New York was my touchstone, the city against which I compare all others.

I was back in *my* city. The city was a gift I needed to give my children. As a family, we were coming full circle, returning to our roots. We'd come so far from the last time I'd been on that street, and it had been an unforgettable journey.

There really *is* no place like home.

Afterword

20/20: Hindsight

Looking back, I think it's funny that we did the reverse of what so many other couples do. They move to New York City and get married and start a family there, but then many decide to leave the hustle and bustle and go home, to their place of comfort, in time for their kids to start school. For me, that hustle and bustle was my place of comfort. I left New York to start raising my kids elsewhere, but I needed them to spend at least part of their childhood in my hometown. I was filled with excitement about what would be in store for my kids and for me.

As I reflected on our time abroad, I came to think of my kids' academic identities in terms of the countries we had lived in during our journey.

I think of James thriving in Shanghai, and his competitive academic personality represents the best of the Chinese education system to me. While he doesn't think of himself as Chinese, he is forever shaped by his experience there.

Victoria's identity is the most Japanese because this is where her memory of schooling began, and the Japanese school system worked well with her personality. She welcomed the nurturing, collective environment. It made her comfortable, a precondition for her academic success. When we returned for her to attend school in Tokyo in the summer of 2017 and 2018, she absolutely loved it. She begged for us to move back.

Charles may be the greatest amalgamation of the three. He is a strong individual who seeks challenges, whether it be reading or sports or astrophysics. He relishes the freedom to do things, but more *his* way. The school systems in China and Japan provided him with countless experiences and structure for his physical and academic energy.

I struggled with the decision of where to send my kids to school in New York. After exploring every option and finding out that there were no appropriate openings in our zoned public schools (in James's grade, the only openings were in the remedial track), I ultimately enrolled the children in different private schools. This was a hard-wrought decision, especially after years of feeling committed to sending my kids to public schools. But I needed to find schools that would challenge my children, where teachers and administrators would recognize where they should be placed academically.

At Charles's New York school, I didn't have to argue about placement or wait for an appropriate track to open up—he would be accelerated in math. I also appreciated the school's approach to integrating physical activity, with the last period of the day dedicated to PE or a sports team. Charles has always been so energetic that I appreciate the inclusion of physical activity in his schedule, without cutting into his study and wind-down time at night.

One of the most beautiful parts of our decision was the outreach and strong feeling of community we found immediately. Soon after we accepted a placement for Victoria, mothers from the school began contacting us to welcome her and get to know us. The first week of school, a boy came and dropped off a bag of brownies for Charles to welcome him. All three grade-level parent leaders reached out to me to introduce themselves, leaders from the families of color group reached out to invite me to a reception, the headmaster at Victoria's school invited me to a "new parents" dinner, and Charles had an assigned "buddy" at school to help him make his transition. The welcoming aspects of the schools weren't directed just at the students but at the whole families. James has always been mature for his age, and he was well suited for a school that is nurturing but more hands-off. His school was the perfect fit for him. A child is a product first and foremost of his or her family, and they are the building blocks of the larger school community.

The truth is that public schools and private schools have much to learn from each other in the United States. Both offer fertile ground for cross-pollination, which will only benefit our children. Andreas Schleicher of the OECD commented as much in our interview: "In the US, private and public schools are parallel systems, so the good ideas from private schools don't feed into the public school system." Within the broad outline of what we know as "public schools," there is so much potential to take heart from what private schools get right. Yet at the moment, it's clear from the research that private schools have a significant advantage in attaining higher levels of education, an advantage that increases with the school's capital. When a school is flush with cash, it can hire teachers with doctoral degrees, keep class sizes small, cater to each individual's needs, provide nutritious meals, bring in esteemed guest speakers, take students on amazing cultural field trips, and so on. This doesn't mean every private school is great—some are lousy, actually—but that's not for lack of opportunity.

I wish all our public schools emulated the same degree of community building. Because private schools ask us to pay tuition, they have to ensure that parents *and* kids are happy at the schools, and they understand that much of it centers around belonging. When you feel that you belong somewhere, you want to stay.

As soon as their school years began, I was able to stop holding my breath: the boys, who had fought me on even going to school in Palo Alto, were both onboard again. The culture at their schools was much more academic, so it was "cool" to study again. When I planned a trip that would require us to take off early on a Friday, Charles protested: "Mama, I can't!" he told me. "I can't miss a day of school! I would be so behind."

This was music to my ears.

While all of this has been a real relief to me, I'm deeply conflicted about the idea that my children are now getting the type of education that requires paying for in this country. It isn't right. I shouldn't be able to buy my children a better education than any other parent. No one should. It doesn't make me happy to know that the deck is still stacked in favor of those with means, and that was part of my inspiration for writing this book. When parents know more, they're better armed to take on the system and demand that it be fixed. *All* schools should be welcoming. *All* schools should be equitably funded. *All* schools should have excellent teachers and high expectations. We can accomplish it; there's no reason for that to be a pipe dream.

I've always believed that you assess your children's education every day and then support them as best you can. I don't know what's in the cards for each of us, but I'm glad that this wild roller coaster of a journey has landed me back on my old front doorstep at last.

It taught me so much, primarily that I will do anything for my kids' education. I will be their relentless advocate, undoubtedly making some mistakes along the way. I will get up and try again the next day.

I also learned some other important lessons:

Compassion for others is paramount, and humility matters.
Be a good guest.
Good friends are the best gifts you can have.
Watch and learn quietly first. Question everything.
Expose your kids to concepts you're not sure they can grasp yet.
Pick and choose your battles.
You often get only one chance. Grab it.
Have older friends to learn from and younger friends to teach.
Parenting hurts. But don't let that impede your kids' growth.
Have your own life.
Make backup plans.
Respect that each child in the family is different.

Learn from the parents around you—all the parents, even the ones you can't stand.

Don't be embarrassed to show you don't know something. It's not worth letting your child miss out because you were afraid to ask questions.

Be aware of your community's resources. Don't leave stones unturned.

Care about the greater good. Pay attention to the dynamics around you.

Teach your kids about the world outside your bubble.

Create contexts for comparisons so you can appreciate what you have.

Find out what your kids know and how well they know it.

Listen to them.

Read, read. Always read.

Acknowledgments

This book is the result of countless interviews, school visits, and heartfelt conversations with some of the smartest people I have had the privilege to meet as a parent, researcher, and first-time author.

I was privileged to meet many inspiring thinkers, scholars, and policymakers, many of whom sat down with me to talk through different aspects of this book. In particular, I would like to thank Jo Boaler, Andreas Schleicher, Joyce Epstein, Joseph Kahne, Cathy Williams, and Stephanie M. Jones for their candid insights. Thanks to Arne Duncan, John King, and Vivek Murthy for our brief but impactful conversations.

During my visits to schools throughout the United States, I took great inspiration from the teachers, principals, and staff who opened their doors to me. Seeing their commitment and passion to our kids gave me many moments of gratitude and hope as I struggled to sort through our US education system.

Thank you to my children's countless teachers in Hong Kong, Shanghai, Tokyo, Palo Alto, and New York, who not only planted seeds for lifelong opportunities but also opened up my eyes to varied pedagogical practices, cultures, and communities. In particular, to Tan Laoshi, Tsoi Laoshi (Happy Pear), and Dong Dong, their patience and ability to bridge worlds helped me to continue learning and growing. Thanks to Ben Stubbings of the *Japan Times*, who gave me my first chance at published writing.

Thank you to my work colleagues Autumn Knowlton, Sarah Bidwell, Jenna Glatzer, Sarah Pelz, and Anna Sproul-Latimer. I consider you family. You have been alongside me throughout this journey and often been supporting me when the task felt daunting. Because of the personal nature of my book, you know me inside and out. Katsumi Watanabe, your commitment to my work since its inception has been invaluable.

To my most influential Drexel professors, whom I pushed and who pushed me right back: Rebecca Clothey, Deanna Hill, and Richard Van Heertum. Your understanding of the field of comparative education and my passion fueled my desire to write this book.

My friends kept me going through the deadlines, travel, parenting, and pressures of writing this book, which I'd been thinking about for years before I put pen to paper. I have been accompanied on this journey by friends from my childhood, as well as new friends. Thank you to Elizabeth Norquist, Roseann Dembeck, Pandora Edmiston, and Yuichiro Eda, close friends since childhood—you have seen me through it all and somehow still managed to stay by my side. Kent Dahn and Kristen Chang Winkler have kept me going since college. Thank you to Marcy Blum, Anna Mark, Sandra Rosenthal, and Alexandra Landeggar, who kept me close to my US roots no matter where in the world I was.

Stacey Morse, whom I met in Hong Kong, has been a model mother and close friend. Jianing Wang, like a sister, will always and forever represent my experiences of friendship and community in Shanghai. Shannon Ellis is another dear friend whose strength helped to keep me sane in Shanghai. I'm still awed by Leslie Wang, a student I advised in Shanghai. In Tokyo, I was most fortunate to cross paths with Melanie Borisoff, Rosemary Hyson, Yuka Irie, and Alexandra Harney—role models and the truest of friends. My shenanigans with Eve Kagimoto on the games committee make me laugh to this day. I relied on Asma

Rabani and Reshma Shah to keep me grounded in the (sometimes surreal) landscape of parenting in Silicon Valley. And Noelia Arteaga, thank you for being the mentee who mentored me.

And to those who passed too early but remind me to keep on going: Justin Rascoff, Pei Lynn Yee, Bob Warren, Candida Silver, and Lee Rizzuto.

Finally, a special thanks to my family: Pa, Yuyu, Ryoko, Kuni, *ojichan* and *obachan*, Larry, Aunt Margaret. You have been the foundation to every success in my life. I love you.

Appendix A

The Ins and Outs of Your Local School District

I n nearly all cases, when there is a problem in a class (for example, bullying, personality conflicts, learning difficulties, inappropriate teaching materials, homework overload), your first step is talking to the teacher. But if you don't get a satisfactory response from the teacher, do you know what to do next?

For anything that matters, don't be afraid to move on fairly quickly. You don't want to waste time when it appears a teacher isn't responsive. For issues related to emotional or learning needs, consider bringing in the school counselor, psychologist, or social worker (there may be overlap in the roles). If at all possible and appropriate, band together with other parents about the issue; there is always strength in numbers. Consult with a child advocate or organization that deals with issues related to yours. Study your state's education laws so you know your child's rights and what the school must provide.

Go to the principal with your prepared talking points and request. If you get no satisfaction there, go to the person on the district level with the title that sounds closest to what you're looking for—for example, district director of educational services, director of special education, curriculum coordinator.

Move on to the assistant superintendent, then the superintendent. And if that's still unsatisfactory, take it to the school board.

Go to meetings with a cool head and as much documentation and written support as possible. If you can't get other parents together on the issue, bring your partner or another ally so you're less likely to be outnumbered. Be doggedly insistent on not leaving without an actual plan for the next steps—not just a vague "We'll look into it" or "We'll take care of it." Ask for specifics: Who will follow up, when and how, and what will happen if it doesn't work? Schedule a follow-up on the spot: either another meeting (preferable) or a phone call to let you know what measures were taken and how things are working out.

Appendix B

Citizenship and Civics Education

Inspired by the challenges in our current polarized political situation, I asked a pointed question at every school I visited while writing this book: "How do students learn about civic participation at your school?" I checked with countless teachers and administrators about it; I was hungry to hear their thoughts on civics, political participation, and national identity in the United States.

When I spoke with student government leaders in a rural high school just outside Binghamton, New York, the most consistent answer I heard when I asked what defined our national identity in the United States was "freedom." Freedom is an important concept in the United States—but where does that freedom start and end? How well does freedom serve us when trying to forge a united national identity?

Joseph Kahne at the University of California, Riverside, shed some light on this for me. We spoke about the state of civics education in the United States, the role of social media in democracy, and the skills children should be learning today in order to participate as citizens now and in the future. With our current climate of increasing inequality and social media becoming the mediator of news, our functioning democracy is under increasing threat. Kahne believes that our schools are doing students and our nation a great disservice by neglecting civics education, since they are the best positioned to do so.

Civics Education Can Lead to More Civility

In the rush to prepare students for standardized tests that focus on reading and math, courses on civics education often get pushed to the side.[1]

Requirements for civics education vary from state to state. But these classes play a unique role in teaching students about the principles and the practice of democracy. In fact, the information immigrants need to know to pass the citizenship exam is being incorporated into civics requirements for students. Twenty-four states currently have requirements or just voted to incorporate content from the naturalization test into civics requirements.[2] Examples of this content include the division of powers among the three branches of government, basic information on the Constitution and the amendments to it, and the rights and responsibilities of citizenship.

In addition to learning this content, civics classes provide students with opportunities to apply critical thinking and debate skills that are transferable to their other classes. Students develop communication skills that don't take center stage in any other specific academic discipline in high school.

These skills also help develop the ability for young people to carry out their responsibilities as adults in the working world, such as writing reports, analyzing research, and making presentations. Speaking persuasively is important in many professions, including for policymakers, who must explain their vision to voters in order to be elected and then be effective. Civics classes help to instill public speaking skills, as well as demonstrate the value of mobilizing people behind a cause.

In addition, civics classes offer students opportunities to develop digital literacy in terms of creating content for the Internet themselves on social media, blogs, or other media; in addition, these skills help them to analyze the credibility of content and perspectives they encounter on the Internet. They can become more aware of their biases. Given the digital landscape young people face today, digital literacy is an important skill for them to develop at home and at school.

For me, though, our national identity in the United States is intertwined with the future of the world. I want my children to understand themselves as US citizens and *global* citizens.

It can be helpful to consider civic participation as an ever-expanding circle. The circle begins with your home, with the values you emphasize through your family's activities and habits. You can emphasize citizenship through taking your kids with you to the voting polls, through the kinds of programming you have on your TV, and through your relationships with your neighbors. You can bring it to the forefront in your discussions about national and world events. What citizenship model do you want your children to adopt? But be mindful that our children tend to parrot us, so let them voice their own opinions.

The next circle of citizenship encompasses your child's school. Do you attend

PTA meetings, volunteer in your child's classroom, or chaperone field trips? Do you initiate activities that resonate with your own values? Do you reach out to other families in the school when they are going through tough times?

Community is the next circle outside your school. Do you volunteer and encourage your children to volunteer? Do you stay informed about local activities and support local organizations?

Do you visit history and other kinds of museums with your children in order to encourage them to envision themselves as part of a broader community? Do they have chances to spend time around people different from themselves, perhaps the single biggest advantage of being a citizen of a diverse nation such as the United States? All parents should review the Declaration of Independence, the Constitution, and US Citizenship Exam with their children starting in early elementary school to impart the value that we are all part of a greater good.

Finally, are they learning compassion and empathy, not only for those living in the United States but for those living all over the world? What are you teaching them about who "we" and "they" are?

As you think about what citizenship means to you, remember that your children pick up on your actions as well as your words. Parents are their most significant model.

Glossary

Blue Ribbon Schools Program (United States)—A US Department of Education program that recognizes high academic achievement or great improvement at public and private schools.

Civics education—Curriculum intended to instill a sense of national identity in students, often based on the rights and responsibilities associated with citizenship of that country.

Common Core (United States)—Standards adopted on a state level to gauge students' proficiency in agreed-on math and language arts standards at each grade, K–12. Adopting Common Core standards has been optional since the initiative was introduced in 2010.

Competency-based grading—Grading based on students' demonstrated mastery of a competency, as compared with a letter-based grading system that offers a range of acceptable options for students to proceed to the next level.

Compulsory education—The number of years of schooling each child is required to attend by law; the number of years varies from country to country.

Cultural Revolution (China)—Policy under Chairman Mao Zedong from 1966 to 1976 that had the stated purpose of eliminating capitalist elements in Chinese society.

Curriculum—The content students are learning in a class or program.

Curriculum alignment—A coordinated approach to curriculum within or across a grade, school, district, or state. Alignment indicates that students are learning similar material over a similar time frame, so that all students have been exposed to the same material.

Deng Xiaoping (1904–1997) (China)—President of the People's Republic of China from 1978 to 1989, well known for implementing market-economy driven reforms. Successor of Mao Zedong.

Dual-language program—Program that teaches students literacy and content in two languages. In the United States, these languages are commonly English and a second language, such as Mandarin or Spanish. These programs are most heavily concentrated in elementary schools.

Early childhood education (ECE)—A subfield of education focused on children from birth to age eight.

Educational accreditation—A quality assurance process for certifying educational institutions and carried out by an external body.

Educational assessment—Assessment with three general purposes: formative (as learning is occurring), summative (to check for learning outcomes), and as an aid in learning. Assessment can be carried out in various forms, such as testing (multiple choice or short answer, for example), oral comprehension checks, and essays.

Elementary school—In the United States, typically kindergarten through fifth or sixth grade. In Japan and China, elementary school starts in first grade.

English Language Learners (ELLs) (United States)—Students learning English as an additional language. They are typically offered additional resources in order to help them learn English while partaking in grade-level curriculum.

Enrichment activities—Educational activities organized outside formal schooling—for example, tutoring, music lessons, and camp.

Every Student Succeeds Act (ESSA) (United States)—Federal education law signed into effect by President Barack Obama on December 10, 2015. The act reauthorizes the Elementary and Secondary Education Act, which had an unprecedented focus on systematically implementing measures for equity in US public schools. The 2015 act also focuses on equity for schoolchildren.

Exmissions—The application process from private preschool to elementary school.

Expatriate (expat)—An individual living outside their country of citizenship.

Free-range parenting—A parenting style characterized by a high level of autonomy for children.

***Gaman* (Japan)**—Japanese phrase that means "be patient and have forbearance."

***Gaokao* (China)**—The national college entrance exam.

Helicopter parenting—A parenting style characterized by intense management of children's daily activities. It is criticized for limiting children's ability to develop self-regulation and autonomy.

Honorifics (Japan)—Linguistic element of Japanese that indicates respect and deference to the person being addressed.

Incentive pay—Pay for teachers (normally only a small percentage) associated with specific performance standards for teachers or students, such as students' test scores or certain measurements of improvement on students' academic performance.

Individualized Education Program (IEP) (United States)—An education program written to meet the individual needs of a child receiving special education services in a public school.

International school—A private school that promotes international education in an international environment that follows a curriculum other than the one dictated by the school's country of residence, such as the International Baccalaureate.

International student—Any student enrolled in a K–12 school or tertiary educational institution outside the country of their citizenship. International students can be enrolled in a short-term program such as an exchange or can complete an entire degree program.

Janken **(Japan)**—A game used to randomly choose among three options. In English, it is commonly called "rock, paper, scissors."

Jiritsu **(Japan)**—A Japanese phrase that refers to self-reliance and independence.

Kikokushijo **(Japan)**—Japanese citizens returning to Japan after a substantial time abroad. They may be singled out as different from other Japanese people because they have adopted foreign customs.

Kodomo no keitai **(Japan)**—Children's cell phones with minimal features, such as emergency calling and basic preprogrammed text messages.

Kuuki o yomu **(Japan)**—Literally translates as "to read the air." It means that an individual is expected to read social cues in order to behave properly.

Laoshi **(China)**—An honorific title in Mandarin to refer to teachers.

Legacy admissions (United States)—Private school and university policy of preferential admission to applicants with a family member (usually a parent or sibling) who attended the same institution.

Magnet schools—Public schools that offer specialized courses or curriculum. They draw from students in a school district or from a broader geographic area; they are not limited by school zones within a school district. They began in the United States in the 1970s as a way to counter racial segregation and exist in other countries as well.

Mao Zedong (1893–1976) (China)—Leader of the Chinese Revolution and chairman of the Communist Party of China from 1949 to 1976; considered the founding father of the People's Republic of China.

Mastery—Comprehensive knowledge of a skill or content area.

Meiwaku o kakenai **(Japan)**—Loosely translates into English as "Be responsible for yourself while also helping the community."

Mindset—A concept developed in the field of psychology that makes a correlation between an individual's approach to learning and her facility for learning and retaining information. A fixed mindset indicates the perspective that an individual's learning is limited by genetics or other predetermined factors. A growth mindset reflects a more open-ended understanding of an individual's ability to learn.

No Child Left Behind (NCLB) (United States)—Enacted in 2002 under President George W. Bush, this act focused on implementing accountability in US public schools, mainly measured through standardized tests. It was replaced in 2015 by the Every Student Succeeds Act.

Organisation for Economic Co-operation and Development (OECD)—An intergovernmental association of thirty-six countries founded in 1961 with the goal of aiding economic growth through world trade. Most of the organization's member countries have highly developed economies.

One-child policy (China)—National policy instituted in 1980 limiting most couples to one child in order to address the country's high population growth. On January 1, 2016, the Chinese government revised the policy to allow every couple to have two children.

Pedagogy—The method or practice of teaching; teaching techniques.

Programme for International Student Assessment (PISA)—An international exam administered to fifteen-year-olds every three years on science, math, reading, collaborative problem-solving, and financial literacy. All members of the Organisation for Economic Co-operation and Development (OECD) administer the test, as well as other participating countries and economies. In 2015, 28 million students in seventy-two countries and economies took PISA.

Parent–Teacher Association (PTA)—A national association based in US public schools that offers opportunities for parents and teachers to advocate for children in their schools through fund-raising and other social activities. These associations also exist in Japan.

Pregnancy rota (Japan)—An informal system used to determine the order in which women in a given workplace "take their turn" getting pregnant.

Professional development (PD)—Activities intended to update teachers' professional skills on a periodic basis.

Private schools—Schools affiliated with a religious institution or operating independently and therefore not operated by the government.

Renrakucho (Japan)—Daily parent-teacher journal.

School board—The local educational authority, mandated with overseeing the standards, budgets, and accountability of local schools. In the United States, these bodies are elected or appointed.

Science, technology, engineering, and math (STEM)—A group of academic disciplines that is commonly viewed as a source of technical innovation and high-paying jobs in the global market.

Secondary school—Typically refers to grades 7 to 12; US junior high or middle school is lower secondary, and high school is upper secondary.

Shinzo Abe (1954–) (Japan)—Prime minister of Japan and leader of the Liberal Democratic Party since 2012.

Shokuiku (Japan)—Public school curriculum on health, nutrition, and well-being.

Shokuin shitsu (Japan)—Teachers' room, where teachers collaborate outside the classroom.

Social-emotional learning (SEL)—An effort to address the social and emotional aspects of child development and learning within the context of the school.

Standardized tests—Multiple-choice tests administered to students at specific milestones in their education. Standardized tests are administered at the district, state, and national levels, depending on the educational authority that measures the outcomes. Standardized tests are administered around the world.

Superintendent (United States)—An administrator in charge of overseeing several schools within a district or the entire district.

Teaching credentials—The academic and professional certifications required for a teacher to be employed. These requirements vary by country. Within the United States, the credentialing requirements vary by state.

Tertiary education—All schooling after secondary school, including at community colleges, vocational or technical colleges, and universities.

Third-culture kids—Children growing up outside the country of their citizenship. They often adopt characteristics of their family's culture, as well as the local cultures in which they are raised, which leads to considering their identity in relation to a "third culture."

Tokkatsu (Japan)—Japanese educational philosophy of collaborative whole child education, which is integrated into the national curriculum. It includes nonacademic activities such as lunch, club activities, and student councils.

Whole child education (United Sates)—An educational approach that addresses academic content as well as students' mental, physical, and social well-being.

"Womenomics" (Japan)—Prime Minister Shinzo Abe's plan, introduced in 2014, to incorporate more women into leadership positions in Japanese corporations.

Xi Jinping (1953–) (China)—President of the People's Republic of China since 2013.

Zhongkao (China)—High school entrance exam.

Notes

Introduction: Three's Company

1. OECD, "Programme for International Student Assessment (PISA): Results from PISA 2012," *OECD Country Note*. https://www.oecd.org/unitedstates /PISA-2012-results-US.pdf.
2. Andrea McCarren, "Parents in Trouble Again for Letting Kids Walk Alone," *USA Today*, April 13, 2015. https://www.usatoday.com/story/news/nation /2015/04/13/parents-investigated-letting-children-walk-alone/25700823/.
3. OECD, "Education GPS, PISA 2015," http://gpseducation.oecd.org/Country Profile?primaryCountry=USA&treshold=10&topic=PI.

Chapter 1: The Wonder Years

1. Matthew Stewart, "The 9.9 Percent Is the New American Aristocracy," *The Atlantic*, June 2018. https://www.theatlantic.com/magazine/archive /2018/06/the-birth-of-a-new-american-aristocracy/559130/?silverid-ref= MzEwMTU3NjM1MjA3S0&utm_campaign=masthead-actives&utm _source=promotional-email&utm_medium=email&utm_content=20180516.
2. Pablo Mitnik and David B. Grusky, "Economic Mobility in the United States." Report from the Pew Charitable Trusts and the Russell Sage Foundation, July 2015.
3. Diane Whitmore Schanzenbach, David Boddy, Megan Mumford, and Greg Nantz, *Fourteen Economic Facts on Education and Economic Opportunity*. Paper published by The Hamilton Project, March 24, 2016.
4. Jill Barshay, "Governments Are Spending Billions More on Education, and It's Making Inequality Worse," *Hechinger Report*, January 15, 2018. https://hech ingerreport.org/three-quarters-u-s-public-school-spending-cuts-restored/.
5. U.S. Census Bureau, *Annual Survey of School System Finances 2016*.
6. Barshay, "Governments Are Spending Billions More on Education."

7. Center on the Developing Child, "Five Numbers to Remember." Brief published by Center on the Developing Child, Harvard University, 2009.

8. OECD, *Education at a Glance 2017: OECD Indicators.* https://read.oecd.i library.org/education/education-at-a-glance-2017_eag-2017-en#page1.

9. Silke Hertel and Nina Jude, "Parental Support and Involvement in School," in S. Kuger, E. Klieme, N. Jude, and D. Kaplan (eds.), *Assessing Contexts of Learning: An International Perspective* (New York: Springer, 2016).

10. Melissa Korn, "How Much Does Being a Legacy Help Your College Admissions Odds?" *Wall Street Journal*, July 9, 2018. https://www.wsj.com/articles /legacy-preferences-complicate-colleges-diversity-push-1531128601.

11. Mark Silva, "Education: 'The Great Equalizer,'" *U.S. News & World Report*, April 5, 2017. www.usnews.com/news/best-states/articles/2017-04-05/ed ucation-the-great-equalizer.

12. Dana McCoy et al., "Impacts of Early Childhood Education on Medium- and Long-Term Educational Outcomes," *Educational Researcher* 46 (8): 474–487.

13. Lynn Karoly, "The Economic Returns to Early Childhood Education." *The Future of Children* 26(2): 37–55.

14. US Department of Labor, "Preschool Teachers." Bureau of Labor Statistics, 2018. https://www.bls.gov/ooh/education-training-and-library/preschool -teachers.htm.

15. Schanzenbach et al., *Fourteen Economic Facts.*

Chapter 2: Gilligan's Island

1. Wei Du, "In Hong Kong, Shortage of Land for Housing Remains a Thorny Issue," *Channel NewsAsia*, September 23, 2017. https://www.channelnews asia.com/news/asia/in-hong-kong-shortage-of-land-for-housing-remains -a-thorny-issue-9223650.

2. Deborah Stipek, Alan Schoenfeld, and Deanna Gomby, "Math Matters, Even for Little Kids," *Education Week*, March 27, 2012. https://www.edweek.org /ew/articles/2012/03/28/26stipek.h31.html.

3. Diane Whitmore Schanzenbach, David Boddy, Megan Mumford, and Greg Nantz, *Fourteen Economic Facts on Education and Economic Opportunity.* Paper published by The Hamilton Project, March 24, 2016.

4. Naja Ferjan Ramírez and Patricia K. Kuhl, "Bilingual Language Learning in Children." Paper published by Institute for Learning & Brain Sciences, University of Washington, June 2, 2016. http://ilabs.uw.edu/Bilingual_Language _Learning_in_Children.

5. Fergus I. Craik, Ellen Bialystok, and Morris Freedman, "Delaying the Onset of Alzheimer Disease: Bilingualism as a Form of Cognitive Reserve," *Neurology* 75(19): 1726–1729.

6. Ramírez and Kuhl, "Bilingual Language Learning in Children."
7. European Commission, "Europeans and their Languages," *Special Eurobarometer* 386, June 2012. http://ec.europa.eu/commmfrontoffice/publicopinion/archives/ebs/ebs_386_en.pdf.

Chapter 3: Mission: Impossible

1. Sophie Williams, "Fluorescent Pork for Dinner?" *Daily Mail*, January 8, 2016, https://www.dailymail.co.uk/news/peoplesdaily/article-3389996/Chinese-man-shocked-meat-bought-market-GLOWING-blue-dark.html.

Chapter 4: Star Trek: The Next Generation

1. Charles M. Achilles et al., "The State of Tennessee's Student/Teacher Achievement Ratio (STAR) project," report, Harvard Dataverse, V1, 2018.
2. Xi Jinping, "Secure a Decisive Victory in Building a Moderately Prosperous Society in All Respects and Strive for the Great Success of Socialism with Chinese Characteristics for a New Era." Report delivered at the Nineteenth National Congress of the Communist Party of China, October 18, 2017. http://www.xinhuanet.com/english/download/Xi_Jinping's_report_at_19th_CPC_National_Congress.pdf.
3. Zhang Jun, "China's Vision for the Next 30 Years." *Nikkei Asian Review*, November 15, 2017. https://asia.nikkei.com/Opinion/China-s-vision-for-the-next-30-years2.

Chapter 5: Get Smart

1. Linda Darling-Hammond et al., *Empowered Educators: How High-performing Systems Shape Teacher Quality Around The World* (San Francisco: Jossey-Bass, 2017).
2. Ibid.
3. OECD, "Programme for International Student Assessment (PISA): Results from PISA 2012." http://www.oecd.org/pisa/aboutpisa/.
4. Manu Kapur, "Examining Productive Failure, Productive Success, Unproductive Failure, and Unproductive Success in Learning," *Educational Psychologist* 51(2): 289–299.
5. Yojana Sharma, "To Fight Unemployment, China Expands Vocational Ed Programs," *Chronicle of Higher Education*, June 18, 2014. https://www.chronicle.com/article/To-Fight-Unemployment-China/147217.
6. Sean H. K. Kang, "Spaced Repetition Promotes Efficient and Effective Learning: Policy Implications for Instruction," *Policy Insights from the Behavioral and Brain Sciences* 3(1): 9–12.
7. Susana Claro and Susanna Loeb, "New Evidence That Students' Beliefs

About Their Brains Drive Learning," *Evidence Speaks Reports* 2(29). Brookings Institution. https://www.brookings.edu/research/new-evidence-that-students-beliefs-about-their-brains-drive-learning/.

8. Jo Boaler and Pablo Zoido, "Why Math Education in the U.S. Doesn't Add Up," *Scientific American*, November/December 2016.

9. David Kember, "Why Do Chinese Students Out-Perform Those from the West? Do Approaches to Learning Contribute to the Explanation?" *Cogent Education* 3(1) 2016.

10. Common Core Standards Initiative, "Mathematics Standards, 2019." http://www.corestandards.org/Math/.

11. Angela L. Duckworth and Martin Seligman, "Self-Discipline Outdoes IQ in Predicting Academic Performance of Adolescents," *Psychological Science* 16(12): 939–44.

12. Centers for Disease Control and Prevention, "Physical Activity Facts," CDC Healthy Schools, 2018. https://www.cdc.gov/healthyschools/physicalactivity/facts.htm.

13. Ellen Winner, Thalia R. Goldstein, and Stéphan Vincent-Lancrin, *Art for Art's Sake? The Impact of Arts Education* (Paris: OECD Publishing, 2013).

Chapter 6: The A-Team

1. *ICEF Monitor*, "Increasing Numbers of Chinese Graduates Returning Home from Overseas," 2018. http://monitor.icef.com/2018/02/increasing-numbers-chinese-graduates-returning-home-overseas/.

2. World Bank, *China—Systematic Country Diagnostic: Towards a More Inclusive and Sustainable Development*. Washington, D.C.: World Bank Group.

3. Evan Osnos, "What Did China's First Daughter Find in America?" *The New Yorker*, April 6, 2015. https://www.newyorker.com/news/news-desk/what-did-chinas-first-daughter-find-in-america.

4. Sam Dillon, "Top Test Scores from Shanghai Stun Educators," *New York Times*, December 7, 2010. https://www.nytimes.com/2010/12/07/education/07education.html.

5. *Times Higher Education*, "World University Rankings, 2018." https://www.timeshighereducation.com/world-university-rankings/2018/world-ranking#!/page/0/length/25/sort_by/rank/sort_order/asc/cols/stats.

6. Ibid.

7. OECD, "How Many Students Study Abroad?" *OECD Factbook 2015–2016: Economic, Environmental and Social Statistics* (Paris: OECD Publishing, 2016). https://doi.org/10.1787/factbook-2015-71-en.

8. Institute of International Education, "Fast Facts," 2017. https://www.iie.org/opendoors.

9. University of California, "Fall Enrollment at a Glance." Accessed September 1, 2018, https://www.universityofcalifornia.edu/infocenter/fall-enrollment-glance.

10. Christine Farrugia, "Globally Mobile Youth: Trends in International Secondary Students in the United States, 2013–2016," New York: International Institute for Education, 2017.

11. Ed Fuller, "Chinese Students Are a Win-Win for U.S. Tourism," *Forbes*, November 13, 2017. https://www.forbes.com/sites/edfuller/2017/11/13/chinas-students-creating-winwin-experience-for-us-tourism/#65065a493cad.

12. "Canada Books 20% Growth in 2017," *ICEF Monitor*, March 21, 2018. http://monitor.icef.com/2018/03/canada-books-20-growth-2017/.

13. Rob Smith, "The World's Biggest Economies in 2018," *World Economic Forum*, April 18, 2018. https://www.weforum.org/agenda/2018/04/the-worlds-biggest-economies-in-2018/.

14. Mario Piacentini, "Developing an International Assessment of Global Competence," *Childhood Education* 93(6): 507–510. doi:10.1080/00094056.2017.1398564.

15. Casey Bayer, "PISA 2018 Test to Include Global Competency Assessment," Harvard Graduate School of Education, December 12, 2017. https://www.gse.harvard.edu/news/17/12/pisa-2018-test-include-global-competency-assessment.

16. Sean Coughlan, "England and US Will Not Take PISA Tests in Tolerance," *BBC News*, January 24, 2018. http://www.bbc.com/news/business-42781376.

17. Niall McCarthy, "The Share of Americans Holding a Passport Has Increased Dramatically in Recent Years," *Forbes*, January 11, 2018. https://www.forbes.com/sites/niallmccarthy/2018/01/11/the-share-of-americans-holding-a-passport-has-increased-dramatically-in-recent-years-infographic/#32f4ff753c16.

18. Institute of International Education, "Fast Facts."

19. OECD, "How Many Students Study Abroad?" 168.

20. OECD, "Education Indicators in Focus," Paris: OECD Publishing, 2013.

21. Institute of International Education, "Fast Facts."

22. *ICEF Monitor*, "Foreign Language Enrolment in the US Trending Downward," March 7, 2018. http://monitor.icef.com/2018/03/foreign-language-enrolment-us-trending-downward/.

23. Institute of International Education, "Fast Facts."

Chapter 7: Growing Pains

1. "The Second Basic Plan for the Promotion of Education," Ministry of Education Culture, Sports, Science and Technology—Japan (MEXT), 2015. http://

www.mext.go.jp/en/policy/education/lawandplan/title01/detail01/__ics
Files/afieldfile/2015/03/06/1355571.pdf.

Chapter 8: Mister Rogers' Neighborhood

1. Ryoto Tsuneyoshi, ed., *The World of Tokkatsu: The Japanese Approach to Whole Child Education* (Tokyo: self-published, 2012), p. 5.
2. Ibid.
3. "Tokyo Population 2019," *World Population Review* http://worldpopulation review.com/world-cities/tokyo-population/.
4. Teru Clavel, "Thinking Outside the Usual White Box," *Japan Times*, March 2, 2014. https://www.japantimes.co.jp/community/2014/03/02/issues/thinking -outside-the-usual-white-box/#.W1uFBi2B0mI.
5. Miriam Evans and Alyssa R. Boucher, "Optimizing the Power of Choice: Supporting Student Autonomy to Foster Motivation and Engagement in Learning," *Mind, Brain, and Education*, 9(2): 87–89. doi:10.1111/mbe.12073.
6. Carol Vogel, "Rock, Paper, Payoff: Child's Play Wins Auction House an Art Sale," *New York Times*, April 29, 2005. https://www.nytimes.com/2005/04 /29/arts/design/rock-paper-payoff-childs-play-wins-auction-house-an-art -sale.html.
7. Chris Weller, "Japan's Mouth-Watering School Lunch Program Is a Model for the Rest of the World," *Business Insider*, March 27, 2017. https://www .businessinsider.com/japans-amazing-school-lunch-program-2017-3#the -end-result-isnt-just-a-satisfied-student-body-but-one-that-learns-respon sibility-and-healthy-eating-habits-japans-life-expectancy-is-among-the -highest-in-the-world-while-its-rate-of-obesity-is-well-below-the-global -average-9.
8. Juliana F. W. Cohen et al., "School Lunch Waste Among Middle School Students," *American Journal of Preventive Medicine* 44(2): February 2013. https:// doi.org/10.1016/j.amepre.2012.09.060.
9. School Nutrition Association. "Sodium Targets in the National School Lunch Program," June 6, 2015. https://schoolnutrition.org/uploadedFiles/5_News _and_Publications/1_News/2015/06_June/Sodium%20Final%20White%20 Paper%206_8_15.pdf.
10. Mary Clare Jalonick, "Government Relaxes Nutrition Standards for School Lunches," *PBS Newshour*, May 1, 2017. https://www.pbs.org/newshour /health/government-relaxes-nutrition-standards-school-lunches.
11. Zhang Jun, "China's Vision for the Next 30 Years," *Nikkei Asian Review*, November 5, 2017. https://asia.nikkei.com/Opinion/China-s-vision-for-the -next-30-years2.
12. "Bullying in Japan Reaches Highest Level on Record," *NHK World—Japan*,

October 27, 2017. https://www3.nhk.or.jp/nhkworld/nhknewsline/backsto ries/bullyinginjapanreaches/.

13. "Japan: Events of 2016," *World Report 2017*, Human Rights Watch. https:// www.hrw.org/world-report/2017/country-chapters/japan.

14. Teru Clavel, "Kikokushijo: Returnees to a Country Not Yet Ready for Them," *Japan Times*, May 4, 2014. https://www.japantimes.co.jp/community/2014/05 /04/issues/kikokushoji-returnees-country-yet-ready/#.W1ub2i2B0mI.

Chapter 9: MacGyver

1. Stephanie Jones, Katharine Brush, Rebecca Bailey, Gretchen Brion-Meisels, Joseph McIntyre, Jennifer Kahn, Bryan Nelson, and Laura Stickle, *Navigating SEL from the Inside Out: Looking Inside and Across 25 Leading SEL Programs: A Practical Resource for Schools and OST Providers*, March 2017. Report, published by Harvard Graduate School of Education.

2. "Quote-Unquote: Xi's Views on Education," *China Daily*, February 28, 2017.

3. Hanna Melnick, Channa Cook-Harvey, and Linda Darling-Hammond, "Encouraging Social and Emotional Learning: Next Steps for States," abstract, Learning Policy Institute. https://learningpolicyinstitute.org/product/en couraging-social-emotional-learning-next-steps-states-brief.

4. MEXT (2015a), "Implementation Status of 2014 Public School Teacher Selection Exams." Tokyo, Japan. http://bit.ly/1O8xVwZ.

5. D. E. Rowe and Richard H. Derrah, "Teacher License Changes and High Schools in Japan," *International Journal of Humanities and Management Sciences*, 4(5) 2016.

6. MEXT (Japan), "Basic School Survey 2018." http://www.mext.go.jp/b_menu /toukei/chousa01/kihon/kekka/k_detail/1407849.htm.

7. National Center on Education and the Economy, "Japan: Teacher and Principal Quality." Accessed September 1, 2018. http://ncee.org/what-we-do/center -on-international-education-benchmarking/top-performing-countries /japan-overview/japan-teacher-and-principal-quality/.

8. Asia Society, "Advice from Asia." Accessed September 1, 2018. https://asiasoci ety.org/global-cities-education-network/advice-asia-invest-teachers.

9. Linda Darling-Hammond et al., *Empowered Educators: How High-Performing Systems Shape Teaching Quality Around the World* (San Francisco: Jossey-Bass, 2017).

10. Asia Society, "Advice from Asia."

11. Dick Startz, "Teacher Pay Around the World," *Brown Center Chalkboard*, The Brookings Institution, June 20, 2016. https://www.brookings.edu /blog/brown-center-chalkboard/2016/06/20/teacher-pay-around-the world/.

12. OECD, *Education at a Glance 2017: OECD Indicators.* https://read.oecd-ilibrary.org/education/education-at-a-glance-2017_eag-2017-en#page1.
13. Darling-Hammond et al., *Empowered Educators.*
14. OECD, "Teaching Hours," *OECD Data, Education at a Glance 2018.* https://data.oecd.org/eduresource/teaching-hours.htm.
15. Darling-Hammond et al., *Empowered Educators.*
16. Ruth Ahn, "Japan's Communal Approach to Teacher Induction: Shokuin Shitsu as an Indispensable Nurturing Ground for Japanese Beginning Teachers," *Teaching and Teacher Education,* 59, 420–430. https://doi.org/10.1016/j.tate.2016.07023.
17. Desiree Carver-Thomas and Linda Darling-Hammond, "Teacher Turnover: Why It Matters and What We Can Do About It." Report published by Learning Policy Institute, August 16, 2017. https://learningpolicyinstitute.org/product/teacher-turnover-report.
18. Richard Ingersoll, Lisa Merrill, and Daniel Stuckey, "The Changing Face of Teaching," *Educational Leadership* 75(8) May 2018.
19. Matthew Ronfeldt, Susanna Loeb, and James Wyckoff, "How Teacher Turnover Harms Student Achievement," *American Educational Research Journal* 50(1): 4–36.
20. Ibid, p. 5.
21. Carver-Thomas and Darling-Hammond, "Teacher Turnover."
22. Ronfeldt, Loeb, and Wyckoff, "How Teacher Turnover Harms Student Achievement," p. 5.
23. Carver-Thomas and Darling-Hammond, "Teacher Turnover."

Chapter 10: Wonder Woman

1. Keiko Sato and Ippei Minetoshi, "Questions Raised as Parents Hire Stand-Ins for PTA Activities," *The Asahi Shimbun,* October 3, 2017. http://www.asahi.com/ajw/articles/AJ201710030001.html.
2. Kirsty Kawano, "All You Need to Know About Tokyo Public School PTAs," *Savvy Tokyo,* October 1, 2015. https://savvytokyo.com/all-you-need-to-know-about-tokyo-public-school-ptas/.
3. Yoko Yamamoto, Susan D. Holloway, and Sawako Suzuki, "Parental Engagement in Children's Education: Motivating Factors in Japan and the U.S.," *School Community Journal* 26(1): 45–66.
4. Ibid.
5. "Statistics of Japan 2013," *e-Stat.* https://www.e-stat.go.jp/stat-search/files?page=1&layout=datalist&toukei=00200522&tstat=000001063455&cycle=0&tclass1=000001063456&tclass2=000001068831&second2=1.
6. Miwa Suzuki, "'Pregnancy Rotas' Add to Working Women's Woes in Japan," *Japan*

Today, June 4, 2018. https://japantoday.com/category/national/%27Pregnancy
-rotas%27-add-to-working-women%27s-woes-in-Japan?.

7. Shoko Oda and Isabel Reynolds, "What Is Womenomics, and Is It Working
for Japan?" *Bloomberg Quick Take,* September 19, 2018. https://www.bloom
berg.com/news/articles/2018-09-19/what-is-womenomics-and-is-it-work
ing-for-japan-quicktake.

8. Alana Semuels, "The Mystery of Why Japanese People Are Having So Few
Babies," *The Atlantic,* July 20, 2017. https://www.theatlantic.com/business
/archive/2017/07/japan-mystery-low-birth-rate/534291/.

9. Matt Turner, "Here's How Much Paid Leave New Mothers and Fathers Get
in 11 Different Countries," *Business Insider,* September 7, 2017. http://www
.businessinsider.com/maternity-leave-worldwide-2017-8.

10. Kaitlin Holmes, Jocelyn Frye, Sarah Jane Glynn, and Jessica Quinter, "Rhetoric vs. Reality: Equal Pay," Center for American Progress, November 7, 2016.
https://www.americanprogress.org/issues/women/reports/2016/11/07
/292175/rhetoric-vs-reality-equal-pay/.

11. "Gender Wage Gap," *OECD Data.* Accessed September 1, 2018 from https://
data.oecd.org/earnwage/gender-wage-gap.htm.

12. Oda and Reynolds, "What Is Womenomics? and Is It working for Japan?"

13. Ibid.

14. Ibid.

15. World Bank, "Proportion of Seats Held by Women in National Parliaments," *The
World Bank Data,* 2018. https://data.worldbank.org/indicators/SG. GEN.PARL.ZS

16. YoonKyung Chung, Barbara Downs, Danielle H. Sandler, and Robert Sienkiewicz, "The Parental Gender Earnings Gap in the United States," Center for
Economic Studies, U.S. Census Bureau, Working Papers 17–68, 2017. https://
ideas.repec.org/p/cen/wpaper/17-68.html.

17. Claire Cain Miller, "The 10-Year Baby Window That Is the Key to the Wom-
en's Pay Gap," *New York Times,* April 9, 2018. https://www.nytimes.com/2018
/04/09/upshot/the-10-year-baby-window-that-is-the-key-to-the-womens
-pay-gap.html.

18. "PISA Scores, by Sex," *OECD Data,* http://www.oecd.org/gender/data/pisa
scoresbysex.htm.

Chapter 11: The Twilight Zone

1. "Top 101 Cities with the Most People Having Master's or Doctorate Degrees,"
City-Data.com. http://www.city-data.com/top2/h182.html.

2. "Palo Alto Home Prices & Values," *Zillow.* Accessed September 1, 2018.
https://www.zillow.com/palo-alto-ca/home-values/.

3. Theodore Schleifer, "There Are 143 Tech Billionaires Around the World, and

Half of Them Live in Silicon Valley," *Recode*, May 19, 2018. https://www.re
code.net/2018/5/19/17370288/silicon-valley-how-many-billionaires-start
-up-tech-bay-area.

4. Ivy Morgan and Ary Amerikaner, "Funding Gaps 2018: An Analysis of School
Funding Across the U.S. and Within Each State," The Education Trust, February 27, 2018. https://edtrust.org/resource/funding-gaps-2018/.

5. "The State of Funding Equity in California," The Education Trust, 2017.
https://edtrust.org/graphs/?sname=California.

6. Ed-Data, "Palo Alto Unified," Education Data Partnership, Santa Clara
County website. Accessed September 1, 2018, http://www.ed-data.org/dis
trict/Santa-Clara/Palo-Alto-Unified.

7. Alexandra Sifferlin, "Degenerative Brain Disease Found in 87 Percent of Former Football Players," *Time*, July 25, 2017. http://time.com/4871597/degen
erative-brain-disease-cte-football/.

8. Polina Marinova, "This University's Athletes Are Dominating the U.S. Olympic Team," *Fortune*, August 9, 2016. http://fortune.com/2016/08/09/stanford
-olympics-athletes-college/.

9. "Universities by Number of Rhodes Scholars," WorldAtlas.com. https://
www.worldatlas.com/articles/universities-by-number-of-rhodes
-scholars.html.

10. Natalie Weiner, "$72 Million for a High School Stadium? In Texas, It's Only
Up from There," *Bleacher Report*, August 25, 2017. https://bleacherreport
.com/articles/2729443-72-million-for-a-high-school-stadium-in-texas-its
-only-up-from-there.

11. Katy Independent School District, "Bond Information," January 18, 2018.
http://www.katyisd.org/dept/bf/Pages/Bond-Information.aspx.

Chapter 12: Who's the Boss?

1. National Center on Education and the Economy, "Japan: Learning Systems."
Accessed September 1, 2018 at http://ncee.org/what-we-do/center-on
-international-education-benchmarking/top-performing-countries/japan
-overview/japan-instructional-systems/.

2. Alana Semuels, "Japan Might Be What Equality in Education Looks Like,"
The Atlantic, August 2, 2017. https://www.theatlantic.com/business/archive
/2017/08/japan-equal-education-school-cost/535611/.

3. Elena Kadvany, "Mayor Alleges 'Culture of Corruption' at Ravenswood
School District," *Palo Alto Online*, February 17, 2018. https://www.paloalto
online.com/news/2018/02/17/mayor-alleges-culture-of-corruption-at-ravens
wood-school-district.

4. California Department of Education, "District Profile: Ravenswood City

Elementary." Accessed September 1, 2018. https://www.cde.ca.gov/sdprofile /details.aspx?cds=41689990000000.

5. Ed-Data, "Palo Alto Unified," Education Data Partnership, Santa Clara County website. Accessed September 1, 2018. http://www.ed-data.org/dis trict/Santa-Clara/Palo-Alto-Unified.

6. Palo Alto Unified School District. "Voluntary Transfer Program." Accessed April 1, 2019 at https://www.pausd.org/programs/voluntary-transfer-pro gram.

7. Sean Coughlan, "Computers 'Do Not Improve' Pupil Results, Says OECD," *BBC News*, September 15, 2015. https://www.bbc.com/news/business -34174796.

8. James Doubek, "Attention, Students: Put Your Laptops Away," NPR.org, April 17, 2016. https://www.npr.org/2016/04/17/474525392/attention-students -put-your-laptops-away.

9. Google for Education, "Giving." Accessed January 11, 2019. https://edu .google.com/giving/?modal_active=none.

10. Michelle R. Davis and Michele Molnar, "Educators Carefully Watch Pearson as It Moves to Sell K-12 Curriculum Business," *Education Week*, March 5, 2018. https://www.edweek.org/ew/articles/2018/03/07/educators-care fully-watch-pearson-as-it-moves.html.

11. See the ClassDojo website: https://www.classdojo.com/about.

Chapter 13: Cheers

1. *Inside Schools*, "The Christa McAuliffe School (I.S. 187)." Accessed May 10, 2019. https://insideschools.org/school/20K197.

2. Utah State Board of Education, "Polk School." Accessed September 1, 2018. https://datagateway.schools.utah.gov/Schools/37167.

3. John Hattie, *Visible Learning for Teachers* (Abingdon, UK: Routledge, 2008).

4. DC Public Schools, "Per Student Funding." Accessed January 11, 2019. http:// dcpsbudget.ourdcschools.org/.

5. Jo Boaler, "How You Can Be Good at Math, and Other Surprising Facts About Learning," TEDx, Stanford, CA, May 2017. https://www.youtube.com/watch ?v=ARWBdfWpDyc.

Appendix B: Citizenship and Civics Education

1. Emily Cardinali, "What Your State Is Doing to Beef Up Civics Education," NPR.org, July 21, 2018, https://www.npr.org/sections/ed/2018/07/21/6242 67576/what-your-state-is-doing-to-beef-up-civics-education.

2. Ibid.

References

Abamu, Jenny. "Believe and You Can Achieve? Researchers Find Limited Gains from Growth Mindset Interventions." *EdSurge*, May 29, 2018. https://www.edsurge.com/news/2018-05-29-believe-and-you-can-achieve-researchers-find-limited-gains-from-growth-mindset-interventions.

————. "'A Deal with the Devil': NPR Reporter Anya Kamenetz on Teaching with 'Addictive Tech' Like Facebook." *EdSurge*, February 27, 2018. https://www.edsurge.com/news/2018-02-27-a-deal-with-the-devil-npr-reporter-anya-kamenetz-on-teaching-with-addictive-tech-like-facebook.

————. "How Can a Student be 'Proficient' in One State But Not Another? Here Are the Graphs." *EdSurge*, May 31, 2018. https://www.edsurge.com/news/2018-05-30-how-can-a-student-be-proficient-in-one-state-but-not-another-here-are-the-graphs.

Abkowitz, Alyssa. "The Cashless Society Has Arrived—Only It's in China." *Wall Street Journal*, January 4, 2018.

Achilles, C. M., Helen Pate Bain, Fred Bellott, Jayne Boyd-Zaharias, Jeremy Finn, John Folger, John Johnston, and Elizabeth Word. "Tennessee's Student Teacher Achievement Ratio (STAR) Project." Harvard Dataverse, V1, 2008. https://dataverse.harvard.edu/dataset.xhtml?persistentId=hdl:1902.1/10766.

Adelstein, Jake. "In Japan, People Are Flipping Out over the Flip-Phone (Galapagos Phone): What's Old Is New Again." *Forbes*, March 5, 2015.

Affeldt, John T. "New Accountability in California Through Local Control Funding Reforms: The Promise and the Gaps." Education Policy Analysis Archives, 2015. https://epaa.asu.edu/ojs/article/view/2023.

Ahn, Ruth. "Japan's Communal Approach to Teacher Induction: Shokuin Shitsu as an Indispensable Nurturing Ground for Japanese Beginning Teachers." *Teaching and Teacher Education* 59 (2016): 420–430.

Ahn, Ruth, Shigeru Asanuma, and Hisayoshi Mori. "Japan's Teachers Earn Tenure on Day One." *Phi Delta Kappan* 97, no. 6 (2016): 27.

Aidman, Barry, and Sarah Nelson Baray. "Leveraging Community Resources: Creating Successful Partnerships to Improve Schools." *Educational Forum* 80, no. 3 (2016): 264–277.

Aitkenhead, Decca. "Best Teacher in the World Andria Zafirakou: 'Build Trust with Your Kids—Then Everything Else Can Happen.'" *Guardian*, March 23, 2018.

Akita, Kiyomi. "Recent Curriculum Reform in Japan: The Future of Everyday-Life-Oriented Curriculum." *International Journal of Early Childhood Education* 17, no. 1 (2011): 33–43.

Alexander, Karl. "Is It Family or School? Getting the Question Right." *RSF: The Russell Sage Foundation Journal of the Social Sciences* 2, no. 5 (2016): 18–33.

Allegretto, Sylvia. "Teachers Across the Country Have Finally Had Enough of the Teacher Pay Penalty." Economic Policy Institute, April 4, 2018. https://www .epi.org/publication/teachers-across-the-country-have-finally-had-enough -of-the-teacher-pay-penalty/.

Allman, John. "Letter to Parents from Trinity School." August 30, 2017. https://trinityschoolnyc.myschoolapp.com/podium/push/default.aspx ?i=177980&s=390&snd=092c7b22-276c-420f-83bf-1d259e37e6b7.

Altintas, Evrim. "The Widening Education Gap in Developmental Child Care Activities in the United States, 1965–2013." *Journal of Marriage and Family* 78, no. 1 (2016): 26–42.

Alves, Tom, and Ellen Bernstein. "Give Teachers a Voice in Education Reform." *Education Week*, November 15, 2017.

American Academy of Pediatrics. "Let Them Sleep: AAP Recommends Delaying Start Times of Middle and High Schools to Combat Teen Sleep Deprivation." August 25, 2014. https://www.aap.org/en-us/about-the-aap/aap-press-room /Pages/Let-Them-Sleep-AAP-Recommends-Delaying-Start-Times-of-Middle -and-High-Schools-to-Combat-Teen-Sleep-Deprivation.aspx.

American School Counselor Association. "State-by-State Student-to-Counselor Ratio Report." States News Service, February 9, 2018. https://www.school counselor.org/asca/media/asca/Publications/ratioreport.pdf.

Andersen, Simon Calmar, Maria Knoth Humlum, and Anne Brink Nandrup. "Increasing Instruction Time in School Does Increase Learning." *Proceedings of the National Academy of Sciences of the United States of America* 113, no. 27 (2016): 7481–7484.

Anderson, Gary L., and Liliana Montoro Donchik. "Privatizing Schooling and Policy Making: The American Legislative Exchange Council and New Political and Discursive Strategies of Education Governance." *Educational Policy* 30, no. 2 (2014): 322–364.

Anderson, James D. "Eleventh Annual Brown Lecture in Education Research: A Long Shadow: The American Pursuit of Political Justice and Education Equality." *Educational Researcher* 44, no. 6 (2015): 319–335.

Anderson, Jenny. "A Stanford Professor Says We Should Teach More Math in Preschool." *Quartz*, November 13, 2017. https://qz.com/1125046/a-stanford -professor-says-we-should-teach-more-math-in-preschool/.

Anderson, Jill. "Coping Skills for Anxious Times." Harvard Graduate School of Education, November 29, 2017. https://www.gse.harvard.edu/news/uk/17/11 /coping-skills-anxious-times.

Anderson, Meg. "Hey, New Teachers, It's OK to Cry in Your Car." NPR.org, October 22, 2015. https://www.npr.org/sections/ed/2015/10/22/450575463/it-s-okay -to-cry-in-your-car-fighting-disillusionment-as-a-first-year-teacher.

Anderson, Michael L., Justin Gallagher, and Elizabeth Ramirez Ritchie. "How the Quality of School Lunch Affects Students' Academic Performance." *Brown Center Chalkboard* (blog), Brookings Institution, 2017. https://www.brook ings.edu/blog/brown-center-chalkboard/2017/05/03/how-the-quality-of -school-lunch-affects-students-academic-performance/.

Ando, Shuntaro, Sosei Yamaguchi, Yuta Aoki, and Graham Thornicroft. "Review of Mental-Health-Related Stigma in Japan." *Psychiatry and Clinical Neurosciences* 67, no. 7 (2013): 471–482.

ASCD. "Six Questions to Consider Before Adding Technology to Your School." *ASCD in Service* (blog), September 21, 2017. http://inservice.ascd.org/six -questions-to-consider-before-adding-technology-to-your-school/.

Asia Society. "Advice from Asia: Invest in Teachers." Asia Society, March 16, 2011. https://asiasociety.org/global-cities-education-network/advice-asia-invest -teachers.

Associated Press. "'Free-Range Parenting' Runs Amok with Push to Legalize Movement." *New York Post*, April 10, 2018.

Atack, Patrick. "China 'Can Use Students as a Valve to Control Their Influence.'" *The Pie News*, October 24, 2017. https://thepienews.com/news/china-can -use-students-as-a-valve-to-control-their-influence-chan/.

———. "32% of CEOs Study Abroad, According to Study, EU Research." *The Pie News*, December 19, 2017. https://thepienews.com/news/32-of-ceos-study-abroad -according-to-study-eu-research/.

Atteberry, Allison, Susanna Loeb, and James Wyckoff. "Teacher Churning: Reassignment Rates and Implications for Student Achievement." *Educational Evaluation and Policy Analysis* 39, no. 1 (2016): 3–30.

Au, Wayne, and Jesslyn Hollar. "Opting Out of the Education Reform Industry." *Monthly Review* 67, no. 10 (2016): 29.

REFERENCES

Auld, Euan, and Paul Morris. "PISA, Policy and Persuasion: Translating Complex Conditions into Education 'Best Practice.'" *Comparative Education* 52, no. 2 (2016): 202–229.

Baker, Bruce D. "School Finance and the Distribution of Equal Educational Opportunity in the Postrecession U.S." *Journal of Social Issues* 72, no. 4 (2016): 629–655.

Baker, Bruce D., and Mark Weber. "State School Finance Inequities and the Limits of Pursuing Teacher Equity Through Departmental Regulation." *Education Policy Analysis Archives* 24 (2016): 47.

Balingit, Moriah. "U.S. High School Graduation Rates Rise to New High." *Washington Post*, December 4, 2017.

Banks, James A. "Failed Citizenship and Transformative Civic Education." *Educational Researcher* 46, no. 7 (2017): 366–377.

Barnett, Erin R., Elizabeth A. Boucher, William B. Daviss, and Glyn Elwyn. "Supporting Shared Decision-Making for Children's Complex Behavioral Problems: Development and User Testing of an Option Grid Decision Aid." *Community Mental Health Journal* 54, no. 1 (2018): 7–16.

Barnett, Erin R., Rebecca L. Butcher, Katrin Neubacher, Mary K. Jankowski, William B. Daviss, Kathleen L. Carluzzo, Erica G. Ungarelli, and Cathleen R. Yackley. "Psychotropic Medications in Child Welfare: From Federal Mandate to Direct Care." *Children and Youth Services Review* 66 (2016): 9–17.

Barnum, Matt. "As Teachers Across the Country Demand Higher Pay, Here's How Much Salaries Have Stalled—and Why It Matters for Kids." *Chalkbeat*, April 3, 2018. https://www.chalkbeat.org/posts/us/2018/04/03/as-teachers-across-the-country-demand-higher-pay-heres-how-much-salaries-have-stalled-and-why-it-matters-for-kids/.

———. "Common Core Tests Were Supposed to Usher in a New Era of Comparing America's Schools. What Happened?" *Chalkbeat*, November 14, 2017. https://www.chalkbeat.org/posts/us/2017/11/14/common-core-tests-were-supposed-to-usher-in-a-new-era-of-comparing-americas-schools-what-happened/.

———. "Do Community Schools and Wraparound Services Boost Academics? Here's What We Know." *Chalkbeat*, February 20, 2018. https://chalkbeat.org/posts/us/2018/02/20/do-community-schools-and-wraparound-services-boost-academics-heres-what-we-know/.

———. "A Surprising Link: When Kids Work Harder on Tests, Their Countries' Economies Grow More." *Chalkbeat*, January 23, 2018. https://chalkbeat.org/posts/us/2018/01/23/a-surprising-link-when-kids-work-harder-on-tests-their-countries-economies-grow-more/.

———. "Want More Young People to Aspire to Become Teachers? Try Paying Teachers More." *Chalkbeat*, October 5, 2017. https://www.chalkbeat.org/posts/us/2017/10/05/want-more-young-people-to-aspire-to-become-teachers-try-paying-teachers-more/.

———. "When Union Protections Disappear, Poor Schools Lose Teachers, New Research Finds." *Chalkbeat*, December 12, 2017. https://www.chalkbeat.org/posts/us/2017/12/12/when-union-protections-disappear-poor-schools-lose-teachers-new-research-finds/.

Barrow, Elizabeth. "No Global Citizenship? Re-Envisioning Global Citizenship Education in Times of Growing Nationalism." *High School Journal* 100, no. 3 (2017): 163.

Barshay, Jill. "Governments Are Spending Billions More on Education, and It's Making Inequality Worse." *Hechinger Report*, January 15, 2018.

———. "New Evidence Indicates That Paying Teachers Bonuses Raises Student Performance by a Small Amount." *Hechinger Report*, January 29, 2018. https://hechingerreport.org/new-evidence-indicates-paying-teachers-bonuses-raises-student-performance-small-amount/.

———. "Teachers Often Ask Youngsters to Learn in Ways That Exceed Even Adult-Sized Attention Spans." *Hechinger Report*, December 4, 2017. http://hechingerreport.org/teachers-often-ask-youngsters-learn-ways-exceed-even-adult-sized-attention-spans/.

———. "Three Lessons from Rigorous Research on Education Technology." *Hechinger Report*, September 25, 2017. http://hechingerreport.org/three-lessons-rigorous-research-education-technology/.

———. "Two Studies Point to the Power of Teacher-Student Relationships to Boost Learning." *Hechinger Report*, May 21, 2018. http://hechingerreport.org/two-studies-point-to-the-power-of-teacher-student-relationships-to-boost-learning/.

———. "The U.S. Might Have Been 19th in the World in Math (Instead of 36th) If We'd Bribed our Students with $25." *Hechinger Report*, November 20, 2017. http://hechingerreport.org/u-s-might-19th-world-math-instead-36th-wed-bribed-students-25/.

Batel, Samantha, and Laura Jimenez. "State Accountability Fact Sheets: Overview and Critical Context." Center for American Progress, August 2017. https://cdn.americanprogress.org/content/uploads/2017/08/03122444/ESSA-Fact sheet-ALL.pdf.

Bayer, Casey. "PISA 2018 Test to Include Global Competency Assessment." Harvard Graduate School of Education, December 12, 2017.

Beck, Taylor. "LA School District Lowers Minimum Grade Needed to Pass College Prep Classes." *Daily Caller*, June 10, 2015. http://dailycaller.com/2015/06/10/la-school-district-lowers-minimum-grade-needed-to-pass-college-prep-classes/.

Bellafante, Ginia. "Can Prep Schools Fight the Class War?" *New York Times*, September 9, 2017.

Berardi, Francesca. "What Does a Program That Costs More Than $40,000 a Year

Get Your Two-Year-Old?" *Hechinger Report*, November 30, 2017. http://hech ingerreport.org/heres-best-child-care-money-can-buy-looks-like/.

Berdik, Chris. "Dealing with Digital Distraction." *Hechinger Report*, January 22, 2018. http://hechingerreport.org/dealing-digital-distraction/.

Berger, Ron, Leah Ruger, and Libby Woodfin. "Making Students Partners in Data-Driven Approaches to Learning." *Mindshift*, September 8, 2014. https://www .kqed.org/mindshift/37598/how-students-can-be-partners-in-data-driven -approaches-to-learning.

Beauvais, Clementine. "An Exploration of the 'Pushy Parent' Label in Educational Discourse." *Discourse: Studies in the Cultural Politics of Education* 38. no. 2 (2015): 159–171.

Beland, Louis-Philippe, and Richard Murphy. "Ill Communication: Technology, Distraction and Student Performance." *Labour Economics* 41 (2016): 61–76.

Benedetti, Christopher. "The Trouble with Grit: Arming Preservice Teachers with Grit and Strategies Is Not the Way to Prepare Them for a Profession They Chose Based on Their Underlying Beliefs and Sense of Creativity." *Phi Delta Kappan* 97, no. 7 (2016): 80.

Benoit, David. "iPhones and Children Are a Toxic Pair, Say Two Big Apple Investors." *Wall Street Journal*, January 8, 2018.

Benus, Matthew J., Leisa A. Martin, and Glenn P. Lauzon. "Does Pledging Allegiance to the Flag Have Educational Value?" *Schools* 13, no. 2 (2016): 312–338.

Bergstein, Rachelle. "Crazy Parenting Tips from Around the World." *New York Post*, January 10, 2018.

Berliner, Wendy. "Why There's No Such Thing as a Gifted Child." *Guardian*, July 25, 2017.

Bhattacharya, Jasodhara, and Kate Anderson. *Measuring Global Citizenship Education*. Washington, DC: Brookings Institution, April 2017. https://www .brookings.edu/research/measuring-global-citizenship-education/.

Bialystok, Ellen. "The Bilingual Adaptation: How Minds Accommodate Experience." *Psychological Bulletin* 143, no. 3 (2017): 233–262.

Bjork, Christopher. *High-Stakes Schooling: What We Can Learn from Japan's Experiences with Testing, Accountability, and Education Reform*. Chicago: University of Chicago Press, 2015.

Blachor, Devorah. "PTA Culture and the Working Mother." *Washington Post*, April 10, 2018.

Blackwell, Lindsay, Emma Gardiner, and Sarita Schoenebeck. "Managing Expectations: Technology Tensions Among Parents and Teens." In *Proceedings of the Nineteenth ACM Conference on Computer-Supported Cooperative Work and Social Computing* (1390–1401). New York: ACM, 2016.

Blad, Evie. "How One District Is Spreading Social-Emotional Learning Across All Its Schools." *Education Week*, March 9, 2018.

————. "Teachers Say Social-Emotional Learning Is Important, But They Can't Do It Alone." *Education Week*, March 13, 2018.

Blom, Erica. "How Many Scholarships Could We Fund If We Eliminated College Sports? Hint: A Lot." Urban Institute, April 11, 2018. https://www.urban.org /urban-wire/how-many-scholarships-could-we-fund-if-we-eliminated -college-sports-hint-lot.

Boaler, Jo. "Designing Mathematics Classes to Promote Equity and Engagement." *Journal of Mathematical Behavior* 41 (2016): 172–178.

Boaler, Jo, and Sarah Kate Selling. "Psychological Imprisonment or Intellectual Freedom? A Longitudinal Study of Contrasting School Mathematics Approaches and Their Impact on Adults' Lives." *Journal for Research in Mathematics Education* 48, no. 1 (2017): 78–105.

Boaler, Jo, and Pablo Zoido. "Why Math Education in the U.S. Doesn't Add Up." *Scientific American Mind*, November 1, 2016.

Boeskens, Luca. *Regulating Publicly Funded Private Schools: A Literature Review on Equity and Effectiveness*. Paris: OECD Publishing, 2016.

Bond, Nathan, and Andy Hargreaves. *The Power of Teacher Leaders: Their Roles, Influence, and Impact*. New York: Routledge, 2017.

Bowman, Kristi L. *The Pursuit of Racial and Ethnic Equality in American Public Schools: Mendez, Brown, and Beyond*. East Lansing: Michigan State University Press, 2014.

Bradbury, Bruce, Miles Corak, Jane Waldfogel, and Elizabeth Washbrook. *Too Many Children Left Behind: The U.S. Achievement Gap in Comparative Perspective*. New York: Russell Sage Foundation, 2015.

Brinded, Lianna. "A Prediction: The World's Most Powerful Economies in 2030." World Economic Forum, February 9, 2017. https://www.weforum.org /agenda/2017/02/a-prediction-the-worlds-most-powerful-economies -in-2030/.

Brody, Leslie. "Alumni from Elite New York City High Schools Unite to Fight Admissions Changes." *Wall Street Journal*, June 20, 2018.

————. "In High-Stress School Admissions Process, Some Students Win in Second Shot." *Wall Street Journal*, May 27, 2018.

————. "New York City Mayor Alters Exam-School Admissions." *Wall Street Journal*, June 4, 2018.

————. "Who Got into Stuyvesant and New York's Other Elite Public High Schools." *Wall Street Journal*, March 7, 2018.

Brooks, David. "Good Leaders Make Good Schools." *New York Times*, March 12, 2018.

Bruni, Frank. "Corporations Will Inherit the Earth." *New York Times*, February 10, 2018.

Bryant, Jake, Emma Dorn, Marc Krawitz, Paul Kihn, Mona Mourshed, and Jimmy Sarakatsannis. *Drivers of Student Performance: Insights from North America*. McKinsey & Company, 2017. https://www.mckinsey.com/industries/social

-sector/our-insights/drivers-of-student-performance-insights-from-north
-america.

Burnette II, Daarel. "ESSA Aims to Shine Brighter Light on Per-Pupil Spending."
Education Week, April 18, 2017.

———. "K–12 Spending in Most States Still Far Below Pre-Recession Levels, Report Says." *Education Week*, November 29, 2017.

———. "State K–12 Funding, Aid Formulas High on Legislators' Radar." *Education
Week*, February 13, 2018.

———. "States Confront New Mandate on School-Spending Transparency." *Education Week*, February 28, 2018.

Burns, Martha S. "Three Ways to Counter the Effects of Stress on the Brain." *ASCD Express* 13, no. 10 (2018). http://www.ascd.org/ascd-express/vol13/1310-burns.aspx.

Burns, Monica. "Cultivating a Love of Reading in the Digital Age." *Edutopia*, November 30, 2017. https://www.edutopia.org/article/cultivating-love-reading
-digital-age.

Butrymowicz, Sarah. "Most Colleges Enroll Many Students Who Aren't Prepared
for Higher Education." *Hechinger Report*, January 30, 2017. http://hechinger
report.org/colleges-enroll-students-arent-prepared-higher-education/.

———. "This Country Spends Billions on Private Schools—and Has a Terrible
Learning Gap Between Poor and Wealthy." *Hechinger Report*, March 1, 2018.
https://hechingerreport.org/can-sending-public-money-private-schools
-improve-equity/.

Cabrera, Julio C., Michael C. Rodriguez, Stacy R. Karl, and Carlos Chavez. "In What
Ways Do Health Behaviors Impact Academic Performance, Educational As-
pirations, and Commitment to Learning?" Minnesota Youth Development
Research Group, April 2018. www.mnydrg.com.

Calarco, Jessica McCrory. "'Free-Range' Parenting's Unfair Double Standard." *The
Atlantic*, April 3, 2018.

California Department of Education. "District Profile: Ravenswood City Elementary." Accessed October 9, 2018. https://www.cde.ca.gov/sdprofile/details
.aspx?cds=41689990000000.

Camera, Lauren. "In Most States, Poorest School Districts Get Less Funding." *U.S.
News & World Report*, February 27, 2018.

Camera, Lauren, and Lindsey Cook. "Title I: Rich School Districts Get Millions
Meant for Poor Kids." *U.S. News & World Report*, June 1, 2016.

Campbell, David E., and Richard G. Niemi. "Testing Civics: State-Level Civic Education Requirements and Political Knowledge." *American Political Science Review* 110, no. 3 (2016): 495–511.

Capps, Kriston. "In the U.S., Almost No One Votes in Local Elections." *CityLab*,
November 1, 2016. http://www.citylab.com/politics/2016/11/in-the-us-almost
-no-one-votes-in-local-elections/505766/.

Cardinali, Emily. "How to Make a Civics Education Stick." NPR.org, August 14, 2018. https://www.npr.org/2018/08/14/632666071/how-to-make-a-civics-edu cation-stick.

———. "What Your State Is Doing to Beef Up Civics Education." NPR.org, July 21, 2018.

Cardoza, Kavitha. "In Canada's Public Schools, Immigrant Students Are Thriving." *Education Week*, February 28, 2018.

Care, Esther, Helyn Kim, and Alvin Vista. "How Do We Teach 21st Century Skills in Classrooms?" *Education Plus Development* (blog), Brookings Institution, October 17, 2017. https://www.brookings.edu/blog/education-plus-develop ment/2017/10/17/how-do-we-teach-21st-century-skills-in-classrooms/.

Carew, Thomas J., and Susan H. Magsamen. "Neuroscience and Education: An Ideal Partnership for Producing Evidence-Based Solutions to Guide 21st Cen tury Learning." *Neuron* 67, no. 5 (2010): 685–688.

Carey, Kevin, and Elizabeth A. Harris. "It Turns Out Spending More Probably Does Improve Education." *New York Times*, December 12, 2016.

Caro, Daniel H., Jenny Lenkeit, and Leonidas Kyriakides. "Teaching Strategies and Differential Effectiveness Across Learning Contexts: Evidence from PISA 2012." *Studies in Educational Evaluation* 49 (2016): 30–41.

Caron, Christina. " 'To Kill a Mockingbird' Removed from School in Mississippi." *New York Times*, October 16, 2017.

Carver-Thomas, Desiree, and Linda Darling-Hammond. "What Can We Do About Teacher Turnover?" *Edutopia*, November 2, 2017. https://www.edutopia.org /article/what-can-we-do-about-teacher-turnover.

———. "Teacher Turnover: Why It Matters and What We Can Do About It." Learning Policy Institute, August 16, 2017.

Cascio, Elizabeth U., and Diane Whitmore Schanzenbach. "The Impacts of Ex panding Access to High-Quality Preschool Education." *Brookings Papers on Economic Activity* 161 (2013): 1–13.

Cavanagh, Sean. "A 'Punishing Decade' for K–12 Education Funding in the States." *EdWeek Market Brief*, December 1, 2017. https://marketbrief.edweek.org/mar ketplace-k-12/punishing-decade-education-funding-states/.

Center for American Progress. "How Cities and States Are Leading the Way on Mental Health." Accessed June 28, 2018. https://www.americanprogress.org /events/2018/02/28/447345/cities-states-leading-way-mental-health/.

Center on the Developing Child at Harvard University. "Brain Architecture." Ac cessed August 16, 2018. https://developingchild.harvard.edu/science/key -concepts/brain-architecture/.

———. "Five Numbers to Remember About Early Childhood Development." 2009. https://developingchild.harvard.edu/resources/five-numbers-to-remember -about-early-childhood-development/.

Centers for Disease Control. "Physical Activity Facts." Accessed October 9, 2018. https://www.cdc.gov/healthyschools/physicalactivity/facts.htm.

Chapman, Ben. "Parental Involvement Improving at NYC Schools: Stats." *New York Daily News*, November 13, 2017.

Chase, Catherine C., and David Klahr. "Invention Versus Direct Instruction: For Some Content, It's a Tie." *Journal of Science Education and Technology* 26, no. 6 (2017): 582–596.

Chavous, Kevin P. *Building a Learning Culture in America*. New Brunswick, NJ: Transaction, 2017.

Chen, Li-Kai, Emma Dorn, Marc Krawitz, Cheryl S. Lim, and Mona Mourshed. "Drivers of Student Performance: Asia Insights." McKinsey & Company, January 2018. https://www.mckinsey.com/industries/social-sector/our-insights/drivers-of-student-performance-asia-insights.

Chetty, Raj, John N. Friedman, and Jonah E. Rockoff. *Measuring the Impacts of Teachers II: Teacher Value-Added and Student Outcomes in Adulthood*. Cambridge, MA: National Bureau of Economic Research, 2013.

China Daily, National Affairs section. "Quote-Unquote: Xi's Views on Education." February 28, 2017. http://www.chinadaily.com.cn/china/2017-02/28/content_28376745.htm.

Chingos, Matthew M. *How Progressive Is School Funding in the United States?* Washington, DC: Brookings Institution, 2017. https://www.brookings.edu/research/how-progressive-is-school-funding-in-the-united-states/.

Chokshi, Niraj. "Do Men Think They're Better at Science Than Women Do? Well, Actually . . ." *New York Times*, April 7, 2018.

Choshi, Daisuke. "Research of Teacher Personnel Changes in Educational Management," *Bulletin of the Graduate School of Education*, University of Tokyo. https://ci.nii.ac.jp/naid/120005763980.

Christensen, Robert K., Richard M. Clerkin, Rebecca A. Nesbit, and Laurie E. Paarlberg. "Are Parent-Teacher Groups Leading? An Exploratory Study of Nonprofit-Government Interactions in the Public School Context." *Journal of Nonprofit Education and Leadership* 6, no. 1 (2016): 47–59.

Chung, YoonKyung, Barbara Downs, Danielle H. Sandler, and Robert Sienkiewicz. "The Parental Gender Earnings Gap in the United States." Center for Economic Studies, November 2017. https://ideas.repec.org/p/cen/wpaper/17-68.html.

Cimpian, Joseph. "How Our Education System Undermines Gender Equity." *Brown Center Chalkboard* (blog), Brookings Institution, 2018. https://www.brookings.edu/blog/brown-center-chalkboard/2018/04/23/how-our-education-system-undermines-gender-equity/.

City-Data.com. "Top 101 Cities with the Most People Having Master's or Doctor-

ate Degrees (Population 50,000+)." Accessed September 1, 2018. http://www
.city-data.com/top2/h182.html#ixzz5TTxcgvuh.

Claro, Susana, and Susanna Loeb. "New Evidence That Students' Beliefs About
Their Brains Drive Learning." Washington, DC: Brookings Institution, 2017.

Claro, Susana, David Paunesku, and Carol S. Dweck. "Growth Mindset Tempers the
Effects of Poverty on Academic Achievement." *Proceedings of the National Academy of Sciences of the United States of America* 113, no. 31 (2016): 8664–8668.

ClassDojo.com. "About Us." Accessed October 9, 2018. https://www.classdojo
.com/about/.

Clavel, Teru. "Kikokushijo: Returnees to a Country Not Yet Ready for Them."
Japan Times, May 4, 2014.

———. "Thinking Outside the Usual White Box." *Japan Times*, March 2, 2014.

Cline, Seth. "Is Summer Breaking America's Schools?" *U.S. News & World Report*,
June 7, 2018.

Coburn, Donald. "The Teenage Smartphone Problem Is Worse Than You Think."
Education Week, February 1, 2018.

Cochrane, Emily. "A Call to Cut Back Online Addictions. Pitted Against Just One
More Click." *New York Times*, February 24, 2018.

Cohen, Julia F. W., Scott Richardson, S. Bryn Austin, Christina D. Economos, and
Eric B. Rimm. "School Lunch Waste Among Middle School Students." *American Journal of Preventive Medicine* 44, no. 2 (2013): 114–121.

Commission on the Abraham Lincoln Study Abroad Fellowship Program. "Global
Competence and National Needs: One Million Americans Studying Abroad."
November 2005. www.nafsa.org/uploadedFiles/NAFSA_Home/Resource
_Library_Assets/CCB/lincoln_commission_report(1).pdf.

Common Core State Standards Initiative. "Mathematics Standards." Accessed
December 18, 2018. http://www.corestandards.org/Math/.

Corcoran, Sean Patrick, and E. Christine Baker-Smith. "Pathways to an Elite
Education: Application, Admission, and Matriculation to New York City's
Specialized High Schools." *Education Finance and Policy* 13 (2015): 256–279.

Coughlan, Sean. "England and US Will Not Take PISA Tests in Tolerance." *BBC
News*, January 24, 2018.

———. "Global Education Rankings to Measure Tolerance." *BBC News*, December
13, 2017. http://www.bbc.com/news/business-42318895.

———. "School Computers 'Do Not Raise Results.'" *BBC News*, September 15,
2015. https://www.bbc.co.uk/news/business-34174796.

Craik, Fergus I. M., Ellen Bialystok, and Morris Freedman. "Delaying the Onset of
Alzheimer Disease: Bilingualism as a Form of Cognitive Reserve." *Neurology*
75, no. 19 (2010): 1726–1729.

Craw, Jennifer. "Graduation Rates Worldwide." National Center on Education and the Economy, May 30, 2018. http://ncee.org/2018/05/graduation-rates-worldwide/.

Crockett, Yvonne. "U.S. Department of Education Budget News." US Department of Education, 2018. Accessed April 10, 2018. https://www2.ed.gov/about/overview/budget/news.html.

Crouse, Karen. "Katie Ledecky Turns Pro After Dominating College Swimming." *New York Times*, March 26, 2018.

———. "Young Swimmers May Have to Wait to Dress Like Katie Ledecky." *New York Times*, May 11, 2018.

Cuban, Larry. "The Khan Lab School in Silicon Valley (Part 1)." *Larry Cuban on School Reform and Classroom Practice*. 2018. https://larrycuban.wordpress.com/2018/05/14/the-khan-lab-school-in-silicon-valley-part-1/.

———. "The Khan Lab School in Silicon Valley (Part 2)." *Larry Cuban on School Reform and Classroom Practice*. 2018. https://larrycuban.wordpress.com/2018/05/17/khan-lab-school-part-2/.

Cummins, Eleanor. "Your Two-Year-Old Is Full of Potential. Here's How to Develop It." *Hechinger Report*, December 1, 2017. http://hechingerreport.org/2-year-old-full-potential-heres-develop/.

Damour, Lisa. "Parenting the Fortnite Addict." *New York Times*, April 30, 2018.

Darling-Hammond, Linda. "The President's 2018 Education Budget Proposal Is Déjà Vu All Over Again." Learning Policy Institute, February 15, 2018. https://learningpolicyinstitute.org/blog/presidents-2018-education-budget-proposal.

———. "Teacher Education Around the World: What Can We Learn from International Practice?" *European Journal of Teacher Education* 40, no. 3 (2017): 291.

———. " 'Teaching Is the Profession On Which All Other Professions Depend': Linda Darling-Hammond on Transforming Education." Stanford Graduate School of Education, July 21, 2018. https://ed.stanford.edu/news/teaching-profession-which-all-other-professions-depend-linda-darling-hammond-transforming.

Darling-Hammond, Linda, Dion Burns, Carol Campbell, A. Lin Goodwin, Karen Hammerness, Ee-Ling Low, Ann McIntyre, Mistilina Sato, and Ken Zeichner. *Empowered Educators: How High-Performing Systems Shape Teaching Quality Around the World.* San Francisco: Jossey-Bass, 2017.

Darlow, Veronica, Jill M. Norvilitis, and Pamela Schuetze. "The Relationship Between Helicopter Parenting and Adjustment to College." *Journal of Child and Family Studies* 26, no. 8 (2017): 2291–2298.

Davis, Michelle, and Michele Molnar. "Educators Carefully Watch Pearson as It Moves to Sell K–12 Curriculum Business." *Education Week*, March 5, 2018.

DC Public Schools. "Per Student Funding." Accessed January 11, 2019. http://dcpsbudget.ourdcschools.org/.

Deardorff, Darla K. "A 21st Century Imperative: Integrating Intercultural Competence in Tuning." *Tuning Journal for Higher Education* 3, no. 1 (2015): 137–147.

Dee, Thomas S., and Dan Goldhaber. *Understanding and Addressing Teacher Shortages in the United States*. Washington, DC: Brookings Institution, April 2017. https://www.brookings.edu/research/understanding-and-addressing-teacher-shortages-in-the-united-states/.

DeNisco, Alison. "School Districts Find Creative Ways to Fund Pre-K." *District Administration Magazine*, November 17, 2017. https://www.districtadministration.com/article/school-districts-find-creative-ways-fund-pre-k.

Desautels, Lori. "Navigating Confrontations with Parents." *Edutopia*, May 21, 2018. https://www.edutopia.org/article/navigating-confrontations-parents.

Desteno, David. "We're Teaching Grit the Wrong Way." *Chronicle of Higher Education*, March 18, 2018.

DeVos, Betsy. "How We Can Catch Up to Other Countries in Education." *Education Week*, June 28, 2018.

DeWitt, Peter. "Do Educators Really Want Parents to Be Held Accountable?" *Education Week*, March 11, 2018.

Dillon, Sam. "Top Scores from Shanghai Stun Experts." *New York Times*, December 7, 2010.

Disare, Monica. "Here's How New York City Divvies Up School Funding—and Why Critics Say the System Is Flawed." *Chalkbeat*, January 20, 2018. https://www.chalkbeat.org/posts/ny/2018/01/29/gov-cuomo-wants-needy-schools-to-get-more-money-here-is-new-york-citys-flawed-system-for-doing-that/.

———. "How One Manhattan District Has Preserved Its Own Set of Elite High Schools." *Chalkbeat*, June 7, 2018. https://chalkbeat.org/posts/ny/2018/06/07/how-one-manhattan-district-has-preserved-its-own-set-of-elite-high-schools/.

———. "'Why Are We Screening Children? I Don't Get That': Chancellor Carranza Offers Harsh Critique of NYC School Admissions." *Chalkbeat*, May 23, 2018. https://www.chalkbeat.org/posts/ny/2018/05/23/why-are-we-screening-children-i-dont-get-that-chancellor-carranza-offers-harsh-critique-of-nyc-school-admissions/.

———. "Why Do Some New York City Schools Get to Choose Their Students? Here's the Case for and Against 'Screening.'" *Chalkbeat*, November 6, 2017. https://www.chalkbeat.org/posts/ny/2017/11/06/why-do-some-new-york-city-schools-get-to-choose-their-students-heres-the-case-for-and-against-screening/.

Donnelly, Joseph E., Charles H. Hillman, Darla Castelli, Jennifer L. Etnier, Sarah Lee, Phillip Tomporowski, Kate Lambourne, and Amanda N. Szabo-Reed. "Physical Activity, Fitness, Cognitive Function, and Academic Achievement in Children: A Systematic Review." *Medicine and Science in Sports and Exercise* 48, no. 6 (2016): 1197–1222.

Doran, Leo, and Benjamin Herold. "One-to-One Laptop Initiatives Boost Student Scores, Study Finds." *Education Week*, May 18, 2016.

Doubek, James. "Attention, Students: Put Your Laptops Away." NPR.org, April 17, 2016.

Doucleff, Michaeleen. "A Lost Secret: How to Get Kids to Pay Attention." NPR .org, June 21, 2018. https://www.npr.org/sections/goatsandsoda/2018/06 /21/621752789/a-lost-secret-how-to-get-kids-to-pay-attention.

Dougherty, Danielle, and Jill Sharkey. "Reconnecting Youth: Promoting Emotional Competence and Social Support to Improve Academic Achievement." *Children and Youth Services Review* 74 (2017): 28–34.

Du, Wei. "In Hong Kong, Shortage of Land for Housing Remains a Thorny Issue." *Channel News Asia*, September 20, 2017. https://www.channelnewsasia.com /news/asia/in-hong-kong-shortage-of-land-for-housing-remains-a-thorny -issue-9223650.

Dubner, Stephen J. "Does 'Early Education' Come Way Too Late?" *Freakonomics Radio*. November 19, 2015. http://freakonomics.com/podcast/does-early-edu cation-come-way-too-late-a-new-freakonomics-radio-podcast/.

———. "How to Fix a Broken High-Schooler, in Four Easy Steps." *Freakonomics Radio*. February 4, 2016. http://freakonomics.com/podcast/fix-broken-high -schooler-four-easy-steps-freakonomics-radio-rebroadcast/.

———. "Is America's Education Problem Really Just a Teacher Problem?" *Freakonomics Radio*. November 27, 2014. http://freakonomics.com/podcast /is-americas-education-problem-really-just-a-teacher-problem-a-new-freak onomics-radio-podcast/.

Duckworth, Angela L., and Martin E. P. Seligman. "Self-Discipline Outdoes IQ in Predicting Academic Performance of Adolescents." *Psychological Science* 16, no. 12 (2005): 939–944.

Duncan Evans, Cristina. "A Teacher's Case Against Summer Vacation." *Education Week*, July 8, 2014.

Dweck, Carol S. "From Needs to Goals and Representations: Foundations for a Unified Theory of Motivation, Personality, and Development." *Psychological Review* 124, no. 6 (2017): 689–719.

———. *Mindset: How You Can Fulfill Your Potential*. London: Constable & Robinson, 2012.

Dwyer, Jim. "Decades Ago, New York Dug a Moat Around Its Specialized Schools." *New York Times*, June 8, 2018.

Dynarski, Susan. "Online Courses Are Harming the Students Who Need the Most Help." *New York Times*, January 19, 2018.

Economist. "Colleges Receive More Applications When Their Basketball Teams Do Well." March 26, 2018.

———. "The Glass-Ceiling Index." February 15, 2018.

————. "How Heavy Use of Social Media Is Linked to Mental Illness." May 18, 2018.

————. "How Indians Triumphed in America." November 26, 2016.

————. "Regulating the Tech Titans: Should the Tech Giants Be More Heavily Regulated?" April 27, 2018.

————. "Why China's Communists Recognise Just 56 Ethnic Groups." July 15, 2018.

EdBuild. "Funded: State Policy Analysis." Accessed January 29, 2018. http://funded.edbuild.org/state/WA.

Education Data Partnership. "Palo Alto." Accessed October 9, 2018. http://www.ed-data.org/district/Santa-Clara/Palo-Alto-Unified.

Edutopia. "Special Series: Nashville District Goes All-In on SEL." February 13, 2018. https://mailchi.mp/edutopia/special-series-nashville-district-goes-all-in-on-sel?e=bd09a7b709.

Egalite, Anna J., and Patrick J. Wolf. "A Review of the Empirical Research on Private School Choice." *Peabody Journal of Education* 91, no. 4 (2016): 441–454.

Egan, Timothy. "Actually, You Can Fix Stupid." *New York Times*, March 30, 2018.

Emerich, Paul. "Why I Left Silicon Valley, Ed Tech, and 'Personalized' Learning." *Larry Cuban on School Reform and Classroom Practice,* 2018. https://larrycuban.wordpress.com/2018/01/20/why-i-left-silicon-valley-ed-tech-and-personalized-learning-paul-emerich/.

Ennis, Gretchen Marie, and Jane Tonkin. "'It's Like Exercise for Your Soul': How Participation in Youth Arts Activities Contributes to Young People's Wellbeing." *Journal of Youth Studies* 21, no. 3 (2018): 340–359.

Espenshade, Thomas J., and Alexandria Walton Radford. "Evaluative Judgments vs. Bias in College Admissions." *Forbes*, August 1, 2010.

European Commission. "Europeans and Their Languages." *Special Eurobarometer* 386 (June 2012). http://ec.europa.eu/commfrontoffice/publicopinion/archives/ebs/ebs_386_en.pdf.

Fabian Romero, Esmeralda. "How Can My Kids Be Honor Roll Students and Still Not Read at Grade Level?" *THTP Blog*, July 12, 2018. Accessed July 16, 2018. https://tntp.org/blog/post/how-can-my-kids-be-honor-roll-students-and-still-not-read-at-grade-level.

Farrugia, Christine. *Globally Mobile Youth: Trends in International Secondary Students in the United States, 2013–2016.* New York: Institute for International Education, 2017.

Ferguson, Maria. "ESSA Is More Than the Latest Acronym on Education's Block." *Phi Delta Kappan* 97, no. 6 (2016): 72–73.

Fiske, Siri. "A Better Way to Teach the Gifted—and Everyone Else." *Wall Street Journal,* January 16, 2018.

Fleer, Marilyn, and Bert Van Oers. *International Handbook of Early Childhood Education.* Dordrecht: Springer Netherlands, 2017.

Florida, Richard. "When Cities Are More Economically Powerful Than Nations." *City Lab*, March 16, 2017. https://www.citylab.com/work/2017/03/the-eco nomic-power-of-global-cities-compared-to-nations/519294/.

Foltos, Les. "Teachers Learn Better Together." *Edutopia*, January 29, 2018. https:// www.edutopia.org/article/teachers-learn-better-together.

Foreman, Leesa M. "Educational Attainment Effects of Public and Private School Choice." *Journal of School Choice* 11, no. 4 (2017): 642–654.

Frakt, Austin. "Worried About Risky Teenage Behavior? Make School Tougher." *New York Times*, April 30, 2018.

Fuller, Ed. "Chinese Students Are a Win-Win for U.S. Tourism." *Forbes*, November 13, 2017.

Gallo, Alberto. "How the American Dream Turned into Greed and Inequal- ity." World Economic Forum, November 9, 2017. https://www.weforum .org/agenda/2017/11/the-pursuit-of-happiness-how-the-american-dream -turned-into-greed-and-inequality/.

Gao, Helen. "Chinese, Studying in America, and Struggling." *New York Times*, De- cember 12, 2017.

Garcia, Emma, and Elaine Weiss. "Education Inequalities at the School Starting Gate: Gaps, Trends, and Strategies to Address." Economic Policy Institute, 2017. https://search.proquest.com/docview/1958456189.

Garcia Mathewson, Tara. "Don't Ask Which Ed Tech Products Work, Ask Why They Work." *Hechinger Report*, February 21, 2018. http://hechingerreport.org /dont-ask-ed-tech-products-work-ask-work/.

———. " States Will Soon Be Free to Transform Standardized Testing, But Most Won't." *Hechinger Report*, November 15, 2017. http://hechingerreport.org /states-will-soon-free-transform-standardized-testing-wont/.

Garcia-Navarro, Lulu, and Michaeleen Doucleff. "Parenting Myths and Facts." NPR.org, May 13, 2018. https://www.npr.org/2018/05/13/610777733/parenting -myths-and-facts.

Gaudelli, William. *Global Citizenship Education: Everyday Transcendence*. New York: Routledge, 2016.

Gelles, David. "Inside a Powerful Silicon Valley Charity, a Toxic Culture Festered." *New York Times*, May 11, 2018.

George, Madeleine J., and Candice L. Odgers. "Seven Fears and the Science of How Mobile Technologies May Be Influencing Adolescents in the Digital Age." *Perspectives on Psychological Science* 10, no. 6 (2015): 832–851.

Gewertz, Catherine. "Peers Guide Ninth Graders Through 'Make-or-Break' Year." *Education Week*, November 11, 2017.

———. "School Counselors Responsible for 482 Students on Average, Report Finds." *Education Week*, February 8, 2018.

Glenn, Heidi. "Confused by Your Public School Choices? Hire a Coach." *NPR Ed*,

November 27, 2017. https://www.npr.org/sections/ed/2017/11/27/551853951/confused-by-your-public-school-choices-hire-a-coach.

Golinkoff, Roberta Michnick, Kathy Hirsh-Pasek, and Jessa Reed. "Learning on Hold: Cell Phones Sidetrack Parent-Child Interactions." *Developmental Psychology* 53, no. 8 (2017): 1428–1436.

Gonser, Sarah. "School Counselors Keep Kids on Track. Why Are They First to Be Cut?" *Hechinger Report,* May 31, 2018. https://hechingerreport.org/school-counselors-keep-kids-on-track-why-are-they-first-to-be-cut/.

Gonzalez-DeHass, Alyssa R., and Patricia P. Willems. "Nurturing Self-Regulated Learners: Teacher, Peer, and Parental Support of Strategy Instruction." *Educational Forum* 80, no. 3 (2016): 294–309.

Gooblar, David. "The Benefits of Doing It Wrong." *Chronicle Vitae,* January 24, 2018. Accessed March 26, 2018. https://chroniclevitae.com/news/1986-the-benefits-of-doing-it-wrong.

———. "Yes, We Should Teach Character." *Chronicle Vitae,* December 21, 2017. https://chroniclevitae.com/news/1969-yes-we-should-teach-character.

Goodall, Janet. *Narrowing the Achievement Gap: Parental Engagement with Children's Learning.* Abingdon, Oxon: Routledge, 2017.

Google for Education. "Giving." Accessed January 11, 2019. https://edu.google.com/giving/?modal_active=none.

Goren, Heela, and Miri Yemini. "The Global Citizenship Education Gap: Teacher Perceptions of the Relationship Between Global Citizenship Education and Students' Socio-Economic Status." *Teaching and Teacher Education* 67 (2017): 9–22.

Gotlieb, Rebecca, Elizabeth Hyde, Mary Helen Immordino-Yang, and Scott Barry Kaufman. "Cultivating the Social-Emotional Imagination in Gifted Education: Insights from Educational Neuroscience." *Annals of the New York Academy of Sciences* 1377, no. 1 (2016): 22–31.

Gottlieb, Derek. *Education Reform and the Concept of Good Teaching.* New York: Routledge, 2014.

Grahame, Jason A. "Digital Note-Taking: Discussion of Evidence and Best Practices." *Journal of Physician Assistant Education* 27, no. 1 (2016): 47–50.

Grissom, Jason A. "Strong Principals Retain Effective Teachers—and Don't Retain Ineffective Ones." *Brown Center Chalkboard* (blog), Brookings Institution, September 28, 2018. https://www.brookings.edu/blog/brown-center-chalkboard/2018/09/28/strong-principals-retain-effective-teachers-and-dont-retain-ineffective-ones/.

Grossman, Joanna L. *Nine to Five: How Gender, Sex, and Sexuality Continue to Define the American Workplace.* New York: Cambridge University Press, 2016.

Gstalter, Morgan. "Utah Becomes First State to Pass 'Free-Range Parenting' Law." *The Hill,* March 27, 2018. http://thehill.com/homenews/state-watch/380485-utah-becomes-first-state-to-pass-free-range-parenting-law.

Gu, Mingyuan, Jiansheng Ma, and Jun Teng. *Portraits of Chinese Schools*. Singapore: Springer, 2017.

Gunter, Helen, David Hall, and Michael W. Apple. *Corporate Elites and the Reform of Public Education*. Bristol, UK: Policy Press, 2017.

Guzman-Lopez, Adolfo. "LAUSD Board Seeking Fix for College Prep Requirements." Southern California Public Radio, May 7, 2015. https://www.scpr.org/news/2015/05/07/51506/lausd-board-weighs-options-as-college-prep-policy/.

Hafner, Marco, Martin Stepanek, and Wendy M. Troxel. "The Economic Implications of Later School Start Times in the United States." RAND.org, October 31, 2017. https://www.rand.org/pubs/external_publications/EP67365.html.

Haimovitz, Kyla, and Carol S. Dweck. "What Predicts Children's Fixed and Growth Intelligence Mindsets? Not Their Parents' Views of Intelligence But Their Parents' Views of Failure." *Psychological Science* 27, no. 6 (2016): 859–869.

Hammond, Christopher D. "Internationalization, Nationalism, and Global Competitiveness: A Comparison of Approaches to Higher Education in China and Japan." *Asia Pacific Education Review* 17, no. 4 (2016): 555–566.

Hardiman, Mariale. "Informing Pedagogy Through the Brain-Targeted Teaching Model." *Journal of Microbiology and Biology Education* 13, no. 1 (2012): 11–16.

Harmon, Amy. "College Admission Is Not a Personality Contest. Or Is It?" *New York Times*, June 15, 2018.

Harris, Elizabeth. "As Calls for Action Crescendo, De Blasio Takes on Segregated Schools." *New York Times*, June 3, 2018.

———. "In School Together, But Not Learning at the Same Rate." *New York Times*, January 31, 2018.

———. "'Smart Is Something You Get': How a Bronx School Succeeds." *New York Times*, February 2, 2018.

Harris, Elizabeth A., and Josh Katz. "Why Are New York's Schools Segregated? It's Not as Simple as Housing." *New York Times*, May 2, 2018.

Harris, Elizabeth A., and Kate Taylor. "Welcome to New York, and Here's a To-Do List." *New York Times*, April 2, 2018.

Hathaway, Ian. "Almost Half of Fortune 500 Companies Were Founded by American Immigrants or Their Children." *The Avenue* (blog), Brookings Institution, December 4, 2017. https://www.brookings.edu/blog/the-avenue/2017/12/04/almost-half-of-fortune-500-companies-were-founded-by-american-immigrants-or-their-children/.

Hattie, John. *Visible Learning*. Abingdon, Oxon: Routledge, 2008.

———. *Visible Learning for Mathematics, Grades K–12: What Works Best to Optimize Student Learning*. Thousand Oaks, CA: Corwin Mathematics, 2017.

Hattie, John, Deb Masters, and Kate Birch. *Visible Learning into Action: International Case Studies of Impact*. London: Routledge, Taylor & Francis Group, 2015.

REFERENCES

Hauser, Christine. "Too Many Children in California Can't Read, Lawsuit Claims." *New York Times*, December 6, 2017.

Hawkins, Beth. "With Churn at the Nation's Three Largest School Districts, Experts Agree: A Good Superintendent Is Hard to Find." *The 74*, January 17, 2018. https://www.the74million.org/with-churn-at-the-nations-3-largest-school-districts-experts-agree-a-good-superintendent-is-hard-to-find/.

Hayman, Suzie. *Parents and Digital Technology: How to Raise the Connected Generation*. London: Routledge, Taylor & Francis Group, 2016.

He, Eric. "Former Palo Altans Trade Silicon Valley Lifestyle for Better 'Quality of Life' Elsewhere." *Palo Alto Online*, August 10, 2018. https://www.paloaltoonline.com/news/2018/08/10/why-they-left.

Hebert, Jon. "Are We Asking Enough of High School Graduates?" *Education Week*, July 19, 2017.

Hechinger Report, Early Education (blog). "Back to School Ideas for Preschool Thru College—and Teachers Too," August 6, 2018. https://hechingerreport.org/back-to-school-ideas-for-preschool-thru-college-and-teachers-too/.

Hempe, Melanie. "Can You Raise a Teen Today Without a Smartphone?" Families Managing Media, February 2, 2018. http://www.familiesmanagingmedia.com/can-raise-teen-today-without-smartphone/.

Hernández, Javier C. "China Tries to Redistribute Education to the Poor, Igniting Class Conflict." *New York Times*, June 12, 2016.

———. "Study Finds Chinese Students Excel in Critical Thinking. Until College." *New York Times*, July 30, 2016.

———. "To Inspire Young Communists, China Turns to 'Red Army' Schools." *New York Times*, October 15, 2017.

Herold, Benjamin. "Computer Science for All and Silicon Valley: Generous Support or Corporate Takeover?" *Education Week*, February 20, 2018.

———. "Multi-Tasking with Mobile Phones: Yep, It's Bad for Learning." *Education Week*, April 17, 2018.

———. "Teachers on Tech: Good for Student Learning, Bad for Student Health." *Education Week*, April 6, 2018.

———. "Chan Zuckerberg Initiative Gives $14M for Personalized Learning in Chicago." *Education Week*, May 4, 2018.

———. "Congress Considering $95 Million for Study of Technology's Effects on Children." *Education Week*, August 15, 2018.

———. "Gates Foundation, Chan Zuckerberg Team Up to Seek 'State of the Art' Ideas for Schools." *Education Week*, May 8, 2018.

Herrington, Christopher M. "Public Education Financing, Earnings Inequality, and Intergenerational Mobility." *Review of Economic Dynamics* 18, no. 4 (2015): 822–842.

Hertel, Silke, and Nina Jude. "Parental Support and Involvement in School." In *As-*

sessing Contexts of Learning: An International Perspective, edited by Susanne Kuger, Eckhard Klieme, Nina Jude, and David Kaplan, 209–225. New York: Springer, 2016.

Hervey, Sheena. "Bring Back Cursive in All Public Schools." *New York Daily News*, November 18, 2017.

Hess, Frederick M., and Maddie Fennell. "Point-Counterpoint: Teacher Professionalism." *Kappa Delta Pi Record* 51, no. 4 (2015): 159.

Hill, Paul T. "Teaching the 'Unwritten Constitution.'" *Brown Center Chalkboard* (blog), Brookings Institution, December 12, 2017. https://www.brookings.edu/blog /brown-center-chalkboard/2017/12/12/teaching-the-unwritten-constitution/.

Hinton, Marva. "Most States Still Don't Require Full-Day Kindergarten, Report Finds." *Education Week*, July 9, 2018.

———. "Should More Early-Childhood Education Centers Offer Extended Hours?" *Education Week*, November 13, 2017.

Hintz, Phil. "Apple Renews Its Commitment to Education." *Tech and Learning*, April 25, 2018.

Hirsh-Pasek, Kathy. "The Enormous Cost of Toxic Stress: Repairing Damage to Refugee and Separated Children." *Future Development* (blog), Brookings Institution, July 9, 2018. https://www.brookings.edu/blog/future-develop ment/2018/07/09/the-enormous-cost-of-toxic-stress-repairing-damage-to -refugee-and-separated-children/.

Hobbs, Tawnell D. "Losing Students, Private Schools Try to Change." *Wall Street Journal*, December 29, 2017.

Holmes, Kaitlin, Jocelyn Frye, Sarah J. Glynn, and Jessica Quinter. "Rhetoric vs. Reality: Equal Pay." Center for American Progress, November 7, 2016.

Howard, Jacqueline. "The Best—and Worst—School Lunches Around the World." CNN, April 9, 2018. https://www.cnn.com/2018/04/09/health/school-lunches -in-other-countries-parenting-without-borders-intl/index.html.

Hoy, Selena. "Why Little Kids in Japan Are So Independent." *City Lab*, September 28, 2015. http://www.citylab.com/commute/2015/09/why-are-little-kids-in -japan-so-independent/407590/.

Hu, Winnie. "In a Twist, Low Scores Would Earn Admission to Select Schools." *New York Times*, June 6, 2018.

Hu, Winnie, and Elizabeth A. Harris. "A Shadow System Feeds Segregation in New York City Schools." *New York Times*, June 17, 2018.

Huang, Xiao, Norman G. Lederman, and Chaojing Cai. "Improving Chinese Junior High School Students' Ability to Ask Critical Questions." *Journal of Research in Science Teaching* 54, no. 8 (2017): 963–987.

Hughes, Charles A., Jared R. Morris, William J. Therrien, and Sarah K. Benson. "Explicit Instruction: Historical and Contemporary Contexts." *Learning Disabilities Research and Practice* 32, no. 3 (2017): 140–148.

REFERENCES

Human Rights Watch. "Japan: Events of 2016." *World Report 2017*.

Hutt, Rosamond. "These Are the Ten Most Magnetic Cities in the World." World Economic Forum, April 5, 2017. https://www.weforum.org/agenda/2017/04/the-top-10-most-powerful-cities-in-the-world/.

Iasevoli, Brenda. "Can Greater Academic Demands Lead to Less Risky Behavior in Teenagers?" *Education Week*, June 1, 2018.

ICEF Monitor. "American Graduate Schools Report Decline in International Applications and Commencements." February 14, 2018. http://monitor.icef.com/2018/02/american-graduate-schools-report-decline-international-applications-commencements/.

————. "Canada Books 20% Growth in 2017." March 21, 2018. http://monitor.icef.com/2018/03/canada-books-20-growth-2017/.

————. "Canada's International Student Enrolment Surged in 2016." November 22, 2017. http://monitor.icef.com/2017/11/canadas-international-student-enrolment-surged-2016.

————. "Foreign Language Enrolment in the US Trending Downward." March 7, 2018. http://monitor.icef.com/2018/03/foreign-language-enrolment-us-trending-downward/.

————. "Increasing Numbers of Chinese Graduates Returning Home from Overseas." February 6, 2018. http://monitor.icef.com/2018/02/increasing-numbers-chinese-graduates-returning-home-overseas/.

————. "Japan Well on Its Way to 300,000 International Students." January 11, 2018. http://monitor.icef.com/2018/01/japan-300000-international-students/.

————. "More Than 200,000 Japanese Students Abroad in 2016." January 31, 2018. http://monitor.icef.com/2018/01/200000-japanese-students-abroad-2016/.

————. "New Study Forecasts Slowing Growth in International Student Mobility." February 7, 2018. http://monitor.icef.com/2018/02/new-study-forecasts-slowing-growth-in-international-student-mobility/.

Imberman, Scott A., and Michael F. Lovenheim. "Incentive Strength and Teacher Productivity: Evidence from a Group-Based Teacher Incentive Pay System." *Review of Economics and Statistics* 97, no. 2 (2015): 364–386.

————. "Does the Market Value Value-Added? Evidence from Housing Prices After a Public Release of School and Teacher Value-Added." *Journal of Urban Economics* 91 (2016): 104.

Ingersoll, Richard M., Lisa Merrill, and Daniel Stuckey. "The Changing Face of Teaching." *Educational Leadership* 75, no. 8 (2018): 44–49.

Ingersoll, Richard M., and Michael Strong. "The Impact of Induction and Mentoring Programs for Beginning Teachers: A Critical Review of the Research." *Review of Educational Research* 81, no. 2 (2011): 201–233.

Institute of International Education. "Fast Facts." 2017. https://www.iie.org/opendoors.

————. "Globally Mobile Youth: Trends in International Secondary Students in the United States, 2013–2016." Institute of International Education, 2017. https://www.iie.org:443/en/Research-and-Insights/Publications/Globally -Mobile-Youth-2013-2016.

————. "Open Doors Data." Accessed August 23, 2018. https://www.iie.org:443 /Research-and-Insights/Open-Doors/Data.

————. "Places of Origin." Accessed August 23, 2018. https://www.iie.org:443 /Research-and-Insights/Open-Doors/Data/International-Students/Places -of-Origin.

Interlandi, Jeneen. "Why Are Our Most Important Teachers Paid the Least?" *New York Times*, January 9, 2018.

Jalonick, Mary Clare. "Government Relaxes Nutrition Standards for School Lunches." *PBS News Hour*, May 1, 2017.

Janta, Barbara. "In Britain's Approach to Free Child Care, Lessons for the U.S." RAND.com, October 27, 2017. https://www.rand.org/blog/2017/10/in-britains -approach-to-free-childcare-lessons-for.html.

Jazynka, Kitson. "Parents Raise Massive Amounts of Money at Some Public Schools. Should They Share It?" *Washington Post*, March 19, 2018.

Jerrim, John, and Lindsey Macmillan. "Income Inequality, Intergenerational Mobility, and the Great Gatsby Curve: Is Education the Key?" *Social Forces* 94, no. 2 (2015): 533.

Jimenez, Laura, and Scott Sargrad. "Are High School Diplomas Really a Ticket to College and Work?" Center for American Progress, April 2, 2018. https://www .americanprogress.org/issues/education-k-12/reports/2018/04/02/447717 /high-school-diplomas/.

Job, Veronika, Malte Friese, and Katharina Bernecker. "Effects of Practicing Self-Control on Academic Performance." *Motivation Science* 1, no. 4 (2015): 219–232.

Jochim, Ashley, and Patrick McGuinn. "The Politics of the Common Core Assessments." *Education Next* 16, no. 4 (2016): 44–62.

Johnson, Greer, and Neil Dempster. *Leadership in Diverse Learning Contexts*. New York: Springer, 2016.

Johnson, Heather Beth. *The American Dream and the Power of Wealth: Choosing Schools and Inheriting Inequality in the Land of Opportunity*, 2nd ed. New York: Routledge, 2014.

Johnson, Rucker, and Sean Tanner. "Money and Freedom: The Impact of California's School Finance Reform." Learning Policy Institute, February 2, 2018. https://learningpolicyinstitute.org/product/ca-school-finance-reform-brief.

Johnson, Sydney. "Public Educators Share Fallout on Personalized Learning, Privatization and Edtech." *EdSurge*, October 16, 2017. https://www.edsurge .com/news/2017-10-16-at-public-education-conference-educators-share -fall-outs-on-personalized-learning-privatization-and-edtech.

Jones, Denisha, Deena Khalil, and R. Davis Dixon. "Teacher-Advocates Respond to ESSA: 'Support the Good Parts—Resist the Bad Parts.'" *Peabody Journal of Education* 92, no. 4 (2017): 445.

Jones, Stephanie, Katharine Brush, Rebecca Bailey, Gretchen Brion-Meisels, Joseph McIntyre, Jennifer Kahn, Bryan Nelson, and Laura Stickle. "Navigating Social and Emotional Learning from the Inside Out." Wallace Foundation, May 2, 2017. https://www.wallacefoundation.org/knowledge-center/pages/navigating-social-and-emotional-learning-from-the-inside-out.aspx.

Journell, Wayne. "We Still Need You! An Update on the Status of K–12 Civics Education in the United States." *PS: Political Science and Politics* 48, no. 4 (2015): 630–634.

Jun, Zhang. "China's Vision for the Next 30 Years." *Nikkei Asian Review*, November 5, 2017.

Kadvany, Elena. "District Grapples with Ongoing Budget Deficit." *Palo Alto Online*, January 19, 2018. https://www.paloaltoonline.com/news/2018/01/19/district-grapples-with-ongoing-budget-deficit.

———. "Mayor Alleges 'Culture of Corruption' at Ravenswood School District." *Palo Alto Online*, February 17, 2018.

———. "Paly Revising Schedule to Address Instructional Minutes Deficit." *Palo Alto Online*, June 12, 2018. https://www.paloaltoonline.com/news/2018/06/12/paly-revising-schedule-to-address-instructional-minutes-deficit.

———. "Should Palo Alto Students Be Required to Study Computer Science?" *Palo Alto Online*, May 23, 2018. https://www.paloaltoonline.com/news/2018/05/23/should-palo-alto-students-be-required-to-study-computer-science.

———. "Teachers' Union Agrees to Reallocate Bonus to Schools." *Palo Alto Online*, February 14, 2018. https://www.paloaltoonline.com/news/2018/02/14/teachers-union-agrees-to-reallocate-bonus-to-schools.

Kahlenberg, Richard D. "Tenure." *American Educator* (Summer 2015). https://www.aft.org/ae/summer2015/kahlenberg.

Kamenetz, Anya. "Six Potential Brain Benefits of Bilingual Education." NPR.org, December 26, 2017. https://www.npr.org/sections/ed/2016/11/29/497943749/6-potential-brain-benefits-of-bilingual-education.

———. "What's Going On in Your Child's Brain When You Read Them a Story?" NPR.org, May 24, 2018. https://www.npr.org/sections/ed/2018/05/24/611609366/whats-going-on-in-your-childs-brain-when-you-read-them-a-story.

Kaneda, Masayo, and Shigeru Yamamoto. "The Japanese School Lunch and Its Contribution to Health." *Nutrition Today* 50, no. 6 (2015): 268–272.

Kang, Sean H. K. "Spaced Repetition Promotes Efficient and Effective Learning: Policy Implications for Instruction." *Policy Insights from the Behavioral and Brain Sciences* 3, no. 1 (2016): 12–19.

Kapur, Manu. "Examining Productive Failure, Productive Success, Unproductive

Failure, and Unproductive Success in Learning." *Educational Psychologist* 51, no. 2 (2016): 289–299.

Karoly, Lynn A. "The Economic Returns to Early Childhood Education." *Future of Children* 26, no. 2 (2016): 37–55.

Katy Independent School District. "Bond Information." Accessed October 9, 2018. http://www.katyisd.org/dept/bf/Pages/Bond-Information.aspx.

Kaufman, Julia H., Elaine Lin Wang, Laura S. Hamilton, Lindsey E. Thompson, and Gerald Hunter. "U.S. Teachers' Support of Their State Standards and Assessments." RAND.org, 2017. https://www.rand.org/pubs/research_reports/RR2136.html.

Kawano, Kirsty. "All You Need to Know About Tokyo Public School PTAs." *Savvy Tokyo*, October 1, 2015.

Kelmon, Jessica. "Ten Tips to Boost Sixth Grade Math Skills." Great Schools.org, July 11, 2018. https://www.greatschools.org/gk/articles/10-tips-boost-6th -grade-math-skills/.

Kember, David. "Why Do Chinese Students Out-Perform Those from the West? Do Approaches to Learning Contribute to the Explanation?" *Cogent Education* 3, no. 1 (2016).

Kim, Ada S., and Katie Davis. "Tweens' Perspectives on Their Parents' Media-Related Attitudes and Rules: An Exploratory Study in the US." *Journal of Children and Media* 11, no. 3 (2017): 358.

Kim, Sung Won, Kari-Elle Brown, Edward J. Kim, and Vanessa L. Fong. " 'Poorer Children Study Better': How Urban Chinese Young Adults Perceive Relationships Between Wealth and Academic Achievement." *Comparative Education Review* 62, no. 1 (2018): 84–102.

Kirp, David L. "What Pre-K Means for Your Pre-Teenager." *New York Times*, December 14, 2017.

Kirsch, Irwin, and Henry Braun. *The Dynamics of Opportunity in America: Evidence and Perspectives.* New York: Springer, 2016.

Klass, Perri. "Taking Playtime Seriously." *New York Times*, January 29, 2018.

Klein, Alyson. "Betsy DeVos: A One-Year Progress Report." *Education Week*, February 6, 2018.

———. "How Do ESSA Plans Stack Up on Using Evidence in School Improvement?" *Education Week*, January 11, 2018.

———. "States, Districts Will Share More Power Under ESSA." *Education Digest* 81, no. 8 (2016): 4.

Kline, David. "Fear American Complacency, Not China." *Wall Street Journal*, November 20, 2017.

Koh, Caroline. *Motivation, Leadership and Curriculum Design: Engaging the Net Generation and 21st Century Learners.* Singapore: Springer, 2015.

Kohli, Sonali. "Students Are More Anxious in the Trump Era, Teachers Say." *Los Angeles Times*, October 25, 2017.

Korn, Melissa. "How Much Does Being a Legacy Help Your College Admissions Odds?" *Wall Street Journal*, July 9, 2018.

Korn, Melissa, and Nicole Hong. "In Harvard Affirmative Action Suit, Filings to Provide Rare Look at Admissions Process." *Wall Street Journal*, June 13, 2018.

Kounang, Nadia. "Repeated Hits, Not Concussions, Linked to CTE." CNN, January 18, 2018. https://www.cnn.com/2018/01/18/health/cte-concussion -repeated-hits-study/index.html.

Kraft, Matthew A., and Todd Rogers. "The Underutilized Potential of Teacher-to-Parent Communication: Evidence from a Field Experiment." *Economics of Education Review* 47 (2015): 49–63.

Kroll, Judith F., and Paola E. Dussias. "The Benefits of Multilingualism to the Personal and Professional Development of Residents of the US." *Foreign Language Annals* 50, no. 2 (2017): 248–259.

Kucirkova, Natalia, and Garry Falloon. *Apps, Technology and Younger Learners: International Evidence for Teaching.* London: Routledge, Taylor & Francis Group, 2016.

Kuger, Susanne, Eckhard Klieme, Nina Jude, and David Kaplan. *Assessing Contexts of Learning: An International Perspective.* New York: Springer, 2016.

Lafortune, Julien. *School Finance Reform and the Distribution of Student Achievement.* Cambridge, MA: National Bureau of Economic Research, 2016.

Lake, Robin. "For Public School Choice, Focus on Reality—Not Rhetoric." *Brown Center Chalkboard* (blog), Brookings Institution, November 9, 2017. https:// www.brookings.edu/blog/brown-center-chalkboard/2017/11/09/for-public -school-choice-focus-on-reality-not-rhetoric/.

Lardieri, Alexa. "Despite Higher Academic Standards, Student Performance Is Lacking." *U.S. News & World Report*, May 23, 2018.

Lareau, Annette, Elliot B. Weininger, and Amanda Barrett Cox. "How Entitled Parents Hurt Schools." *New York Times*, June 24, 2018.

Larsen, Marianne A. *Internationalization of Higher Education.* New York: Palgrave Macmillan US, 2016.

Larson, Satu, Susan Chapman, Joanne Spetz, and Claire D. Brindis. "Chronic Childhood Trauma, Mental Health, Academic Achievement, and School-Based Health Center Mental Health Services." *Journal of School Health* 87, no. 9 (2017): 675–686.

Leachman, Michael, Kathleen Masterson, and Eric Figueroa. "A Punishing Decade for School Funding." Center on Budget and Policy Priorities, November 27, 2018. https://www.cbpp.org/research/state-budget-and-tax/a-punishing-dec ade-for-school-funding.

Lechtenberg, Suzie, and David Herman. "Is America's Education Problem Really Just a Teacher Problem?" *Freakonomics Radio*, 2016. http://freako nomics.com/podcast/americas-education-problem-really-just-teacher -problem-freakonomics-radio-rebroadcast/.

REFERENCES

Lee, Jacqueline. "Palo Alto Parents Join Fight Against New Sex-Ed Curriculum." *Mercury News*, April 20, 2017.

Leonhardt, David. "Lost Einsteins: The Innovations We're Missing." *New York Times*, December 3, 2017.

Levin, Henry M., and Clive R. Belfield. *Privatizing Educational Choice: Consequences for Parents, Schools, and Public Policy*. London: Routledge, Taylor and Francis, 2015.

Li, Haibin. "The 'Secrets' of Chinese Students' Academic Success: Academic Resilience Among Students from Highly Competitive Academic Environments." *Educational Psychology* 37, no. 8 (2017): 1–14.

Lijadi, Anastasia Aldelina, and Gertina J. Van Schalkwyk. "'The International Schools Are Not So International After All': The Educational Experiences of Third Culture Kids." *International Journal of School and Educational Psychology* 6, no. 1 (2016): 50–61.

Lin-Siegler, Xiaodong, Carol S. Dweck, and Geoffrey L. Cohen. "Instructional Interventions That Motivate Classroom Learning." *Journal of Educational Psychology* 108, no. 3 (2016): 295–299.

Lloyd, Sterling C. "Nation's Schools Stuck in 'Average' Range on Annual Report Card." *Education Week*, January 17, 2018.

Lloyd, Sterling C., and Alex Harwin. "Nation's Schools Get Middling Grade on Quality Counts Report Card; Overall, the Nation's Schools Earn a C on the Latest Quality Counts Report Card, with Variations Among Some States." *Education Week*, December 30, 2016.

Loeb, Susanna. "Continued Support for Improving the Lowest-Performing Schools." Brookings Institution, *Evidence Speaks Reports* 2, no. 8 (2017): 1–5.

Longhurst, Max L., Suzanne H. Jones, and Todd Campbell. "Factors Influencing Teacher Appropriation of Professional Learning Focused on the Use of Technology in Science Classrooms." *Teacher Development* 21, no. 3 (2017): 323–365.

Los Angeles Times Editorial Board. "What's Really in LAUSD's Online Credit Recovery Courses?" *Los Angeles Times*, June 19, 2016.

Loveless, Tom. "2016 Brown Center Report on American Education: How Well Are American Students Learning?" *Brown Center Report on American Education* 3, no. 5 (2016). https://search.proquest.com/docview/1787807518.

Mackie, Vera. "Closing the Gender Gap in Japan." East Asia Forum, August 1, 2016. http://www.eastasiaforum.org/2016/08/01/closing-the-gender-gap-in -japan/.

Maclean, Rupert. *Life in Schools and Classrooms: Past, Present and Future*. New York: Springer, 2017.

Mader, Jackie. "New Research Finds It Hasn't Gotten Easier for Poor Kids to Catch Up." *Hechinger Report*, October 31, 2017. http://hechingerreport.org/new -research-finds-hasnt-gotten-easier-poor-kids-catch/.

Maier, Anna, Julia Daniel, Jeannie Oakes, and Livia Lam. *Community Schools as an Effective School Improvement Strategy: A Review of the Evidence.* Learning Policy Institute, December 14, 2017. https://learningpolicyinstitute.org/product/community-schools-effective-school-improvement-report.

Mann, Elizabeth, and Logan Casey. "New Survey of Minorities Adds Dissenting View to Public Satisfaction with Schools." *Brown Center Chalkboard* (blog), Brookings Institution, 2018. https://www.brookings.edu/blog/brown-center-chalkboard/2018/01/11/new-survey-of-minorities-adds-dissenting-view-to-public-satisfaction-with-schools/.

Maranto, Robert. "Civic Disengagement." *Academic Questions* 30, no. 2 (2017): 123–125.

Maranto, Robert, Julie Trivitt, Malachi Nichols, and Angela Watson. "No Contractual Obligation to Improve Education: School Boards and Their Superintendents." *Politics and Policy* 45, no. 6 (2017): 1003–1023.

Marcus, Jon. "New, MIT-Based Program Proposes Transforming Physicists, Engineers into Teachers." *Hechinger Report*, January 18, 2018. http://hechingerreport.org/new-mit-based-program-proposes-transforming-physicists-engineers-teachers/.

Marinova, Polina. "This University's Athletes Are Dominating the U.S. Olympic Team." *Fortune*, August 9, 2016.

Marope, P. T. M., and Yoshie Kaga. *Investing Against Evidence: The Global State of Early Childhood Care and Education.* Paris: UNESCO Publishing, 2015.

Marples, Roger. "What's Wrong with Private Schools." *Journal of Philosophy of Education* 52, no. 1 (2018): 19–35.

Mast, Richard. "How Culture Affects How Chinese Students Approach Learning in Western Education Environments." *International Schools Journal* 36, no. 1 (2016): 40.

Materazzo, Miranda. "State Education Department Promotes Social/Emotional Learning." *Watertown Daily Times*, May 13, 2018.

Mathews, David. *Leaders or Leaderfulness? Lessons from High-Achieving Communities: A Cousins Research Group Report on Community in Democracy.* Kettering Foundation, 2016. https://www.kettering.org/catalog/product/leaders-or-leaderfulness.

Maxwell, Ryan. "Citizens Are Made, Not Born: How Teachers Can Foster Democracy." *ASCD Express* 13, no. 6 (2017).

Mayer, Richard E. "How Can Brain Research Inform Academic Learning and Instruction?" *Educational Psychology Review* 29, no. 4 (2016): 835–846.

McCarren, Andrea. "Parents in Trouble Again for Letting Kids Walk Alone." *USA Today*, April 13, 2015.

McCarthy, Niall. "The Share of Americans Holding a Passport Has Increased Dramatically in Recent Years." *Forbes*, January 11, 2018.

REFERENCES

McCombs, Jennifer S., Anamarie Whitaker, and Paul Y. Yoo. *The Value of Out-of-School Time Programs.* Santa Monica, CA: RAND Corporation, 2017.

McCoy, Dana Charles, Hirokazu Yoshikawa, Kathleen M. Ziol-Guest, Greg J. Duncan, Holly S. Schindler, Katherine Magnuson, Rui Yang, Andrew Koepp, and Jack P. Shonkoff. "Impacts of Early Childhood Education on Medium- and Long-Term Educational Outcomes." *Educational Researcher* 46, no. 8 (2017): 474–487.

McDaniel, Brandon T., and Jenny S. Radesky. "Technoference: Parent Distraction with Technology and Associations with Child Behavior Problems." *Child Development* 89, no. 1 (2018): 100–109.

McGee, Kate, and Acacia Squires. "Students Across D.C. Graduated Despite Chronic Absences, an Investigation Finds." NPR.org, January 16, 2018. https://www.npr.org/sections/ed/2018/01/16/578310510/students-across-d-c-graduated-despite-chronic-absences-an-investigation-finds.

McGuinn, Patrick. "From No Child Left Behind to the Every Student Succeeds Act: Federalism and the Education Legacy of the Obama Administration." *Publius* 46, no. 3 (2016): 392–415.

McGurn, William. "An Asian-American Awakening." *Wall Street Journal,* June 11, 2018.

McMahon, Walter W. "Financing Education for the Public Good: A New Strategy." *Journal of Education Finance* 40, no. 4 (2015): 414–437.

Medina, John. "Is Technology Bad for the Teenage Brain? (Yes, No and It's Complicated.)" *EdSurge,* April 3, 2018. https://www.edsurge.com/news/2018-04-03-is-technology-bad-for-the-teenage-brain-yes-no-and-it-s-complicated.

Melnick, Hanna, Channa Cook-Harvey, and Linda Darling-Hammond. *Encouraging Social and Emotional Learning: Next Steps for States.* Learning Policy Institute, June 15, 2018.

Melville, Kathleen. "The Future of Teacher Leadership Is the Union." *Education Week,* October 25, 2017.

MEXT. "Implementation Status of 2014 Public School Teacher Selection Exams." 2015. http://bit.ly/1O8xVwZ.

———. "Basic School Survey 2018." Accessed January 11, 2019. http://www.mext.go.jp/b_menu/toukei/chousa01/kihon/kekka/k_detail/1407849.htm.

———. "The Second Basic Plan for the Promotion of Education." June 14, 2013. http://www.mext.go.jp/en/policy/education/lawandplan/title01/detail01/_icsFiles/afieldfile/2015/03/06/1355571.pdf.

Michnick Golinkoff, Roberta, Erika Hoff, Meredith Rowe, Catherine Tamis-LeMonda, and Kathy Hirsh-Pasek. "Talking with Children Matters: Defending the 30 Million Word Gap." *Education Plus Development* (blog), Brookings Institution, May 21, 2018. https://www.brookings.edu/blog/education-plus-development/2018/05/21/defending-the-30-million-word-gap-disadvantaged-children-dont-hear-enough-child-directed-words/.

Mikulyuk, Ashley B., and Jomills H. Braddock. "K–12 School Diversity and Social Cohesion: Evidence in Support of a Compelling State Interest." *Education and Urban Society* 50, no. 1 (2018): 5–37.

Miles, Matt. "Tech Companies Are Buying Their Own Education Research. That's a Problem." *Education Week*, February 6, 2018.

Miller, Clair Cain. "The 10-Year Baby Window That Is the Key to the Women's Pay Gap." *New York Times*, April 9, 2018.

Miller, Claire Cain, and Kevin Quealy. "Where Boys Outperform Girls in Math: Rich, White and Suburban Districts." *New York Times*, June 13, 2018.

Minero, Emelina. "Parent Engagement in the Digital Age." *Edutopia*, November 22, 2017. https://www.edutopia.org/article/parent-engagement-digital-age.

Mitchell, Josh, and Melissa Korn. "Targeting China, Trump Threatens Student Visas. That Would Hit a Big U.S. Export." *Wall Street Journal*, March 16, 2018.

Molnar, Margit, and Vincent Koen. "Providing the Right Skills to All in China: From 'Made in China' to 'Created in China.'" OECD Economic Department Working Papers 1219 (2015).

Molnar, Michele. "Educators Identify 'Good Guys/Bad Guys' in How Schools Use Ed Tech." *Market Brief*, 2018. https://marketbrief.edweek.org/marketplace-k-12/educators-identify-good-guysbad-guys-schools-use-ed-tech/.

———. "Giving Families an 'Equal Shot' at Finding the Right School." *Education Week*, February 21, 2018.

———. "Investors Pressure Pearson CEO for Details on Sale of U.S. K–12 Curriculum." *Market Brief*, July 27, 2018. https://marketbrief.edweek.org/marketplace-k-12/still-sale-analysts-ask-pearsons-u-s-k-12-curriculum-business/.

———. "Struggling to Compete in the K–12 Market, Apple Makes Big Product Announcement at a School." *Market Brief*, 2018. https://marketbrief.edweek.org/marketplace-k-12/struggling-compete-k-12-market-apple-makes-big-product-announcement-school/.

Mongeau, Lillian. "How a Growing Number of States Are Hoping to Improve Kids' Brains: Exercise." *Hechinger Report*, February 21, 2018. http://hechingerreport.org/growing-number-states-hoping-improve-kids-brains-exercise/.

———. "Universal Preschool Is Most Cost-Effective, Study Finds." *Hechinger Report*, April 10, 2018. http://hechingerreport.org/universal-preschool-is-most-cost-effective-study-finds/.

———. "What Happens When a Regular High School Decides No Student Is a Lost Cause?" *Hechinger Report*, August 11, 2017. http://hechingerreport.org/what-happens-when-a-regular-high-school-decides-no-student-is-a-lost-cause/.

Mongeau, Lillian, Ryan Alexander-Tanner, and John Osborn D'Agostino. "How to Find a Good Preschool? It's Not as Easy as You Might Think." *Hechinger Report*, April 30, 2018. http://hechingerreport.org/how-to-find-a-good-preschool/.

Mongeau, Lillian, and Stephen Smiley. "Regardless of Income Level, Access to

Quality Care for Two-Year-Olds Is Tight." *Hechinger Report*, November 28, 2017. http://hechingerreport.org/regardless-income-level-access-quality-care-2-year-olds-tight/.

Monroe, Heather. "How Nutrition Affects Teens' Mental Health." *U.S. News & World Report*, May 10, 2018.

Morgan, Ivy, and Ary Amerikaner. "Funding Gaps 2018." Education Trust, February 27, 2018. https://edtrust.org/resource/funding-gaps-2018/.

Mosca, Nick. "Seven Easy Steps to Personalized Mindfulness in Schools." *ASCD Express* 13, no. 10 (2018).

Mueller, Pam A., and Daniel M. Oppenheimer. "The Pen Is Mightier Than the Keyboard: Advantages of Longhand over Laptop Note Taking." *Psychological Science* 25, no. 6 (2014): 1159–1168.

———. "Technology and Note-Taking in the Classroom, Boardroom, Hospital Room, and Courtroom." *Trends in Neuroscience and Education* 5, no. 3 (2016): 139–145.

Mullen, Carol A. *Creativity and Education in China*. New York: Routledge, 2017.

Mundy, Karen E., Andy Green, Bob Lingard, and Antoni Verger. *The Handbook of Global Education Policy*. Malden, MA: Wiley, 2016.

Murphy, Katy. "Is California Ready for a Proposition 13 Overhaul?" *Mercury News*, February 6, 2018.

Myers, John. "Don't Expect Jerry Brown to Tackle Proposition 13 in His Final Year As Governor." *Los Angeles Times*, January 14, 2018.

Myers, Linda. "What Happened to the Teacher Workday?" *Education Week*, February 28, 2018.

Nakayasu, Chie. "School Curriculum in Japan." *Curriculum Journal* 27, no. 1 (2016): 134–150.

National Center for Education Statistics. "Education Expenditures by Country." Accessed September 1, 2018. https://nces.ed.gov/programs/coe/indicator_cmd.asp.

———. "Digest of Education Statistics, 2016." Accessed August 16, 2018. https://nces.ed.gov/programs/digest/d16/tables/dt16_310.20.asp?current=yes.

———. "Foreign Students Enrolled in Institutions of Higher Education in the United States, by Continent, Region, and Selected Countries of Origin: Selected Years, 1980–81 Through 2015–16." 2017.

———. "Japan: Teacher and Principal Quality." Accessed October 9, 2018. http://ncee.org/what-we-do/center-on-international-education-benchmarking/top-performing-countries/japan-overview/japan-teacher-and-principal-quality/.

———. "Japan: Learning Systems." Accessed September 1, 2018. http://ncee.org/what-we-do/center-on-international-education-benchmarking/top-performing-countries/japan-overview/japan-instructional-systems/.

———. "Round-Up: International Education News from the World's Top Performing Education Systems." Accessed September 1, 2018. http://ncee.org/what -we-do/center-on-international-education-benchmarking/round-up/.

National Commission on Social, Emotional, and Academic Development. "The Evidence Base for How We Learn: Supporting Students' Social, Emotional, and Academic Development." Aspen Institute, 2017. https://www.aspeninstitute .org/publications/evidence-base-learn/.

National Parent Teacher Association. "National Standards for Family-School Partnerships." Accessed September 1, 2018. https://www.pta.org/home/run -your-pta/National-Standards-for-Family-School-Partnerships.

Nedelman, Michael. "Screen Time: Mental Health Menace or Scapegoat?" CNN, February 28, 2018. https://www.cnn.com/2018/01/22/health/smartphone -screen-time-happiness-study/index.html.

Newcomb, Tim. "Applying to HS in NYC Is More Like Applying to Med School. This App Can Help Students Find the Right School for Them." *The 74*, March 13, 2018. https://www.the74million.org/article/applying-to-hs-in-nyc-is-more -like-applying-to-med-school-this-app-can-help-students-find-the-right -school-for-them/.

New York Post Editorial Board. "Why New York Schools Spend So Much for Such Mediocre Results." *New York Post*, May 23, 2018.

New York Times letters. "The Battle over Elite High Schools." *New York Times*, June 6, 2018.

———. "The Battle over Screen Time." *New York Times*, February 24, 2018.

———. "What's Right, and Wrong, with Social Media." *New York Times*, April 5, 2018.

NHK Newsline from Tokyo. "Bullying in Japan Reaches Highest Level on Record." *NHK World—Japan*, October 27, 2017. https://www3.nhk.or.jp/nhkworld/nhk newsline/backstories/bullyinginjapanreaches/.

Nicoladis, Elena, and Simona Montanari. *Bilingualism Across the Lifespan: Factors Moderating Language Proficiency*. Washington, DC: American Psychological Association, 2016.

Nishino, Mayumi. "The Challenge of Developing Meaningful Curriculum Initiatives for Moral Education in Japan." *Journal of Moral Education* 46, no. 1 (2017): 46–57.

Noddings, Nel. *A Richer, Brighter Vision for American High Schools*. New York: Cambridge University Press, 2015.

Noguchi, Sharon. "California Earns a D+ in Teacher Training, Below Most States." *Mercury News*, December 27, 2017.

Novoa, Cristina. "Families Can Expect to Pay 20 Percent of Income on Summer Child Care." Center for American Progress, June 11, 2018. https://www.ameri canprogress.org/issues/early-childhood/news/2018/06/11/451700/families -can-expect-pay-20-percent-income-summer-child-care/.

Nutt, Amy Ellis. "Why Kids and Teens May Face Far More Anxiety These Days." *Washington Post*, May 10, 2018.

Oberoi, Naira. "Singapore Teens Have Social Skills as Well as Smarts, Study Suggests." CNN, November 21, 2017. http://www.cnn.com/2017/11/21/world /education-social-skills-singapore/index.html.

Oda, Shoko, and Isabel Reynolds. "What Is Womenomics, and Is It Working for Japan?" *Bloomberg Quick Take*, September 19, 2018.

OECD. "Earnings and Wages: Gender Wage Gap." Accessed October 9, 2018. http://data.oecd.org/earnwage/gender-wage-gap.htm.

———. "Education at a Glance 2017: OECD Indicators." Accessed August 17, 2018. https://read.oecd-ilibrary.org/education/education-at-a-glance-2017_eag -2017-en#page1.

———. "Education GPS, PISA 2015." http://gpseducation.oecd.org/CountryProf ile?primaryCountry=USA&treshold=10&topic=PI.

———. "Education Indicators in Focus." July 2013. https://www.oecd.org/educa tion/skills-beyond-school/EDIF%202013—N%C2%B014%20(eng)-Final.pdf.

———. *Global Competency for an Inclusive World.* Paris: OECD Publishing. Accessed September 1, 2018. https://www.oecd.org/education/Global-competency-for -an-inclusive-world.pdf.

———. "How Does Japan Compare?" In *The Pursuit of Gender Equality: An Uphill Battle*. Paris: OECD Publishing, 2017. https://www.oecd.org/japan/Gender 2017-JPN-en.pdf.

———. "How Many Students Study Abroad?" In *OECD Factbook 2015–2016: Economic, Environmental and Social Statistics*. Paris: OECD Publishing, 2016.

———. "PISA Scores, by Sex." Accessed October 18, 2018. http://www.oecd.org /gender/data/pisascoresbysex.htm.

———. "PISA 2015 Results." 2017. http://www.fachportal-paedagogik.de/fis_bil dung/suche/fis_set.html?FId=1126734.

———. "Programme for International Student Assessment (PISA) Results from 2012." Accessed September 1, 2018. https://www.oecd.org/unitedstates/PISA -2012-results-US.pdf.

———. *Providing the Right Skills to All*. Paris: OECD Publishing, 2015.

———. *Supporting Teacher Professionalism: Insights from TALIS 2013*. Paris: OECD Publishing, 2016.

———. "Teaching Hours." Accessed September 1, 2018. https://data.oecd.org /eduresource/teaching-hours.htm.

———. "What Is PISA?" Accessed September 1, 2018. http://www.oecd.org/pisa /aboutpisa/.

O'Hehir, Andrew. "NYC's High School Wars: Helicopter Parenting Hits a New Peak." Salon.com, December 9, 2017. https://www.salon.com/2017/12/09 /nycs-high-school-wars-helicopter-parenting-hits-a-new-peak/.

Okano, Kaori H. *Nonformal Education and Civil Society in Japan*. London: Routledge, 2015.

REFERENCES

Oliver, John. "Charter Schools." *Last Week Tonight with John Oliver* (HBO). 2016. https://www.youtube.com/watch?v=l_htSPGAY7I&t=2s&app=desktop.

———. "Standardized Testing." *Last Week Tonight with John Oliver* (HBO). 2018. https://www.youtube.com/watch?v=J6lyURyVz7k.

Olsen, Brad, and Rebecca Buchanan. "'Everyone Wants You to Do Everything': Investigating the Professional Identity Development of Teacher Educators." *Teacher Education Quarterly* 44, no. 1 (2017): 9.

Ornstein, Allan C. *Excellence Vs. Equality: Can Society Achieve Both Goals?* London: Routledge, 2015.

Osnos, Evan. "What Did China's First Daughter Find in America?" *New Yorker*, April 6, 2015.

Owens, Ben. "Do You Know Your School's Vision? Tips on Making a Meaningful Mission Statement." *Education Week*, November 22, 2017.

Palmadessa, Allison L. *American National Identity, Policy Paradigms, and Higher Education: A History of the Relationship Between Higher Education and the United States, 1862–2015*. New York: Palgrave Macmillan, 2017.

"Palo Alto Unified." Ed Data. Accessed September 1, 2018. http://www.ed-data .org/district/Santa-Clara/Palo-Alto-Unified.

Palo Alto Unified School District. "Voluntary Transfer Program." Accessed April 1, 2019. https://www.pausd.org/programs/voluntary-transfer-program.

Parker, Stephen, Kalervo N. Gulson, and Trevor Gale. *Policy and Inequality in Education*. Singapore: Springer, 2017.

Parkhouse, Hillary, Ariel Tichnor-Wagner, Jessie Montana Cain, and Jocelyn Glazier. "'You Don't Have to Travel the World': Accumulating Experiences on the Path Toward Globally Competent Teaching." *Teaching Education* 27, no. 3 (2016): 267–285.

Partelow, Lisette, Meg Benner, Michael Dannenberg, and Charles Barone. *Trickle-Down Cuts to Education*. Washington, DC: Center for American Progress, 2017. https://www.americanprogress.org/issues/education-k-12/reports/2017 /10/26/441418/trickle-down-cuts-to-education/.

Passaris, Constantine. "The Word Globalization Is Out of Date. This Is What Should Replace It." World Economic Forum, December 22, 2017. https://www .weforum.org/agenda/2017/12/forget-globalization-internetization-sums -up-our-global-economy-better/.

Pathways to Education. "Pathways Post." Summer 2017. https://www.pathway stoeducation.ca/pathways-post-summer-2017.

Pellissier, Hank. "Stress and Your Child's Brain." *Great Schools*, June 13, 2018. https://www.greatschools.org/gk/articles/how-stress-affects-your-child/.

———. "Why Early Math Is Just as Important as Early Reading." *Great Schools*, September 22, 2017. https://www.greatschools.org/gk/articles/early-math -equals-future-success/.

Perkins, Tasha. "School-Community Partnerships, Friend or Foe? The Double-speak of Community with Educational Partnerships." *Educational Studies* 51, no. 4 (2015): 317–336.

Petersen, Andrea. "The Overprotected American Child." *Wall Street Journal*, June 1, 2018.

———. *The Palgrave International Handbook of Education for Citizenship and Social Justice*. London: Palgrave Macmillan, 2016.

———. "The Right Way for Parents to Help Anxious Children." *Wall Street Journal*, December 8, 2017.

Peterson, Paul E. "The End of the Bush-Obama Regulatory Approach to School Reform: Choice and Competition Remain the Country's Best Hope." *Education Next* 16, no. 3 (2016): 23–32.

Pham, Minh-Ha T. "De Blasio's Plan for NYC Schools Isn't Anti-Asian. It's Anti-Racist." *New York Times*, June 13, 2018.

Piacentini, Mario. "Developing an International Assessment of Global Competence." *Childhood Education* 93, no. 6 (2017): 507–510.

Piccoli, Sean, and Elizabeth A. Harris. "New York City Offers Free Lunch for All Public School Students." *New York Times*, September 6, 2017.

Picha, Gina. "STEM Education Has a Math Anxiety Problem." *Education Week*, August 7, 2018.

Pierce, David. "Your Smartphone Is the Best Computer You Own." *Wall Street Journal*, May 23, 2018.

Pillet-Shore, Danielle. "Being a 'Good Parent' in Parent-Teacher Conferences." *Journal of Communication* 65, no. 2 (2015): 373.

Pitts, Jamilah. "Have Your Feelings for Black and Latino Students Lowered Your Expectations for Them?" *Education Week*, May 23, 2018.

Prats Monné, Xavier. "What Is Learning for? The Promise of a Better Future." *European Journal of Education* 50, no. 1 (2015): 25–28.

Procon.org. "Teacher Tenure: Background of the Issue." 2016. https://teachertenure.procon.org/view.resource.php?resourceID=006636.

PricewaterhouseCoopers. "The World in 2050." Accessed August 24, 2018. https://www.pwc.com/gx/en/issues/economy/the-world-in-2050.html.

Project Play. "The Problem." Accessed July 17, 2018. http://youthreport.project play.us/the-problem/.

Proulx, Natalie. "Does Your School Need More Money?" *New York Times*, April 17, 2018.

Public Policy Institute of California. "Financing California's Public Schools." Accessed September 1, 2018. http://www.ppic.org/publication/financing-cali fornias-public-schools/.

Quart, Alissa. "Here Come the Public-School Consultants." *Atlantic*, December 8, 2015.

Quealy, Kevin, and Margot Sanger-Katz. "Is Sushi 'Healthy'? What About Granola? Where Americans and Nutritionists Disagree." *New York Times*, July 5, 2016.

Quinn, Rand, and Nicole Mittenfelner Carl. "Teacher Activist Organizations and the Development of Professional Agency." *Teachers and Teaching* 21, no. 6 (2015): 745–758.

Quinn, Rand, Megan Tompkins-Stange, and Debra Meyerson. "Beyond Grantmaking: Philanthropic Foundations as Agents of Change and Institutional Entrepreneurs." *Nonprofit and Voluntary Sector Quarterly* 43, no. 6 (2014): 950–968.

Radesky, Jenny S., Staci Eisenberg, Caroline J. Kistin, Jamie Gross, Gabrielle Block, Barry Zuckerman, and Michael Silverstein. "Overstimulated Consumers or Next-Generation Learners? Parent Tensions About Child Mobile Technology Use." *Annals of Family Medicine* 14, no. 6 (2016): 503–508.

Ramírez, Naja Ferjan, and Patricia K. Kuhl. "Bilingual Language Learning in Children." Seattle: University of Washington, Institute for Learning and Brain Sciences, June 2, 2016.

Raths, David. "Smarter Tech Spending for Schools." *District Administration Magazine*, April 11, 2018.

Rattan, Aneeta, Krishna Savani, Dolly Chugh, and Carol S. Dweck. "Leveraging Mindsets to Promote Academic Achievement: Policy Recommendations." *Perspectives on Psychological Science* 10, no. 6 (2015): 721–726.

Ravitch, Diane. *The Death and Life of the Great American School System: How Testing and Choice Are Undermining Education*. New York: Basic Books, 2011.

———. "Five Risks Posed by the Increasing Misuse of Technology in Schools." *EdSurge*, December 29, 2017. https://www.edsurge.com/news/2017-12-29 -5-risks-posed-by-the-increasing-misuse-of-technology-in-schools.

Real-World Literacy Summit 2019. "Data: U.S. Graduation Rates by State and Student Demographics." *Education Week*, December 7, 2017.

Redden, Elizabeth. "NSF Report Documents Declines in International Enrollments After Years of Growth." *Inside Higher Ed*, January 22, 2018. https://www .insidehighered.com/news/2018/01/22/nsf-report-documents-declines -international-enrollments-after-years-growth.

———. "U.S. Universities Report Declines in Enrollments of New International Students; Study Abroad Participation Increases." *Inside Higher Ed*, November 13, 2017. https://www.insidehighered.com/news/2017/11/13/us-universities -report-declines-enrollments-new-international-students-study-abroad.

Reeves, Glenn. "Collegiate Destinations Are Heavy on Academic Prestige." *Palo Alto Online*, April 25, 2018. https://www.paloaltoonline.com/news/2018/04 /25/collegiate-destinations-are-heavy-on-academic-prestige.

Reeves, Richard V. "Happy Mother's Day! Here's the Bill." Brookings Institution, May 11, 2018. https://www.brookings.edu/blog/social-mobility-memos/2018 /05/11/happy-mothers-day-heres-the-bill/.

REFERENCES

Reynolds, Gretchen. "How Exercise May Help the Memory Grow Stronger." *New York Times*, February 21, 2018.

Rich, Motoko. "Why Don't More Men Go into Teaching?" *New York Times*, September 6, 2014.

Rich, Motoko, Amanda Cox, and Matthew Bloch. "Money, Race and Success: How Your School District Compares." *New York Times*, April 29, 2016.

Richey, Jeremiah. "Heterogeneous Trends in U.S. Teacher Quality, 1980–2010." *Education Economics* 23, no. 5/6 (2015): 645–649.

Rimfeld, Kaili, Yulia Kovas, Philip S. Dale, and Robert Plomin. "True Grit and Genetics: Predicting Academic Achievement from Personality." *Journal of Personality and Social Psychology* 111, no. 5 (2016): 780–789.

Robinson, Cheska. "Growth Mindset in the Classroom." *Science Scope* 41, no. 2 (2017): 18.

Robinson, Ken, and Lou Aronica. "What Happens to Student Behavior When Schools Prioritize Art." KQED, April 9, 2018. https://www.kqed.org/mind shift/50874/what-happens-to-student-behavior-when-schools-prioritize-art.

Robinson, Savannah. "Inside a Bronx Middle School Where Students Rarely Apply to Attend Specialized High Schools." *Chalkbeat*, June 19, 2018. https:// www.chalkbeat.org/posts/ny/2018/19/inside-a-bronx-middle-school-where -students-rarely-apply-to-attend-specialized-high-schools/.

———. "The Scene at Stuyvesant: Students Who've Succeeded at SHSAT Wary of New Plan, Though Some Want Change." *Chalkbeat*, June 6, 2018. https:// www.chalkbeat.org/posts/ny/2018/06/06/the-scene-at-stuyvesant-stu dents-whove-succeeded-at-shsat-wary-of-new-plan-though-some-want -change/.

Ronfeldt, Matthew, Susanna Loeb, and James Wyckoff. "How Teacher Turnover Harms Student Achievement." *American Educational Research Journal* 50, no. 1 (2013): 4–36.

Rowe, D. E., and Richard H. Derrah. "Teacher License Changes and High Schools in Japan." *International Journal of Humanities and Management Sciences* 4, no. 5 (2016): 470–471.

Saltman, Kenneth J. *Scripted Bodies: Corporate Power, Smart Technologies, and the Undoing of Public Education*. New York: Routledge, 2016.

Samuels, Christina. "New Analysis Finds Long-Lasting Benefits from Early-Childhood Education." *Education Week*, November 16, 2017.

Sanchez, Claudio. "The Gap Between the Science on Kids and Reading, and How It Is Taught." NPR.org, February 12, 2018. https://www.npr.org/sections /ed/2018/02/12/582465905/the-gap-between-the-science-on-kids-and-read ing-and-how-it-is-taught.

Sanders, Jana M. "Focus on Family: Teachers as Parents: Using Technology to Facilitate Parent Involvement." *Childhood Education* 92, no. 1 (2016): 95–96.

Sato, Keiko, and Ippei Minetoshi. "Questions Raised as Parents Hire Stand-Ins for PTA Activities." *Asahi Shimbun*, October 3, 2017.

Satpathy, Sakshi. "New SELF Program at Gunn Builds Student Connection and Support." *Palo Alto Pulse*, February 2, 2018. http://www.paloaltopulse .com/2018/02/02/new-self-program-at-gunn-builds-student-connection -and-support/.

Saul, Stephanie. "As Flow of Foreign Students Wanes, U.S. Universities Feel the Sting." *New York Times*, January 2, 2018.

Sawchuk, Stephen. "Staffing Schools in No-Stoplight Towns." *Education Week*, January 24, 2018.

———. "What Happens to Student Learning When Teachers Change Positions in Schools?" *Education Week*, August 10, 2017.

———. "When the Curriculum Standards Change and the Teaching Lags Behind." *Education Week*, June 29, 2017.

Scafidi, Benjamin. "The Dismal Productivity Trend for K–12 Public Schools and How to Improve It." *Cato Journal* 36, no. 1 (2016): 121.

Scapp, Ron. *Reclaiming Education: Moving Beyond the Culture of Reform*. New York: Palgrave Macmillan US, 2014.

Schaefer Riley, Naomi. "America's Real Digital Divide." *New York Times*, February 11, 2018.

Schaffhauser, Dian. "When Do States Share Assessment Data?" *The Journal*, February 21, 2018. https://thejournal.com/articles/2018/02/21/how-states -share-assessment-data.aspx.

Schanzenbach, Diane Whitmore, David Boddy, Megan Mumford, and Greg Nantz. *Fourteen Economic Facts on Education and Economic Opportunity*. Washington, DC: Brookings Institution, 2016.

Schanzenbach, Diane Whitmore, and Stephanie Howard Larson. "Is Your Child Ready for Kindergarten?" *Education Next* 17, no. 3 (2017): 18–24.

Schiffman, Richard. "Can Kindness Be Taught?" *New York Times*, December 14, 2017.

Schiffrin, Holly H., and Miriam Liss. "The Effects of Helicopter Parenting on Academic Motivation." *Journal of Child and Family Studies* 26, no. 5 (2017): 1472.

Schleicher, Andreas. "School Technology Struggles to Make an Impact." *BBC News*, September 15, 2015. https://www.bbc.com/news/business-34174795.

Schleicher, Andreas, and Pablo Zoido. "Global Equality of Educational Opportunity: Creating the Conditions for All Students to Succeed: Global Equality of Educational Opportunity." *Journal of Social Issues* 72, no. 4 (2016): 696–719.

Schleifer, Theodore. "There Are 143 Tech Billionaires Around the World, and Half of Them Live in Silicon Valley." *Recode*, May 19, 2018.

Schmoker, Mike. "Why I'm Against Innovation in Education." *Education Week*, May 2, 2018.

School Nutrition Association. "Sodium Targets in the National School Lunch Program," June 6, 2015. Accessed September 1, 2018. https://schoolnutri tion.org/uploadedFiles/5_News_and_Publications/1_News/2015/06_June /Sodium%20Final%20White%20Paper%206_8_15.pdf

Schreiner, Laurie A. "The Privilege of Grit." *About Campus: Enriching the Student Learning Experience* 22, no. 5 (2017): 11–20.

Schwartz, Sarah. "Educators Battle 'Fortnite' for Students' Attention." *Education Week*, May 3, 2018.

Schwartz, Zane. *Rote Learning? It's Just Wrong*. Toronto: Rogers Media, 2015.

Scott, Janelle, and Rand Quinn. "The Politics of Education in the Post-Brown Era: Race, Markets, and the Struggle for Equitable Schooling." *Educational Administration Quarterly* 50, no. 5 (2014): 749–763.

Scott, Lisa S. "This Is the Importance of Books to a Baby's Brain Development." World Economic Forum, December 12, 2017. https://www.weforum.org /agenda/2017/12/why-the-books-you-read-your-baby-could-be-critical-to -their-learning/.

Semuels, Alana. "Japan Might Be What Equality in Education Looks Like." *The Atlantic*, August 2, 2017.

———. "The Mystery of Why Japanese People Are Having So Few Babies." *The Atlantic*, July 20, 2017.

Serino, Louis. *A Portrait of Civics Education in the United States: The 2018 Brown Center Report*. Washington, DC: Brookings Institution, 2018.

———. "What Do International Students Think of American Schools?" *Brown Center Chalkboard* (blog), Brookings Institution, 2017. https://www.brook ings.edu/blog/brown-center-chalkboard/2017/03/29/what-do-inter national-students-think-of-american-schools/.

SHAPE America. "Shape of the Nation 2016: Status of Physical Education in the USA." https://www.shapeamerica.org/uploads/pdfs/son/Shape-of-the-Nation -2016_web.pdf.

Sharma, Yojana. "To Fight Unemployment, China Expands Vocational Ed Programs." *Chronicle of Higher Education*, June 18, 2014.

Sherman, Rachel. "Conflicted Cultivation: Parenting, Privilege, and Moral Worth in Wealthy New York Families." *American Journal of Cultural Sociology* 5, no. 1–2 (2017): 1–33.

———. *Uneasy Street: The Anxieties of Affluence*. Princeton: Princeton University Press, 2017.

Shields, Liam. "Private School, College Admissions and the Value of Education." *Journal of Applied Philosophy* 35, no. 2 (2018): 448–461.

Shin, Sarah J. *Bilingualism in Schools and Society: Language, Identity, and Policy*, 2nd ed. London: Routledge, 2017.

Shuffelton, Amy. "Parental Involvement and Public Schools: Disappearing Mothers in Labor and Politics." *Studies in Philosophy and Education* 36, no. 1 (2017): 21–32.

Shyong, Frank. "Asian Americans Surpass Whites in San Gabriel Valley, Marking a Demographic Milestone." *Los Angeles Times*, August 21, 2018.

Sidorkin, Alexander M., and Mark K. Warford. *Reforms and Innovation in Education.* New York: Springer, 2017.

Sifferlin, Alexandra. "Brain Disease Is Common in Former Football Players: Study." *Time*, July 25, 2017.

Silva, Mark. "Education: 'The Great Equalizer.'" *U.S. News & World Report*, April 4, 2017.

Singer, Natasha. "Tech's Ethical 'Dark Side': Harvard, Stanford and Others Want to Address It." *New York Times*, February 12, 2018.

Singer, Natasha, and Danielle Ivory. "How Silicon Valley Plans to Conquer the Classroom." *New York Times*, November 3, 2017.

Singleton, John. "Charter School Growth Puts Fiscal Pressure on Traditional Public Schools." *Brown Center Chalkboard* (blog), Brookings Institution, 2018. https://www.brookings.edu/blog/brown-center-chalkboard/2018/05/01/charter-school-growth-puts-fiscal-pressure-on-traditional-public-schools/.

Sisk, Victoria F., Alexander P. Burgoyne, Jingze Sun, Jennifer L. Butler, and Brooke N. Macnamara. "To What Extent and Under Which Circumstances Are Growth Mindsets Important to Academic Achievement? Two Meta-Analyses." *Psychological Science* 29, no. 4 (2018): 549–571.

Sleeter, Christine E., La Vonne Isabelle Neal, and Kevin K. Kumashiro. *Diversifying the Teacher Workforce: Preparing and Retaining Highly Effective Teachers.* New York: Routledge, 2014.

Smith, Rob. "The World's Biggest Economies in 2018." World Economic Forum, April 18, 2018.

Smith, Tovia. "A School's Way to Fight Phones in Class: Lock 'Em Up." NPR.org, January 11, 2018. https://www.npr.org/2018/01/11/577101803/a-schools-way-to-fight-phones-in-class-lock-em-up.

Sparks, Sarah D. "The 'Brain' in Growth Mindset: Does Teaching Students Neuroscience Help?" *Education Week*, August 7, 2018.

———. "Could Schools Be Doing More with Title I Money?" *Education Week*, April 16, 2018.

———. "Getting Feedback Right: A Q&A with John Hattie." *Education Week*, June 20, 2018.

———. "Is Curiosity as Good at Predicting Children's Reading, Math Success as Self-Control? Study Says Yes." *Education Week*, May 1, 2018.

———. "Principal-Training Secrets Shared by the World's Top School Systems." *Education Week*, October 19, 2017.

———. "Yes, School Does Permanently Boost IQ, Study Finds." *Education Week*, June 25, 2018.

Spring, Joel H. *The Business of Education: Networks of Power and Wealth in America*. New York: Routledge, 2017.

———. *Globalization of Education: An Introduction*, 2nd ed. New York: Routledge, 2014.

———. *Political Agendas for Education: From Make America Great Again to Stronger Together*, 6th ed. New York: Routledge, 2017.

Startz, Dick. "Teacher Pay Around the World." *Brown Center Chalkboard* (blog), Brookings Institution, June 20, 2016.

"The State of Funding Equity in California." Education Trust. Accessed September 1, 2018. https://edtrust.org/graphs/?sname=California.

"Statistics of Japan 2013." *e-Stat*. https://www.e-stat.go.jp/stat-search/files?page =1&layout=datalist&toukei=00200522&tstat=000001063455&cycle=0&tclass 1=000001063456&tclass2=000001068831&second2=1.

Steinberg, Matthew P., and Rand Quinn. "Education Reform in the Post-NCLB Era: Lessons Learned for Transforming Urban Public Education." *Cityscape* 19, no. 1 (2017): 191–216.

Steiner-Khamsi, Gita. "Standards Are Good (for) Business: Standardised Comparison and the Private Sector in Education." *Globalisation, Societies and Education* 14, no. 2 (2016): 161–182.

Stewart, Matthew. "The 9.9 Percent Is the New American Aristocracy." *The Atlantic*, June 2018.

Stewart, Vivien. "Survey Shows Rise of Asia." *Phi Delta Kappan Magazine* 92, no. 6 (2011): 97–98.

Stipek, Deborah, Alan Schoenfeld, and Deanna Gomby. "Math Matters, Even for Little Kids." *Education Week*, March 28, 2012.

Stitzlein, Sarah Marie. *American Public Education and the Responsibility of Its Citizens: Supporting Democracy in the Age of Accountability*. New York: Oxford University Press, 2017.

———. "Does School Choice Put Freedom Before Equity?" *Education Week*, May 8, 2018.

Stoltzfus, Kate. "No More Easy A's: Classroom Can Be a Breeding Ground for Grit (Q&A)." *Education Week*, November 21, 2017.

Stronge, James, and Xianxuan Xu. "A Leak in the Pipeline: Teacher Shortage Crisis." Frontline Institute, 2018. https://www.frontlineinstitute.com/reports /leak-pipeline-recruiting-report/.

Suzuki, Miwa. "'Pregnancy Rotas' Add to Working Women's Woes in Japan." *Japan Today*, June 4, 2018.

Svinicki, Marilla. "Supporting the Cognitive Skills Behind Note-Taking." *National Teaching and Learning Forum* 26, no. 2 (2017): 11–12.

REFERENCES

Swalwell, Katy. "Mind the Civic Empowerment Gap: Economically Elite Students and Critical Civic Education." *Curriculum Inquiry* 45, no. 5 (2015): 491–512.

Szymanski, Mike. "Some LA Parents Say Paperwork and New Fees Are Forcing Them to Quit Volunteering at Their Schools and Jeopardizing Extracurricular Programs." *LA School Report*, December 19, 2017. http://laschoolreport .com/some-la-parents-say-paperwork-and-new-fees-are-forcing-them-to -quit-volunteering-at-their-schools-and-jeopardizing-extracurricular-pro grams/.

Tamborini, Christopher R., ChangHwan Kim, and Arthur Sakamoto. "Education and Lifetime Earnings in the United States." *Demography* 52, no. 4 (2015): 1383–1407.

Tan, Dali, and Elizabeth Barbour. "Building Global Communities: Working Together Toward Intercultural Competence." *NECTFL Review* 79 (2017): 197.

Tang, Ailin. "The World's Biggest Starbucks Opens in Shanghai. Here's What It Looks Like." *New York Times*, December 6, 2017.

Taylor, Kate. "Caught Sleeping or Worse, Troubled Teachers Will Return to New York Classrooms." *New York Times*, October 13, 2017.

———. "New York City Planned to Put 400 Teachers in Jobs. It's Placed 41." *New York Times*, December 7, 2018.

———. "Unions Sue to Block 'Watered Down' Rules for Charter Teacher Training." *New York Times*, October 12, 2017.

Times Higher Education. "World University Rankings 2018." Accessed September 1, 2018. https://www.timeshighereducation.com/world-university-rankings /2018/world-ranking#!/page/0/length/25/sort_by/rank/sort_order/asc /cols/stats.

———. "World University Rankings 2019." Accessed October 9, 2018. https:// www.timeshighereducation.com/world-university-rankings/2019/world -ranking.

Timsit, Annabelle. "Why the Best Teacher in the World Says Other Countries Should Be More Like China." *Quartz*, May 21, 2018. https://qz.com/1283322 /why-the-best-teacher-in-the-world-says-other-countries-should-be-more -like-china/.

"Tokyo Population 2019." *World Population Review*, December 27, 2018. http:// worldpopulationreview.com/world-cities/tokyo-population/.

Tracy, Marc. "Top Private Schools Bring in the Power Elite (and the Power Forwards)." *New York Times*, March 30, 2018.

Trujillo, Jesus Leal. *Redefining Global Cities.* Washington, DC: Brookings Institution, 2016.

Tsuboya-Newell, Ikuko. "Clear Regulations Needed for International Schools." *Japan Times*, December 24, 2017.

REFERENCES

Tsuneyoshi, Ryoko. *Globalization and Japanese "Exceptionalism" in Education: Insiders' Views into a Changing System*. New York: Routledge, 2017.

———. "The World of Tokkatsu: An Introduction." In *The World of Tokkatsu: The Japanese Approach to Whole Child Education*, edited by Ryoko Tsuneyoshi. Singapore: World Scientific, 2012.

Tucker, Marc. "Most Students Aren't on Grade Level, Here's What to Do About It." *Education Week*, May 30, 2018.

———. "The U.S. Education System Is Very Inefficient: Fact or Fiction?" *Education Week*, February 1, 2018.

Turner, Cory. "America's Schools Are 'Profoundly Unequal,' Says U.S. Civil Rights Commission." NPR.org, January 11, 2018. https://www.npr.org/sections/ed/2018/01/11/577000301/americas-schools-are-profoundly-unequal-says-u-s-civil-rights-commission.

———. "Here's How Much Paid Leave New Mothers and Fathers Get in Eleven Different Countries." *Business Insider*, September 7, 2017.

———. "Why Children Aren't Behaving, and What You Can Do About It." NPR.org, June 2, 2018. https://www.npr.org/sections/ed/2018/06/02/611082566/why-children-arent-behaving-and-what-you-can-do-about-it.

Twenge, Jean. "Smartphones Are Damaging This Generation's Mental Health." World Economic Forum, November 17, 2017. https://www.weforum.org/agenda/2017/11/smartphones-are-damaging-this-generations-mental-health/.

UCLA Pritzker Center for Strengthening Children and Families. "About." Accessed June 28, 2018. https://pritzkercenter.ucla.edu/about/.

Ullberg, Eskil. *New Perspectives on Internationalization and Competitiveness Integrating Economics, Innovation and Higher Education*. Cham: Springer, 2014.

US Census Bureau. *Annual Survey of School System Finances 2016*. Accessed October 9, 2018. https://www.census.gov/programs-surveys/school-finances.html.

US Department of Agriculture. "Extension Notice: Request for Exemptions from the School Meal's Whole Grain-Rich Requirement for School Year 2016–2017." April 29, 2016. https://fns-prod.azureedge.net/sites/default/files/cn/SP33-2016os.pdf.

US Department of Labor, Bureau of Labor Statistics. "Preschool Teachers." In *Occupational Outlook Handbook*. 2018. https://www.bls.gov/ooh/education-training-and-library/preschool-teachers.htm.

U.S. News & World Report. "U.S. News Ranks the 50 States: 2018." Usnews.com. Accessed April 10, 2018. https://www.usnews.com/news/best-states/rankings.

Utah State Board of Education. "Polk School." Accessed September 1, 2018. https://datagateway.schools.utah.gov/Schools/37167.

Veiga, Christina. "Caught in the Upper West Side Integration Debate, Educators at This Middle School Say Test Scores Don't Tell the Whole Story." *Chalkbeat*, May 14, 2018. https://www.chalkbeat.org/posts/ny/2018/05/14/at-west-prep

-academy-officials-say-the-upper-west-side-integration-debate-misses-the
-larger-issue-how-students-are-sorted-into-middle-schools/.

———. "To Integrate Specialized High Schools, Are Gifted Programs Part of the Problem or the Solution?" *Chalkbeat*, July 17, 2018. https://www.chalkbeat.org/posts/ny/2018/07/17/to-integrate-specialized-high-schools-are-gifted-programs-part-of-the-problem-or-the-solution/.

———. "Push to Curb Academic Segregation on the Upper West Side Generates a Backlash—and Support." *Chalkbeat*, April 25, 2018. https://www.chalkbeat.org/posts/ny/2018/04/25/push-to-curb-academic-segregation-on-the-upper-west-side-generates-a-backlash-and-support/.

———. "When Diversity Backfires: How Schools Can Lose Funding as They Try to Integrate." *Chalkbeat*, February 12, 2018. https://www.chalkbeat.org/posts/ny/2018/02/12/when-diversity-backfires-how-schools-can-lose-funding-as-they-try-to-integrate/.

Veiga, Christina, and Sam Park. "Where Specialized High School Students Come from (and Where They Don't)." *Chalkbeat*, June 14, 2018. https://www.chalkbeat.org/posts/ny/2018/06/14/where-specialized-high-school-students-come-from-and-where-they-dont/.

Versel, Leo. "As Cell Phones Proliferate in K–12, Schools Search for Smart Policies." *Education Week*, February 8, 2018.

Vogel, Carol. "Rock, Paper, Payoff: Child's Play Wins Auction House an Art Sale." *New York Times*, April 29, 2005.

Vota, Nicole. "Keeping the Free-Range Parent Immune from Child Neglect: You Cannot Tell Me How to Raise My Children." *Family Court Review* 55, no. 1 (2017): 152–167.

Waite, Duncan, and Ira Bogotch. *The Wiley International Handbook of Educational Leadership*. Hoboken, NJ: Wiley Blackwell, 2017.

Wallace, Jennifer Breheny. "How to Raise More Grateful Children." *Wall Street Journal*, February 2, 2018.

Walsh, Bari. "The Brain-Changing Power of Conversation." Harvard Graduate School of Education, February 14, 2018. https://www.gse.harvard.edu/news/uk/18/02/brain-changing-power-conversation.

Wamsley, Laurel. "France Moves to Ban Students from Using Cellphones in Schools." NPR.org, December 12, 2017. https://www.npr.org/sections/thetwo-way/2017/12/12/570145408/france-moves-to-ban-students-from-using-cellphones-in-schools.

Watson, Sara K. "A Look at Social Media Finds Some Possible Benefits for Kids." NPR.org, June 19, 2018. https://www.npr.org/sections/health-shots/2018/06/19/621136346/a-look-at-social-media-finds-some-possible-benefits-for-kids.

Weber, Catherine M., and Taffy E. Raphael. "Constructing a Collective Identity:

Professional Development for Twenty-First Century Pedagogy." In *International Handbook of Research on Children's Literacy, Learning, and Culture*, eds. Kathy Hall, Teresa Cremin, Barbara Comber, and Luis C. Moll (469–484). Oxford, UK: Wiley, 2013.

Weber, Lauren. "Working Women Often Underestimate Motherhood Costs." *Wall Street Journal*, June 26, 2018.

Weiner, Natalie. "$72 Million for a High School Stadium? In Texas, It's Only Up from There." *Bleacher Report*, August 25, 2017.

Weinstein, Boaz. "No Ethnic Group Owns Stuyvesant. All New Yorkers Do." *New York Times*, June 13, 2018.

Weller, Chris. "Japan's Mouthwatering School Lunch Program Is a Model for the Rest of the World." *Business Insider*, March 27, 2017.

Whitaker, Todd. *Dealing with Difficult Parents*. New York: Routledge, 2015.

Whitehurst, Grover J. "What Is the Market Price of Daycare and Preschool?" Washington, DC: Brookings Institution, 2018. https://www.brookings.edu/research/what-is-the-market-price-of-daycare-and-preschool/.

West, Martin R., Matthew A. Kraft, Amy S. Finn, Rebecca E. Martin, Angela L. Duckworth, Christopher F. O. Gabrieli, and John D. E. Gabrieli. "Promise and Paradox: Measuring Students' Non-Cognitive Skills and the Impact of Schooling." *Educational Evaluation and Policy Analysis* 38, no. 1 (2015): 148–170.

Wilde, Marian. "Are We Stressing Out Our Kids?" Great Schools.org, June 22, 2018. https://www.greatschools.org/gk/articles/stressed-out-kids/.

Will, Madeline. "Here Are Six Strategies for States to Build Stronger Teacher Pipelines." *Education Week*, November 21, 2017.

Will, Madeline, and Stephen Sawchuk. "Teacher Pay: How Salaries, Pensions, and Benefits Work in Schools." *Education Week*, March 30, 2018.

Williams, Sophie. "Fluorescent Pork for Dinner? Chinese Man Finds Meat He Bought GLOWING Blue in the Dark." *Daily Mail*, January 8, 2016.

Willingham, Daniel T. "How to Get Your Mind to Read." *New York Times*, November 25, 2017.

Winner, Ellen, Thalia R. Goldstein, and Stéphan Vincent-Lancrin. *Art for Art's Sake? The Impact of Arts Education*. Paris: OECD Publishing, 2013.

Winthrop, Rebecca, and Eileen McGivney. *Skills for a Changing World: Advancing Quality Learning for Vibrant Societies*. Washington, DC: Brookings Institution, 2016. https://www.brookings.edu/research/skills-for-a-changing-world/.

Wiseman, Alexander W., and Gerald K. LeTendre. *Promoting and Sustaining a Quality Teacher Workforce*. Bingley: Emerald Group, 2015.

WorldAtlas.com. "Universities by Number of Rhodes Scholars." Accessed October 9, 2018. https://www.worldatlas.com/articles/universities-by-number-of-rhodes-scholars.html.

World Bank. *China— Systematic Country Diagnostic: Towards a More Inclusive and Sustainable Development*. Washington, DC: World Bank Group, 2018.

————. "Proportion of Seats Held by Women in National Parliaments (%)." Accessed October 9, 2018. https://data.worldbank.org/indicator/SG.GEN.PARL.ZS.

————. *World Development Report 2018: Learning to Realize Education's Promise*. Washington, DC: World Bank Group, 2018.

World Economic Forum. *The Global Human Capital Report 2017*. http://wef .ch/2xVDayK.

World Happiness Report. "World Happiness Report 2018." Accessed June 29, 2018. http://worldhappiness.report/ed/2018/.

World Population Review. "Tokyo Population 2018." http://worldpopulationreview .com/world-cities/tokyo-population/.

Worthen, Molly. "The Misguided Drive to Measure 'Learning Outcomes.'" *New York Times*, February 23, 2018.

Wrege, Louise. "Working Collaboratively: Teachers Need to Learn to Better Connect with Parents." *Herald Palladium*, January 28, 2018.

WSJ Opinion. "Are Smartphones for Kids a Devil's Bargain?" *Wall Street Journal*, January 19, 2018.

————. "Dumbing Down New York's Public Schools." *Wall Street Journal*, June 12, 2018.

————. "Progressive Education Today." *Wall Street Journal*, June 6, 2018.

Xi, Jingping. "Secure a Decisive Victory in Building a Moderately Prosperous Society in All Respects and Strive for the Great Success of Socialism with Chinese Characteristics for a New Era." Speech, Nineteenth National Congress of the Communist Party of China, October 18, 2017.

Ximenez, Maximilian. "Will New York's Mayor Erase Real Diversity?" *Wall Street Journal*, July 2, 2018.

Yamamoto, Yoko, Susan D. Holloway, and Sawako Suzuki. "Parental Engagement in Children's Education: Motivating Factors in Japan and the U.S." *School Community Journal* 26, no. 1 (2016): 45–66.

Yeh, Stuart S. *Solving the Achievement Gap: Overcoming the Structure of School Inequality*. New York: Palgrave Macmillan, 2016.

Yemini, Miri. *Internationalization and Global Citizenship: Policy and Practice in Education*. Secaucus, NJ: Palgrave Macmillan, 2016.

Yettick, Holly. "Can Preschool Really Narrow Achievement Gaps?" *Education Week*, October 2, 2017.

Yogman, Michael, and Kathy Hirsh-Pasek. "A Prescription for Play." *Education Plus Development* (blog), Brookings Institution, August 21, 2018. https://www .brookings.edu/blog/education-plus-development/2018/08/21/a-prescription -for-play/.

Yuhas, Daisy. "Science of Learning: Has Video Grading Killed the Dreaded Red

Pen?" *Hechinger Report*, May 23, 2018. http://hechingerreport.org/has-video
-killed-the-red-grading-pen/.

Zhao, Yong. "From Deficiency to Strength: Shifting the Mindset about Education
Inequality." *Journal of Social Issues* 72, no. 4 (2016): 720–739.

———. "A World at Risk: An Imperative for a Paradigm Shift to Cultivate 21st
Century Learners." *Society* 52, no. 2 (2015): 129.

Zheng, Siqi, Wanyang Hu, and Rui Wang. "How Much Is a Good School Worth
in Beijing? Identifying Price Premium with Paired Resale and Rental Data."
Journal of Real Estate Finance and Economics 53, no. 2 (2016): 184–199.

Zhou, Jinghao. "China's Path to Achieve World-Class Education." *ASIA Network
Exchange* 24, no. 2 (2017): 27–55.

Zhou, Kai. "Non-Cognitive Skills: Potential Candidates for Global Measurement."
European Journal of Education 52, no. 4 (2017): 487–497.

Zhou, Youyou. "Chinese Students Are Blanketing the World, But Americans
Still Barely Make It Past Europe." *Quartz*, December 9, 2017. https://qz
.com/1144889/chinese-students-blanket-the-world-but-americans-barely
-get-past-europe/.

Zillow. "Palo Alto CA Home Prices and Home Values." Zillow.com. Accessed October 9, 2018. https://www.zillow.com:443/palo-alto-ca/home-values/.

Zimmerman, Alex. "Mental Health Crises Are Major Cause of Police Interventions
in New York City Schools, New Data Show." *Chalkbeat*, November 15, 2017.
https://chalkbeat.org/posts/ny/2017/11/15/mental-health-crises-are-major
-cause-of-police-interventions-in-new-york-city-schools-new-data-show/.

Index

INDEX

About the Author

Teru Clavel is a comparative education expert, author, and speaker who has shared her insights on education and globalization on the *Today* show, *CBS This Morning*, and CNN's *Fareed Zakaria GPS*. She holds a degree in comparative international education as well as in Asian studies, and has spent more than a decade as an education journalist. Teru has been a vocal advocate for students, parents, and educational institutions in the areas of equity, school governance, community building, teacher training, and empowered parenting for our increasingly interconnected world. She can be found on social media @TeruClavel.

World Class

TERU CLAVEL

Reading Group Questions for
World Class

Introduction

1. In the opening to the book, Teru receives a phone call from the Palo Alto school of her oldest son James saying that he has been absent, even though he was there. Has anything like this ever happened to you with your child's school?

2. Teru mentions that she wants her kids to "develop empathy for different ways of thinking" (p. xii). Can you think of any ways you've tried to do this with your child?

3. One of Teru's main points of comparison between United States and East Asian education systems is their different ideas about memorization as a learning strategy. Can you remember negative or positive experiences with this kind of learning when you were a kid? How does your child respond to memorization in their schooling experiences?

4. Teru opens the book by sharing her educational "lens" (p. xiv). Think for a second about *your* lens. How have your own experiences with education affected the way you view it today? If you have children, how have your experiences affected the way you are involved in your child's education?

5. Teru's experience as a child was greatly shaped by being raised by a single Japanese immigrant mother (p. xv). What aspects of Teru's stories resonate with your own upbringing?

6. One of the biggest messages in Teru's book is her belief that education can be "the great equalizer" in the United States (p. xvii). Do you believe that this should be one of our goals for education, as a country? What are the most important aspects of education, in your mind?

Chapter 1

1. In this chapter Teru shares her experience with the application process for preschool in New York City. Have you ever had an experience where you felt that children were unfairly expected to act like adults? Have you had any experiences with competition for children (either you or your children) to attend certain schools? If so, what happened?

2. Teru feels torn about whether she should participate in this competitive application process in order for her son to attend preschool. If you were in her shoes, do you think you would focus on your own child or would you try to find another solution, like she does (p. 5)?

3. Teru includes some research in the book about the impact attending preschool has on a child's outcomes throughout their whole life. Can you think of something a child would learn in preschool that could help set them up for their future?

4. In your opinion, what are the main things that children should be learning in preschool (values, skills, content, and so on)?

5. Teru decides that one of the important values for her children's education is giving them "experiences money can't buy" (p. 18). Can you think of some examples of this kind of experience?

Chapter 2

1. One of the first situations Teru has to confront when she moves to Hong Kong is the expectation that everyone has one or more helpers living in their home. What are the good and bad points about having someone living in your home? Do you think you would feel uncomfortable in that situation?

2. One of Teru's favorite educational thinkers is Joyce Epstein, who has done a lot of research on parental involvement. In Chapter 2, Teru shares Epstein's thoughts on six types of parental involvement: parenting, communicating, volunteering, learning at home, decision-making, and collaborating with community. What are the main ways you're involved with your child's education on a daily basis?

3. When describing her new life in Hong Kong, Teru talks about dealing with her own feelings of entitlement as well as trying to raise her children to not act entitled. Have you ever struggled with your own feelings of entitlement or wondered how you can help to raise your child so they don't feel entitled?

4. When Teru first enrolls James in preschool in Hong Kong she is surprised that he has nightly homework. Eventually she concludes it's good that he got into a routine from an early age. Do you think there's an age at which kids are too young to do homework?

5. James quickly picks up Mandarin once he is in an immersion program. Teru doesn't speak much Mandarin at this time, so she sup-

ports James with his English language skills. How do you fill in for gaps you see in your child's learning at school? Do you work on skills at home, hire a tutor, talk to the teacher, or do something else to help supplement your child's learning in those moments?

Chapter 3

1. When Teru and her family arrive in Shanghai from Hong Kong, they're in for a period of adjustment. In particular, she mentions that they constantly battle cockroaches and rats in their new apartment while hoping for hot running water. Have you ever been in a situation like that? How did you respond to living in a challenging living environment?

2. One memorable moment in Chapter 3 is when the Clavel family is shopping for electronics all day at Gome, an electronics superstore. James's Mandarin skills come in handy as they negotiate the price of every item they want to purchase. Would you be embarrassed to have your child negotiating on your behalf in this situation?

3. When they arrive in Shanghai, Teru knows that she wants to enroll her kids in neighborhood public schools. The family's relocation agent tries to talk her out of her decision, but Teru persists. Do you think Teru should have considered all the available options before making her decision about schools in a new city? Have you ever been in the position of trying to find schools in a new place and being unsure about what to do?

4. James's new school is bare-bones, without any indoor plumbing or technology beyond the classrooms' light bulbs. Teru ultimately decides that she appreciates the focus on paying teachers well over the school's physical appearance. What would you view as the

minimum standards for your child's school? What items do you consider to be "extras" and which things are absolutely necessary?

5. One of the major themes of *World Class* is creating support networks for parents in order to address daily challenges in their children's schooling. Meeting fellow mom Jianing comes at a crucial moment in Teru's time in Shanghai, when she feels like she'll always be an outsider among the other parents. Share an experience when you welcomed a new parent, or when you yourself were welcomed by other parents. What was the context, and why did this moment impact you?

Chapter 4

1. At the beginning of Chapter 4, James proudly announces that he joined a club: the Young Seedlings of the Chinese Communist Party. Teru's response is to conclude that this represented China asking for some "gratitude in return" for educating James. Would you be comfortable with your child joining an organization like this in another country? Would you see it as a learning experience to let them participate, or would you be opposed to it?

2. When she first moves to Shanghai, Teru is surprised to see that there are larger class sizes, with thirty-five students or more per teacher. In the United States, these class sizes would be considered far too big for giving each student enough attention. How does Teru explain why Chinese classrooms are so effective, even with larger class sizes? Do you think this same approach could work in US classrooms? Why or why not?

3. When her middle child, Charles, gets diagnosed with leukemia, Teru goes into a tailspin. She panics and is unable to communicate

with the doctors in the hospital. In this dark moment, Teru's new community in Shanghai comes to the rescue, bringing them food and offering support during Charles's hospital stay. Share a moment where you have found yourself part of a community without even knowing it.

4. Teru describes the testing process for Charles when she applies for him to attend a local private school. She remembers it as a very competitive process, where children were rejected and accepted without much concern for the children's feelings. Do you think that competition is a healthy part of the schooling experience, or do you think it should be avoided? Are there certain ages where competition is more appropriate for children?

Chapter 5

1. Teru opens Chapter 5 with a story about James being held after class for receiving less than a 95 on his math quiz. At the time, Teru is appalled that he is singled out. Later, she comes to appreciate the fact that this moment represents the very high standards that every student is expected to meet in Chinese classrooms. No student is allowed to fall behind, even for a day. How do you think you would respond in a similar situation? Do you think 95 is too high of a standard, or would you be happy for your child to have to meet such high expectations?

2. At first, Teru has concerns that her children will simply be "just a number" in classrooms with so many students. However, when she sees James's forty-six-page report card, she changes her mind. She appreciates the time each teacher dedicates to assessing every area of James's performance, from academics to social skills. How do you feel when you receive your child's report card? Do

you feel you receive adequate information to assess their performance? Does your family have consequences—either positive or negative—for specific grades?

3. As Teru is sorting through her mixed feelings about enrolling her children in Shanghai's public schools, the Organisation for Economic Co-operation and Development (OECD) releases the scores from the international PISA tests. Fifteen-year-olds scored at the top of science, reading, and math among test takers all over the world. Teru feels like these scores are proof that she is making the right decision to enroll her children in public schools in Shanghai. Do you agree that test scores are a good reflection of how good a school system is?

4. Teru mentions that she remembers learning expectations being higher in US schools when she was younger; it was a challenge to get an "A." Now, many students expect an "A" just for showing up and are allowed to take tests multiple times. Do you think this is true? What have you observed?

5. Teru observes that in China every student is expected to master the day's material; she doesn't encounter students who think they're "bad at math." She attributes this to a mastery mindset, which means that students are encouraged to believe they can master any new material with work. How does the mastery mindset compare with the messages you received about learning when you were in school? How does this compare to your child's experiences today?

6. One of the biggest critiques Teru has heard from people in the United States about the Chinese education system is that there is an overreliance on drills and memorization. She observes her children doing drills and loving it, and then being able to apply those

skills to more complex problems. Do you think that the positives of drills and memorization outweigh the negatives? If so, why?

Chapter 6

1. While she's living in Shanghai, Teru decides to work with local high school students who aspire to go to US universities. What do you think would be the most challenging things about applying to US universities when you live in another country? Do you think that students who live in the United States should get a priority in US universities? Why or why not?

2. US universities continue to attract students from all over the world. What is the secret to these high-ranking universities?

3. Would you encourage your child to attend university in another country, either for their entire degree program or for a short amount of time (a semester or year, for example)?

4. Learning Mandarin was a big part of what Teru's children gained during their stay in Shanghai. Do you speak multiple languages in your family? If you don't, how much access do your children have to languages other than English?

5. When Teru's family plans to leave Shanghai, what things does she remember fondly about their time there?

Chapter 7

1. When Teru's family arrives in Tokyo, she has to face the fact that she has never taught her children any Japanese, so much of the

language and culture is foreign to them. Do you think that Teru was right to focus on her children learning English and Mandarin until that moment? Why or why not?

2. Returning to Japan as an adult makes Teru realize how complicated it was for her to grow up with one foot in the United States and one foot in Japan. What examples do you remember about difficulties she had in either country growing up? Have you ever had any similar experiences of not fitting in?

3. When trying to find a place for her daughter, Victoria, at a local preschool, the process is time consuming and agonizing. What are some details you remember about the preschool application process for Victoria? What moments made you laugh and which ones made you cringe?

4. When Victoria finally gets accepted at a preschool, the headmaster expresses that she is wary of having a foreign family in the school. Can you understand the headmaster's concerns in this case?

Chapter 8

1. In Japan there is a big focus on raising young children to be autonomous from a young age. Teru recounts Victoria's overnight class trip at age five. Would you be comfortable letting your child sleep overnight away from home at that age? Why or why not?

2. Japanese children travel to and from school on their own starting in first grade, even in a big city like Tokyo. The whole community looks after children to make sure that everything goes smoothly. Did you travel to school on your own as a child? Are your children able to travel to school on their own, or do they take a bus?

3. Teru describes that the game *Janken* (Rock, Paper, Scissors) is a common practice in Japan in order to make decisions in an unbiased way. Do you agree? Does your family have other ways of making decisions when there are different opinions?

4. Teru describes being impressed with the attention paid to school lunches in Japan. For one thing, students are integral to preparing and serving food to their classmates. For another, students learn about nutrition with each meal. As well, students are encouraged to try new things. How does this approach to school lunch compare with your own experiences growing up? And with your children's experiences now?

5. Teru shares experiences of being bullied in Japan as a young girl. Because Japan is such a homogenous country, every difference stands out. What do you think are the roots of bullying among children in the United States? Were you ever bullied?

Chapter 9

1. Teru opens this chapter with a parent observation day she attended in Tokyo where the teachers dressed as poop to teach children about healthy bowel movements. Have you ever seen anything like this in a US classroom? What did you see?

2. Does your child's school have parent observation days? If so, what have you observed? If not, would you like the opportunity to visit your child's class during the day?

3. Teaching is a competitive profession to get into in Japan. Only around 20 percent of teachers who apply for openings in public schools get hired. What do you think of the status of the teaching

profession in the United States? Do you think it attracts the strongest candidates or should we do more to recruit the best and the brightest as teachers?

4. What could we do to make teaching a more attractive profession in the United States?

5. Teru mentions that teachers in Japan work together after school in a teachers' room. She ties their efforts at communication with better alignment among all teachers; teachers know more about what the other teachers are doing in their classrooms, so they can make sure all students get the support they need each year. Do you feel like you child's teachers communicate about what students are learning (and not learning) each year?

6. Every two to three years teachers in Japan rotate schools and or which grades they teach in order to keep school quality equal. Do you think that US school districts should have a similar policy in place to rotate teachers among schools?

Chapter 10

1. In many Japanese schools, women are expected to serve on the school PTA one year for each child they have enrolled. They do not typically volunteer in their children's classroom, so this is their main contribution to the school. Do you think this is a fair expectation? Would your family struggle to meet this requirement?

2. What ways do you see yourself contributing to your child's school?

3. Women's roles in Japan are changing, from women mainly staying at home to care for their children to many more younger women

working full time. Teru describes the challenges mothers face in trying to both work and raise their children. Do you think that these pressures are contributing to Japan's low birth rate? What can, or should, the government do to encourage more women to have children?

Chapter 11

1. When Teru's family leaves Tokyo, they move to Palo Alto in large part because it has highly ranked public schools. While the district's public schools are well funded by local tax dollars, Teru notices other things about the district's priorities that are surprising. What are some things the she noticed in her first few weeks in Palo Alto?

2. One thing that catches Teru's attention immediately is the way the teachers openly state that they have low learning expectations for the students; students who know the material already will receive an "A," whether they challenge themselves or not. Have you seen schools or teachers with low learning expectations for students? What can parents do when their children are in classes like that?

3. Teru notes that most people living in Palo Alto are of a similar high socioeconomic status, and also that there is a lot of ethnic and cultural diversity. Is there a lot of diversity in your child's school or in your neighborhood? How does diversity (or lack thereof) impact your family's experience in your child's school.

4. In Teru's experience in China and Japan, schools only focus on academics; school sports are almost nonexistent. However, in

Palo Alto Teru notices a big focus on athletics, even at the middle school level. She worries that her children will get swept up in this mentality and place less importance on their studies. What do you think is the right balance between academics and athletics for children? How do you keep that balance in your family?

5. James arrives in Palo Alto two years ahead of his classmates in math because his instruction in China and Japan was so rigorous. In Palo Alto, Teru has to work to convince administrators and teachers to place James in the appropriate level class. What do you think you would do if you were in Teru's position? Would you accept the school's placement in a lower level class or would you try to find another solution?

Chapter 12

1. Teru's son Charles receives an iPad from his teacher, which Teru only discovers by accident. The teacher had not communicated with parents about the device. The iPad is just one example of the ways that technology comes to play a big role in Teru's family, after years of having very little technology in her children's schools in China and Japan. What is your experience with technology in your children's schools?

2. Teru is struck by the lack of equity in public schools in California. She visits schools in districts neighboring Palo Alto and sees bars on windows and classes without enough textbooks for all the students. Do you think there should a certain minimum quality of education and resources for all students, no matter where they live?

3. Another aspect Teru notes when she returns to the States is the presence of corporations in public schools. Some of the examples she mentions are textbook companies, technology companies, testing companies, and funding for short-term afterschool programs. How can schools take advantage of offers of support from corporations without letting these corporations take over the education system?

4. One of the biggest differences between Teru's experiences with her children's schooling in Tokyo and Palo Alto is that in Tokyo she is comfortable leaving the school in charge of her children's learning. In Palo Alto, she feels like she's supplementing their learning at home and that school mainly serves as a place for her kids to learn to be social and to learn more about US culture. Which elements does your child's school do well? Are you comfortable with the role your child's school takes in various aspects of your child's well-being (social, emotional, physical, academic)?

Chapter 13

1. In this chapter Teru shares her experiences of visiting schools all over the United States to get a better sense of whether the issues at her children's schools are unique or taking place all over the country. She pays special attention to the topic of mastery to see how different schools implement mastery. What do you think of when you hear the term "mastery"?

2. At the Science Academy STEM Magnet School in Los Angeles, Teru is impressed by the school's focus on mastery. For example, she mentions that 99 percent of the school's students exceeded the state's standards on their math exam, and 97 percent did so on the English exam. Do you think that test scores are a good measure-

ment of mastery? What other ways can we assess for children's mastery of material?

3. At the public magnet high school School Without Walls in Washington, DC, Teru notices some things that make the school exceptional. For example, the school has a 12–1 teacher-student ratio. One way they are able to do this is by taking advantage of teaching resources at nearby George Washington University, where students can earn an associate degree while they are still in high school. Do you think that magnet schools are a good way to give more students access to a specialized high school? Are there any magnet schools in your district?

4. In her interview with Stanford professor Dr. Jo Boaler, the topic of a mastery mindset comes up. Boaler mentions that the concept of being a "math person" leads some students to have very low standards for their own abilities. Have you ever referred to yourself using these terms, like "being a word person" or "not being a math person"? Do you remember when you first started developing ideas about the limitations of your own learning?

5. At the end of the chapter, Teru decides it's time to move her family to the only place she thinks of as home: New York City. She mentions that she wants to live in a big city, where hundreds of languages are spoken, and where her children can access experiences different from any they have known in their previous homes. What other things make this move unique?

Afterword

1. In the afterword, Teru identifies her three children—James, Charles, and Victoria—with three different countries where they've lived. Which child represents which country and why?

2. What factors went into Teru's decision about where to enroll each of her children in New York City?

3. Teru ends the book with the main lessons she has learned on her parenting journey. Which lessons stand out as important for your personal experience? Why?